Development and the Developing World

To my parents
Suhasini and Ramakrishna

Development and the Developing World

Uma S. Kambhampati

polity

First published in 2004 by Polity Press in association with Blackwell Publishing Ltd

Editorial office:
Polity Press
65 Bridge Street
Cambridge CB2 1UR, UK

Marketing and production:
Blackwell Publishing Ltd
108 Cowley Road
Oxford OX4 1JF, UK

Blackwell Publishing Inc.
350 Main Street
Malden, MA 02148, USA

ISBN: 0-7456-1550-3
ISBN: 0-7456-1551-1 (pb)

A catalogue record for this book is available from the British Library and has been applied for from the Library of Congress.

Typeset in 10 on 11.5 pt Times
by Kolam Information Services Pvt. Ltd, Pondicherry, India
Printed and bound in the United Kingdom by TJ International Ltd, Padstow, Cornwall

For further information on Polity, visit our website: www.polity.co.uk

Contents

Figures and Tables

Figures

Tables

Boxes

Acknowledgements

I first started work on this book in 1996, although my interest in development has been a long-standing one. Over the years, I have worked on it intermittently, taking breaks along the way. I started writing it during a sabbatical granted to me by the School of Development Studies at the University of East Anglia. DEV, as the School is otherwise known, was also my first formal introduction into the inter-disciplinary nature of development and many were the debates and discussions we had at the School regarding the merits or otherwise of disciplinarity vs. inter-disciplinarity within development studies. My years in DEV, and my interaction with both the staff and the students there, have influenced this book enormously. I would also like to express my gratitude to friends I made while at East Anglia.

While this book is the end product of many years of interest in development, much of the writing was done while I was visiting the London School of Economics in 1996, 1999 and 2002. These visits provided me with excellent resources, as well as the space in which to think and write. I am grateful to Athar Hussain and John Harriss for making these visits possible, and to Jean Dreze, whom I first met while on one of these visits.

Although it is many years since I was a student at Cambridge, I must acknowledge my debt to Ajit Singh, who has had a significant impact on many of my attitudes and approaches to development. The manuscript has gone through several versions and many people have commented on it over the years. I have also had useful and interesting discussions regarding the book with a number of people. Ha-Joon Chang, Susanna Franco, Haris Gazdar, Ramkrishna Kambhampati, Steve Morse and Sarah White all commented on the various drafts. Charu Chakravarty, Jude Howell and Eleanor O'Gorman discussed many of the themes with me over the years. I am also extremely grateful for the very able assistance offered to me by Raji Rajan, for whom no task was too big (or too small!) to undertake.

An anonymous reviewer at Polity made a number of constructive comments, particularly on the structure of the book. I am extremely grateful to him for these comments as well as for his encouragement at various stages. I would also like to thank all those on the editorial and production team at Polity for their patience during the entire process.

I have been lucky enough to have received the encouragement of my parents and my parents-in-law through the years. They have facilitated and supported my work in many ways. I would especially like to thank my father, who has indulged my academic whims and has encouraged me to keep going with this project when it looked never-ending. The real costs of the project have been borne by my husband, Vijay, and my children, Aparajita and Akhilesh. Their presence has grounded me and for this I will always be grateful to them.

Introduction and Argument

This book is about development: its causes, characteristics and the way in which it affects different aspects of life in the developing world. While this seems straightforward enough, it is complicated by the fact that the countries constituting the developing world are not clear. Nor is the definition of the term 'development' known with any precision. Most students and practitioners of development accept that it must mean progress of some kind. But what exactly are the dimensions of this progress? Do industrialization and 'modernization' reflect progress, for instance? While there are those who see industrialization as a necessary prerequisite for growth, and therefore for development, others like the environmentalists question whether industrialization actually means progress (chapter 6). Similarly, while some writers maintain that the move towards individuality and rationality, and away from communitarianism and subjectivity, are necessary for industrialization, and therefore are necessary for development, others (especially within the participatory and gender approaches) question the desirability of such 'modernization'.

In this book, we will consider the traditional views of development as well as new views and debates within the field. We consider the theories relating to development, the major actors involved in the process, the impact that it has on the structure of production in developing countries, different aspects of the labour market, the international economy, and rural development. Given this very wide remit, I have had to be very selective regarding the issues that I deal with in this book. What draws these topics together? Is there a theme that runs through them? To begin with, of course, all these topics relate to development and the experiences of the developing world. The book also subscribes to the received wisdom that development is about progress across a wide range of sectors and areas, rather than economic progress alone. In this context, I have attempted to choose topics that reflect both the breadth and the complexity of the notion of development as well as the factors that stand out as universally significant, irrespective of the ideology that one subscribes to.

We will begin by briefly considering the themes that draw the book together. It is worth emphasizing that this book is not about these themes. Instead, these themes recur from time to time throughout the book. Identifying them helps us to identify issues that have emerged as significant in development over the years.

Themes

Three themes stand out as significant in this book. First, while development is itself an inherently complex (and broad) notion, one of the factors that complicates analysis is the difficulty of distinguishing between the causes and the consequences of this process. Second, the state has been and, in spite of globalization and the spread of neo-liberal ideology, continues to be the most important economic actor in the development process. The significance of its role is apparent time and again throughout the book. Third, links with the international economy have been discussed as influencing growth from the time of the classical and Marxist analyses of development. In the context of increasing globalization today, they are becoming even more significant. In what follows, we will look at each of these themes and the way in which they recur in this book.

Development: cause or effect?

As already indicated, one of the main objectives of the book is to analyse the causes and consequences of development. We consider, for instance, the extent to which industrialization, exports, education, population control, political stability and a host of other factors contribute to development. What will emerge from our analysis is that while all of these factors are significant in *leading* to development, many of them are also significant *consequences* of development. Thus, it seems reasonable to say that a country that is stable politically is likely to develop faster (in spite of the exceptions to this rule). However, it is equally reasonable to argue that political stability will follow from economic development. This dual causality is clear in many discussions of development and it is what makes development inherently complicated to analyse.

Similarly, it is well known that high levels of education contribute to development. However, achieving high levels of education requires resources that may not be available in an underdeveloped economy. Which comes first? And is this important? If education proves to be a prerequisite for development (as many models of growth and development indicate), then this is an important issue in which policy-makers need to consider where, if at all, they can cut into the circle (chapter 13). In a similar vein, women's education is said to help control birth rates. But birth rates in their turn need to be controlled if girl children are to be educated. Thus, women's education helps development, but development is required if women are to be educated (chapter 14). This circularity is inherent in a number of aspects of development, and makes an analysis of cause and effect considerably more complicated. While this finding is not new, the book highlights it by considering both directions of causality in a wide number of cases.

- Does development lead to democracy, or does democracy encourage development (chapter 9)?
- Does population control help (or hinder) development? Is development, in its turn, required if population is to be controlled (chapter 11)?
- Does good export performance lead to development, or is development necessary to extract good export performance from an economy (chapter 7)?
- Does foreign direct investment (FDI) lead to growth and development, or does an economy have to be developed to attract FDI to begin with (chapter 8)?
- Does industrialization lead to growth and development, or does fast growth cause industrialization (chapter 2)?
- Does education lead to development, or vice versa (chapter 13)?

And so on. Such questions are endless, but in this book I have attempted to consider some of them in detail so as to indicate the web of interconnections that characterize the development process. Amidst such uncertainty regarding causality, clear prescriptions regarding what might (or might not) lead to development are hard to provide. At best, we can indicate what conditions coexist with development (high levels of industry, exports, education or democracy, for instance).

Dirigisme or laissez-faire?

The second theme that recurs in this book is the significance of the state in the process of development. Once Britain became the first industrial nation, and set the target for other countries to aspire to, development became a project of the nation-state, rather than a process that was spontaneously entered into. Early development economics (born in the late 1940s when a number of colonies were gaining independence) was concerned, therefore, with the kinds of policy that 'an active state and the international community could adopt to accelerate a country's rate of development' (Meier and Rauch, 2000, p. 69). The role of the state therefore has long been seen as central to the process of development.

In spite of this centrality, or maybe because of it, the role of the state in development has been an area of considerable controversy in the last decades of the twentieth century (as we will see in this book). Writers like Lal (1983) have argued that development as a discipline has been dogged by *dirigisme*. In a book entitled *The Poverty of Development Economics*, Lal argues forcefully that the state is harmful for economic development. The 1980s marked a neo-liberal revival in Development Studies. Just as early development economists had emphasized market failures and distortions, so neoclassical developmentalists criticized government failure and policy-induced distortions. The emphasis of these writers was on the market and on getting prices right. The breakthrough made by the East Asian countries has been claimed by both sides: as a victory of market forces by the neo-liberals and as a victory of strategic and focused government intervention by others.

The change of emphasis in the 1980s was reinforced by a number of changes within the developing world. The debt crisis and the need for IMF stabilization support in many countries in Latin America and Africa resulted in an increasing acceptance of neo-liberal policy prescriptions across the world. The rolling back of the state under these policies coincided with an increase in the speed and intensity of globalization, and undermined the importance of the nation-state in the international arena. In spite of these changes, however, the state remains a major player in the development process, as we will see.

Open or closed economy?

The terms 'developed' and 'underdeveloped' are used in relation to the position of certain 'developed' countries. In this sense, international relationships are inherent in the notion of development. International links have also been seen as important sources of finance, aid, markets and knowledge. The early focus, however, was largely on trade and aid relations.

The optimal level of openness has always been an issue for debate in development. Marxist theories saw international linkages as providing an opportunity to postpone under-consumptionist crises at home while helping recipient economies themselves to progress. This is in contrast to dependency theories, which saw international links as the main factor *leading* to *under*development. They focused on the extent to which funds flowed out of the underdeveloped countries as profits or other returns. Though dependency theories were criticized for being limited in scope, they did help to focus on the negative effects of international exposure.

Since the Industrial Revolution in Britain, countries (first in Europe and North America and then throughout the world) have been torn

between the need to protect their infant/fledgling economics from competition with more mature, competitive economies and the need to maintain
some links so as to benefit from financial and knowledge flows from more
advanced economies as well as from access to wider markets. ECLA and
the import-substituting industrialization (ISI) school (chapter 7) in the
1960s emphasized the need for the former, maintaining as they did that
incumbent leaders rarely allowed finance and knowledge to flow in such a
way as to benefit newcomers. The 1960s and the 1970s, therefore, were
decades when most developing countries practised ISI and maintained
highly protected, if not closed, economies. With the onset of the debt
crisis and the ensuing structural adjustment programmes, however, the
pendulum swung perforce towards greater openness (together with decreased government involvement in economies). This has been reinforced
by the increased levels of globalization engendered by trade, financial
and, most importantly, knowledge flows during the last few decades.
This book explores some of these debates and events.

Structure of the book

The book builds up the notion of development, from growth through
industrialization and sustainability, on the one hand, through equity
(between households, sectors and regions as well as within households),
on the other. In the process, it brings out the complexity of the notion of
development and the interrelationships between different aspects of development (as we saw above). It also highlights the role played by the
state and by international links.

Part I of the book begins by defining development in terms of growth,
structural change and equity. It argues that development requires growth,
but is also more than growth. This is first put forward in our discussion of
growth and the basic needs approach to human development, in chapter 1.
Chapter 2 extends this by arguing that while growth is necessary for
development, so too is structural change. This chapter considers the shift
of production and employment towards industry in developing countries.
We note also that structural change does not simply involve industrialization, but also involves, over time, a shift towards more sophisticated
industry and finally towards services. The social and cultural analogue
of such structural change is rural–urban migration and urbanization,
which we discuss in chapter 11. Though initially it was expected that the
benefits of growth would automatically trickle down to the poor, it has
long been accepted that this process is not automatic. Chapter 3 looks at
the role of equity in development. Equity is both part of the definition of
development and a cause and consequence of this process. We consider
all three aspects in this chapter, and note that while the initial consensus
was that equity would worsen prospects for growth, there is now more

disagreement regarding this. We consider also the impact that growth has on equity, and conclude that equity is a necessary component of development, not just a cause or even a consequence.

Thus, Part I of the book establishes that development requires growth, structural change and some measure of equity. In Part II, I introduce the notion that for growth to be truly developmental, it also has to be sustainable. This awareness was reinforced in the 1970s by fears regarding the exhaustion of the earth's natural resources and more recently by fears that current levels of consumption will exhaust the ability of the earth's atmosphere to absorb its pollutants. Such sustainability is required *vis-à-vis* all resources – land, water, fuel and other aspects of the environment. We consider this and the literature relating to it in chapter 6.

Chapter 6 also argues that equity cannot be an *inter*-household concept alone. Until the 1970s, it had been assumed that so long as the benefits of growth were equitably distributed *between* households, altruism within households would ensure an equitable distribution of benefits across members. This was increasingly questioned after the late 1970s by gender theorists, who argued that the assumption of altruism was flawed. These writers maintained that across the world, intra-household inequity was unfavourable to women. They therefore argued that true development, which requires equity, also requires *intra*-household equity, and therefore an improvement in women's rights.

Parts I and II of the book thus build up a cumulative notion of development – growth and industrialization (chapters 1 and 2), class and gender equity (chapters 3 and 6), and environmental sustainability (chapter 6). Thus, the concept becomes bigger and more complex as we go along, and would become even more so if human rights were factored in. A preliminary step in broadening the concept (though only slightly) is taken in chapter 9, when we consider the role of the state and more particularly of democracy in the process of development. While the chapter deals with many aspects of a state's involvement in development, the section on democracy and development indicates that the definition of the term 'development' is open – it could include political rights (so that democracy is part of development), human rights, or an environment in which all individuals can fulfil their true potential. While this sounds like utopia, it is of course the ultimate goal of development. We do not, however, go this far in our analysis in this book. Instead, we limit ourselves to the inclusion of political rights in our analysis in chapter 9.

As seen above, Part II of the book extends the definition of development to include sustainability and gender equity (chapter 6). It also discusses development theorizing along the same lines. Thus, in chapter 4, we consider theories of growth, while in chapter 5, we consider theories of development more broadly. The theories considered in these chapters have helped to identify the factors that are important to development, even while they (together with their critiques) have shown why a precise definition of the term is not possible. In spite of considerable *ex post* criticism, these theories provide a useful starting-point for any analysis of development. They help us to identify a body of existing knowledge, both accepted and criticized, which we can build upon. They also help us to identify, in a highly debated and controversial field, certain factors that are more generally accepted than others. The main contribution of modernization theories was in highlighting the notion that development is not only about economic progress but also about a more general transition from the 'traditional' to the 'modern'. These theories, together with the Keynesian consensus in development economics in the 1960s and 1970s, also highlight the central role of the state in the development process.

Part III on development, the state and the international economy, considers development strategies *vis-à-vis* the role of the state and exposure to the international economy. In chapter 7, we begin by considering issues relating to globalization and its patterns over time. Chapters 7 and 8 also consider the different types of international links that contribute to globalization – trade, aid, commercial loans and foreign direct investment – as well as arise from it. The role of international trade has been a bone of contention amongst development economists for the last four decades at least. Although many economists and policy-makers initially felt that international trade disadvantaged the late starters, the neo-liberal consensus of the 1980s has encouraged a more optimistic attitude to international trade and globalization, for which the East Asian experience has been largely responsible. Of course, the international sector influences not only trade and the balance of payments but also many aspects of the domestic economy (Part IV). Its role is discussed in the specific context of the development experience of Britain, South Korea and China (chapter 10). International links have also helped agriculture, through the import of new technology and markets for agricultural produce (chapter 12). They have disadvantaged the agricultural sector in many countries in Africa, where food production has dipped to historic lows due to the production of commercial crops (for export), government exchange-rate policies, and so on. That international links influence the industrial sector is almost self-evident and requires little elaboration. We see the various impacts in chapters 7, 8 and 12. Finally, international migration in search of employment and education (chapter 11) is also considered.

Traditional wisdom maintained that each country could, and should, specialize in producing items in which it has a comparative advantage. This, however, reinforces the *status quo*, compelling developing countries to continue producing low value-added primary products. Comparative advantage in producing industrial products (which are higher value-added) is rarely ever God-given. Instead, it requires considerable investment, which in turn requires state intervention in capital-constrained economies (chapters 2, 9 and 12). Through a series of licensing, funding and regulatory measures, states in different parts of the developing world have supported their 'infant' industrial sectors. They have made decisions regarding capital- or labour-intensive industries, small- versus large-scale industries, import-substituting versus export-promoting industries (chapter 2), and so on.

Chapter 9 deals with the role of the state both in a centrally planned economy and in the developmental states of East Asia. It also considers the impact of state type on development. While this chapter concentrates on the state, the importance of state intervention is reflected throughout the book, highlighting the fact that, for good or ill, the state permeates all aspects of life in developing countries. Thus, in Part IV the role of the state in administering land reforms as well as in initiating technological change in agriculture (through the import of high-yielding varieties (HYV) of seeds or the funding of inputs to enable these HYVs to be grown) is considered. We also note that the state's decisions regarding pricing, public distribution systems, and exchange rates have influenced the performance of the agricultural sector in many countries in Africa (chapter 12).

Part III concludes (in chapter 10) by analysing three cases – Britain, South Korea and China – in the context of these strategies. The macro role of the state in South Korea (strategic role), China (planning role) and in Britain (supportive role) is compared. We find that the role of the state varied in each of the three cases, from specifically directed intervention in Britain, to focused, strategic intervention in South Korea, to detailed, comprehensive intervention in China. Each of these countries, however, has been relatively successful in its own way. It becomes clear that it is not the amount of intervention but the strength and the focus displayed in such intervention that is significant in their success. The main lesson (especially from South Korea and China) is that strong, focused state intervention is necessary. The chapter also shows that in each case some initial protection was followed up by an eventual opening up of the economy to trade and financial flows. While export-led growth is often highlighted in recent literature, it is clear that international protection has been a necessary condition for this in South Korea, China and also, arguably, in Great Britain.

Part IV deals with the impact of development on the domestic sector. Chapter 11 focuses on population growth as being both a cause and a consequence of development. It also analyses the social and cultural consequences of structural change – rural–urban migration and urbanization. In chapter 12, the impact of structural adjustment on the agricultural sector is considered. We mentioned earlier that structural change in the process of development favours the industrial sector (which grows). Does this imply that the agricultural/rural sector declines, or does it prosper in the process? The chapter explores this through an analysis of the changes that have taken place in an attempt to maintain the prosperity of this sector. Thus, land reforms and technological change are considered in detail. We note that these measures have not been successful in Africa, where famines have been very common in recent years. Of course, famines are caused not merely by the breakdown of the agricultural sector, but also by the lack of opportunities in the other sectors (which have also not grown).

Chapter 13 discusses health and education, and asks whether they are part of human capital formation (and therefore determinants of growth) or components of human welfare (and therefore a consequence, and part, of development). In the process, it extends the notion of development to include health and education, which increase an individual's ability to fulfil their own potential. We note that health and education were first included in the definition of development by the basic needs approach (chapter 1).

Finally, in chapter 14, we consider employment and labour markets. A wide range of employment opportunities is a distributive necessity, and spreads the benefits of any growth that occurs. The role played by the urban informal sector as well as by trade unions in this process is considered, together with women's employment and the extent to which it helps to improve equity in the economy.

In conclusion, we note that this book provides one possible way in which the notion of development, its causes and consequences and the processes leading to, and emerging from, it can be considered. The book also provides an introduction (albeit brief) to the theories of development, which, it is hoped, will provide an insight into the state of the art in the field and will help to prevent a 'reinvention of the wheel'. Three themes unify the book, if such a book can be unified. These include the omnipresence of the state and of the international economy in the process of development. This is reflected in debates about development (and more recently globalization), which have revolved around whether the state and international links (through exports) have a benign influence on development or a harmful one. A third theme that unifies much of the discussion in the book is the circularity in the process of development. This theme has been highlighted as posing one of the major problems for policy-makers and development-practitioners alike. It also helps the reader to understand why the notion of development is so inherently complicated and intangible.

Part I

Defining Development

How can one recognize a developing country? Is it characterized by low incomes per head? If so, how would one class the economies of the Middle East, which are relatively rich? Or is it the significance of industry in these economies? If so, where do the countries of Eastern Europe stand? As these questions indicate, simple one-dimensional definitions of development will not stand up to scrutiny. Development is a multi-dimensional process, one that changes the economy, polity and society of the countries in which it occurs.

Attempts have been made from time to time, however, to find simple patterns that may explain development and describe developing countries. Thus, in 1966 Horowitz described the Third World as a 'self-defined and self-conscious association of nation states', which had the following characteristics:

> First, it tends to be politically independent of both power centres, the United States–NATO complex and the Soviet–Warsaw Pact group. Second, the bulk of the Third World was in a colonial condition until World War II. Third, it draws its technology from the First World while drawing its ideology from the Second World. Thus, the Third World is non-American, ex-colonial, and thoroughly dedicated to becoming industrialised, whatever the economic costs. (Horowitz, 1966, p. 17)

Though dated, and far too general to be useful in practice, this definition does provide a flavour of the persuasions of, and contradictions within, the peoples of the Third World. A similar, broad characterization of development was put forward by Kuznets (1973), who maintained that development required high rates of growth of per capita Gross National Product (GNP), of population and of total factor productivity (especially labour productivity). It also required high rates of structural transformation from agriculture to industry as well as high rates of social, ideological and political transformation (through modernization). This in turn involves increased rationality, planning, equality and improved institutions and attitudes. It also requires greater international economic links through increased exports and greater international influence.

The building blocks for development

In Part I, we will build up the concept of development. We begin with the premiss that development means progress in a range of areas. It must mean economic progress, of course, but it must also involve social and political progress, as well as the fulfilment of basic human needs – material, emotional and cerebral. Each of these components is itself not easy to define. Economic progress itself is not uni-dimensional: it requires growth (discussed in chapter 1), structural change (chapter 2) and distributive equity (chapter 3). In addition to this, social and political progress also need to be included. These aspects of progress are hard to define because they are subjective, and therefore influenced by ideology, ethics and principles. In fact, what constitutes progress in social terms has become controversial (see chapter 6). Is it really progressive to lead independent lives in cities rather than dependent, community-based lives in rural areas? While most writers would agree that, *ceteris paribus*, more income is better than less, there is considerable disagreement about whether more urbanization is better than less. These issues are dealt with in later parts of the book.

In what follows, we will set out a number of stylized facts relating to development, which will sequentially build up the concept. These stylized facts stem from the development experience of the developed countries and are, in this sense, Eurocentric. While they provide us with a starting-point for our analysis of development, they cannot be seen as forecasts of what will happen in today's developing countries. This will be seen as we go further in this book. In fact, there is considerable debate about each of these 'facts', and the book deals with many of these debates in greater detail in the chapters that follow.

Growth and structural change

Development requires growth as well as structural change. A large majority of the population of developing countries tends to be involved in non-manufacturing activities, and in the beginning at least, a large proportion of their GNP is produced by the primary sector. However, as productivity in agriculture increases, fewer people can be employed within this sector, leading to a shift of workers towards the industrial sector. In developing countries, however, insufficient opportunities for employment in manufacturing have meant that though the output of the agricultural sector is increasing and its share in overall Gross Domestic Product (GDP) is decreasing (showing that the share of manufacturing is increasing), the proportion of people employed within this sector is still relatively high.

Distributive equity

In general, countries at lower income levels have higher levels of inequality than richer countries. Development requires a relatively even distribution of income, and initial expectations were that growth would result in improved incomes for all. However, the relationship between growth and equity is not linear (see chapter 3). In fact, there seems to be some evidence to suggest that inequality might increase and then decrease as we move from lower to higher income levels (Kuznets, 1955). This is the inverted U-relationship found by Kuznets, and there is considerable controversy regarding its existence.

'Modernization'

It is generally accepted that developing countries tend to be traditional rather than 'modern', in that they have significant extra-economic distinctions based on caste, religion and language, all of which still matter in these countries. In developed countries, many of these differences have been subsumed under the economic distinction. Additionally, while there is more emphasis on individuality in the latter, there is greater emphasis on communitarian living in the former (see chapter 5). While modernization theories have been strongly criticized in the past two to three decades, many writers and policy-makers continue to see development requiring a shift towards the 'modern' and away from the 'traditional' (chapter 5). The desirability of such change, however, is questioned (chapter 6).

Political transformation

Drawing from Western development experience, it is often argued that political freedom must accompany growth, if it is to be termed development. Thus, many writers maintain that freedom is greatest within democracies, and therefore development requires democracy. This argument has influenced the transitions taking place in the East European countries, for instance, and has begun to bear fruit in East Asia, where political freedoms are increasing. However, the exact dimensions of such political change are debated – is freedom really so great in democracies? are all developed countries democracies of the same kind? These are both questions which have attracted attention. We consider them further in chapter 7.

Demographic characteristics

Development implies improvements in hygiene and sanitation, and a corresponding decrease in death rates. Further development results in the emancipation of women, and increases parental aspirations *vis-à-vis* their children. These changes lead to a decrease in birth rates, resulting in a demographic transition from high birth and death rates, to high birth and low death rates, and finally to low birth and low death rates at the highest stages of development. This demographic transition is based on the experiences of the developed economies. In today's developing world, death rates have fallen faster than before, but birth rates are taking longer to decrease, as we will see.

Rural–urban migration

Allied to the change in the structure of the economy is a shift in population from the rural to the urban sector as development takes place. This shift also results in expanding cities, and further reinforces individuality and rational thinking, as the modernization theorists argued. In reality, of course, urbanization in developing countries has not accompanied development in the same way as it did in the developed countries. The characteristics of the former are very different, as we will see in chapter 11.

Education and health

Development implies fulfilment of basic human needs, including those for education and health. In most developed countries, the demographic and epidemiological transitions have resulted in an ageing population with very high rates of life expectancy. Similarly, there is almost universal primary and secondary education. Whether this comes prior to development, or after it, is still a question that needs to be answered.

Employment

Development requires the benefits of growth to trickle down, and employment provides the surest way of achieving this. In developed countries, such employment is also largely in the industrial or productive tertiary sector. In developing countries, employment is largely rural or in the unproductive tertiary sector (which merely provides ways of surviving in the face of poverty).

The above stylized facts present a picture wherein development requires growth and structural change, some measure of distributive equity, modernization in social and cultural attitudes, a degree of political transformation and stability, an improvement in health and education so that population growth stabilizes, and an increase in urban living and employment. Of course, this is a stylized picture, which reflects an ethnocentric version of development, drawing on the experiences of today's developed countries. We have already touched upon ways in which the experiences of developing countries do not mirror these exactly. We will consider these in more detail as we go along.

1

Growth and Development

As indicated earlier, simple one-dimensional definitions of development do not stand up to scrutiny. Development requires the growth of output as well as structural, social and, possibly, cultural change. Since quantifying such change is not easy, development has often been equated with economic growth. The assumption underlying this was that growth would 'trickle down', but experience has taught us that this is inadequate. Later definitions therefore turned to considering the 'quality of life' more directly instead. Attempts have been made to quantify the 'quality of life' by means of multi-dimensional indices. The most popular and up to date of these is the Human Development Index (HDI), which is based on the level of output, life expectancy (a proxy for health) and adult literacy (a proxy for education).

This chapter considers the Human Development Index and other measures of development in more detail. It also describes the evolution of the term 'development' and its shift away from 'economic growth' through 'basic needs' towards even broader definitions. We note that in spite of moving away from an exclusive focus on the economic dimensions of development, growth remains a very significant aspect of development. We will therefore begin by considering how growth is measured, and the shortcomings of this measure, before we consider the relationship between growth and development.

Growth as a measure of development

Growth is a measure of sustained increases in output or Gross Domestic Product (GDP). It therefore helps to provide an indication of potential improvements in living standards and quality of life in the future. People's standards of living depend upon their incomes, which in turn are related to GDP per capita (see box 1.1). The significance of growth for development was summarized succinctly by Robert Lucas when he said:

> Rates of growth of real per capita income are so diverse, even over sustained periods...Indian incomes will double every 50 years; Korean every 10. An Indian will, on average, be twice as well off as his grandfather; a

---

Box 1.1   The measurement of growth

Growth is usually measured as the rate of change in Gross Domestic Product (GDP) of a country over a specified time period. The GDP is the total quantity of goods and services produced in an economy in a given period of time, usually one year. When comparing countries of different sizes, this measure has to be normalized by the size of population to give the GDP *per capita*. To compare GDP per capita across countries, we need to find some way of converting it into a common measure. One way is to express the national income figures in a common currency. However, this will still not provide a realistic comparison because many products could be cheaper in a country like India than, say, in the UK[1]. Since £1 will buy more products in India, for instance, than it will in the UK, we need to take the purchasing power parity[2] or real exchange rate[3] between countries. While there are many ways to calculate such a measure, they all involve selecting a comparable basket of goods and services from each country and constructing international prices by averaging the prices of each good and service across countries. The national incomes of each country can then be valued at these international prices, making them comparable because they are now in the same currency and at comparable prices.

However, even after these adjustments, the GDP measure remains problematic, especially in developing countries. First, GDP per capita does not include estimates for non-marketed[4] output. Since output from subsistence farms, food, fuel and other items gathered from forests can be quite high in developing countries, GDP per capita might significantly underestimate real income levels in these economies.

Second, GDP per capita is an average measure and does not take differences in distribution into account. This is especially important when one's concern is the economic well-being of the majority. It is also important when income distributions are skewed, as in many developing countries. Attempts to correct this measure for unequal income distributions have included the introduction of 'poverty weights' which would place more weight on the growth of incomes for the lowest 40% (Ahluwalia, 1974) or the use of the absolute income level of the lower 40%. However, even these suggestions do not take the intra-household[5] distribution of incomes and consumption into account or the extent to which people fall below the poverty line (i.e. do they miss one meal a day or two?).

Finally, of course, GDP itself (or its dynamic counterpart, growth) does not reflect welfare in the economy. The latter depends upon other factors like leisure, health, education and the environment.

[1] These differences in price are not captured in different exchange rates, because exchange rates only take traded goods into account. However, there are a large number of non-traded goods that people tend to purchase regularly, and their prices will also be important. Additionally, the range of non-traded goods is likely to be higher in a less developed country. In such a case, there will be a downward bias to the developing countries' income figures.

[2] Purchasing power parity (PPP) is a condition that holds when the prices of goods in different countries are equalized once adjustments are made for the exchange rate.

[3] The real exchange rate is an index that gives the opportunity cost of foreign-produced goods in terms of domestically produced goods.

[4] This includes output from gardens, subsistence farms, work done at home without monetary payments. In short, it includes all output that is not traded through the market.

[5] Intra-household distribution implies distribution within a single household. Thus, while a household may not be poor from the point of view of its income, some members within it may be disadvantaged with regard to consumption. It is often claimed, for instance, that female household members consume less than male members, and that less is invested in female education and health.

Korean 32 times... I do not see how one can look at figures like these without seeing them as representing possibilities. Is there some action a government of India could take that would lead the Indian economy to grow like Indonesia's or Egypt's? If so, what exactly? If not, what is it about the 'nature of India' that makes it so? The consequences for human welfare involved in questions like these are simply staggering: Once one starts to think about them, it is hard to think about anything else. (Lucas, 1988, p. 4)[1]

In spite of early acceptance that growth was necessary for economic development, it was also recognized that it was not sufficient. If growth is to lead to economic development, the benefits of growth must trickle down to everybody, increasing economy-wide living standards and eradicating poverty. Growth is therefore simply the means to an end. In many countries where high GDP growth rates have not translated into improved living conditions for the poor, this measure cannot be seen as a proxy for development. On the other hand, some countries with low incomes have managed, through skilful government intervention, to achieve better conditions of life for their poor. Thus, the assumption of 'trickle down' underlying the use of GDP as a measure of development has been falsified by the experience of developing countries themselves. By the early 1970s, the search was on for broader measures of development.

Broader measures of development

In 1968, under the presidency of Robert McNamara, a World Bank study came to the conclusion that though many developing countries had achieved high rates of growth, poverty and inequality had worsened (Morawetz, 1977). This led to a policy shift within the Bank towards direct attempts to tackle poverty rather than relying on trickle-down.

In the 1970s, the World Bank and others within the development community began to prioritize basic sectors like housing, education and agriculture directly. The strategy continued to emphasize incomes and growth (i.e. it was income-centred) as the means to these ends. It sought to increase incomes sufficiently to allow all groups to purchase these necessities from the market. The state was expected to step in and provide what could not be purchased. The approach was gradualist, and expected improvements to occur over time.

It retained many problems of the income-based approaches, and faced considerable criticism. These criticisms led to the International Labour Organization (ILO) placing 'the satisfaction of basic human needs' and the generation of employment at the centre of its 1976 World Employment Conference. The conference concluded that if the aim of development was to make the basic necessities of life available to a majority of the population, then a concentration on these 'ends', rather than on GDP as the 'means' to achieve them, would yield better results.[2] It therefore saw basic needs as including two main elements: 'first, they include certain minimum requirements of a family for private consumption: adequate food, shelter and clothing, as well as certain household equipment and furniture. Second, they include essential services provided by and for the community at large, such as safe drinking water, sanitation, public transport and health, educational and cultural facilities' (ILO, 1976b). Thus, there was an individual aspect to basic needs and a communitarian or state-related aspect. In addition to basic needs, the conference also recognized the need for employment and for the participation of people in decision-making processes.

While this approach was welcomed as focusing on the 'ends' of decreasing poverty, there was concern within the countries of the Third World that exclusive concentration on this in international funding policies would discourage industrialization, and therefore reduce their chances of economic progress (Singh, 1979). Before long, however, it was seen that providing basic needs on a *sustainable* basis would require economic growth (and therefore probably industrialization). Thus, the basic needs approach led back to the income-centred approach. The difference was in the priority given to growth. Whereas the latter saw income growth as the priority and assumed that it would trickle down, the basic needs approach saw income growth as simply instrumental in achieving the primary goal – the alleviation of poverty.

Once this dual relationship was established, many studies attempted to analyse whether GDP and basic needs satisfaction were empirically correlated with each other. Such a correlation, if it existed, would allow analysts to concentrate on the simpler GDP measure without loss of generality. However, the results were contradictory, and varied considerably according to the measures used for basic needs, the sample of countries being studied, and the level of aggregation of the economic indicators used. Thus, Morawetz (1977) found a weak correlation between the level of GNP[3] and indicators of basic needs fulfilment, and even less correlation between the growth of GNP and improvements in basic needs. Sheehan and Hopkins (1978), on the other hand, concluded that GNP per capita was the most important variable explaining the level of basic needs satisfaction. More recently, in a paper entitled 'Identifying the Poor in Developing Countries: Do Different Definitions Matter?', Glewwe and van der Gaag (1990) compared a number of commonly used measures of poverty – per capita income, household consumption, per capita food consumption, food ratio (proportion of household budget spent on food), calories, medical data and basic needs indicators – using data on Côte d'Ivoire. They found that the groups identified as poor vary depending on the definitions used. More specifically, while income and consumption measures are quite closely correlated, the other (medical/educational) measures have little or no correlation with these.

Since no conclusive relationship could be proved between GNP/GDP and basic needs, the former could not be used as a simple proxy for the latter. Attempts were therefore made to develop a single basic needs index to enable comparison between countries. The first of these was the 'level of living' index (Drewnowski and Scott, 1966), which was followed by the 'development index' developed by McGranahan et al. (1972). The approach became popular as the 'physical quality of life' index (PQLI) developed by Morris and Liser (1977). The PQLI was composed of three indicators – life expectancy at age 1, infant mortality and literacy – each of which was given an equal weight. This arbitrary weighting mechanism received much criticism, with Hicks and Streeten (1979) concluding that 'analytical work can be undertaken using the component indices almost as easily as with the composite index' (p. 576). Larson and Wilford (1979) also criticized the PQLI composite, because they found that the three indicators were very highly correlated with each other, and that any one on its own would serve equally well to rank countries. In addition to this, the PQLI suffered from all the problems of an index (scaling, weighting, changes over time, and limitations to the number of indicators included).

Notwithstanding these criticisms, the United Nations Development Programme (UNDP) has attempted to improve and extend the

PQLI to develop a more comprehensive and detailed index called the 'Human Development Index' (HDI) and its poverty analogue, the 'Human Poverty Index' (HPI). The HDI focuses on the capability perspective on poverty – 'poverty represents the absence of some basic capabilities to function', ranging from physical ones like food, clothing and shelter to more complex ones like participating in community life. This capability approach 'reconciles the notions of absolute and relative poverty, since relative deprivation in incomes and commodities can lead to an absolute deprivation in minimum capabilities' (UNDP, 1997, p. 16).

The human development index measures the average achievements of countries in three basic dimensions of human development – longevity, knowledge and a decent standard of living. Life expectancy levels are used to measure longevity, while adult literacy and enrolment in primary, secondary and tertiary education are taken together to reflect educational achievements. Finally, real GDP per capita is used to measure the standard of living (in PPP–purchasing power parity–dollars). The HDI has also been extended to allow for inequalities of achievement between men and women (the gender-related development index), and between different classes and geographical regions.

Thus, the measurement of development has come a long way since growth was seen as a proxy for development. While it is accepted that there are many problems with indices of this kind (see UNDP, 1997), and the UNDP itself is trying to improve the HDI and HPI, these are the only available measures for comparing development across countries in quantitative terms. As such, they provide a reasonable summary of levels of development, though they may not be accurate in the detail or as comprehensive as desired.

The Millennium Development Goals (MDGs) put forward at the United Nations Millennium Summit (2000) indicate a further extension of the definition of development. These goals aim to halve extreme poverty by the year 2015, achieve universal primary education, promote gender equality and empower women, reduce child and maternal mortality, combat AIDS, malaria and other diseases, ensure environmental sustainability, and develop a global partnership for development. Thus, they bring the role of gender equality and environmental sustainability (see chapter 6) into definitions of development. The UNDP itself has published a variant of the HDI, which takes the position of women into account. However, the MDGs highlight their significance by providing specific targets regarding these goals. We will consider these issues further in chapter 6. In the next section we will consider the figures relating to growth and development to see what insights they have to offer.

Empirical evidence on growth

Table 1.1 provides basic growth and development figures for a selection of high-, low- and middle-income countries. It allows us to compare the different measures as well as to consider some basic facts about the growth process across the world. The countries are sorted on the basis of the GNP per capita column.

From table 1.1, we note that Ethiopia had the lowest GNP per capita, while Japan had the highest in 1995 (see column 3). Once this is transformed into a PPP measure, the picture changes somewhat. Ethiopia still has the lowest PPP GNP, but Japan no longer has the highest. Instead, the USA has the highest PPP GNP, with 26,980 relative to 22,110 for Japan (see column 5). Similarly, Sri Lanka has approximately one-half of the GNP per capita of Kazakhstan but a higher PPP GNP figure (3,250 relative to 3,010). Likewise Venezuela has a lower GNP per capita figure than Brazil, but a considerably higher PPP figure (7,900 relative to 5,400). In spite of these exceptions, however, the rankings with respect to GNP per capita are very similar to the PPP rankings.

Comparing the rankings of countries on the GNP and HDI measures (last column, table 1.1), we find that Sri Lanka, Chile, Costa Rica, Tanzania and Thailand do far better on the HDI scale than on the GNP scale. Thus, they have been able, through government intervention and redistributive policies, to spread the benefits of growth to a wide proportion of the population. On the other hand, countries like Saudi Arabia are unable to translate income growth into corresponding levels of human development and consequently perform worse on human development than on GNP.

One of the most striking findings from table 1.1 is that countries like Korea, Singapore and Hong Kong that were considered developing not so long ago have now graduated to the ranks of the 'high-income' countries. This has been achieved through their very high rates of growth (column 4). Thus, Korea (7.7 per cent), Singapore (6.2 per cent), Hong Kong (4.8 per cent), Malaysia (5.7 per cent), Thailand (8.4 per cent), Indonesia (6 per cent) and China (8.3 per cent) have all grown very fast. On the other hand, many countries in Africa and Eastern Europe have grown very slowly. In the latter case, the transition to a market economy has been largely responsible for the poor growth performance. Finally, some of the Latin American countries have fared very badly, with Brazil and Mexico both showing very slow rates of growth. This can be explained as the aftermath of the debt crisis (the 1980s has often been called 'the lost decade' in Latin American development (C. Edwards, 1992)).

Table 1.1 Growth and development indicators

Country	Population (millions), mid-1995	GNP per capita, 1995 $[a]	GNP growth (%), 1985–95[b]	PPP GNP, 1995[c]	'L.E.B at birth (yrs), 1995	Adult literacy (%), 1995	HDI	GNP–HDI[e]
Low income								
Ethiopia	56.4	100	−0.3	450	49	65	0.244	4
Tanzania	29.6	120	1.0	640	51	32	0.357	21
Sierra Leone	4.2	180	−3.6	580	40	—	0.176	−4
Burkina Faso	10.4	230	−0.2	780	49	81	0.221	−9
Bangladesh	119.8	240	2.1	1,380	58	62	0.368	0
Uganda	19.2	240	2.7	1,470	42	38	0.328	−19
Kenya	26.7	280	0.1	1,380	58	22	0.463	5
India	929.4	340	3.2	1,400	62	48	0.446	5
Ghana	17.1	390	1.4	1,990	59	—	0.468	−8
Pakistan	129.9	460	1.2	2,230	60	62	0.445	−19
China	1200.2	620	8.3	2,920	69	19	0.626	3
Sri Lanka	18.1	700	2.6	3,250	72	10	0.711	9
Middle income								
Egypt	57.8	790	1.1	3,820	63	49	0.614	−20
Indonesia	193.3	980	6.0	3,800	64	16	0.668	−7
Bulgaria	8.4	1,330	−2.6	4,480	71	—	0.78	9
Kazakhstan	16.6	1,330	−8.6	3,010	69	33	0.709	6
Tunisia	9.0	1,820	1.9	5,000	69	—	0.748	−12
Russian Federation	148.2	2,240	−5.1	4,480	65	—	0.792	7
Costa Rica	3.4	2,610	2.8	5,850	77	5	0.889	27
Thailand	58.2	2,740	8.4	7,540	69	6	0.833	−8
Poland	38.6	2,790	1.2	5,400	70	—	0.834	14
Botswana	1.5	3,020	6.1	5,580	68	30	0.673	−30
Venezuela	21.7	3,020	0.5	7,900	71	9	0.861	1
Upper-middle income								
South Africa	41.5	3,160	−1.1	5,030	64	18	0.716	−10
Croatia	4.8	3,250	—	—	74	—	0.76	10
Mexico	91.8	3,320	0.1	6,400	72	10	0.853	0

(Continued)

Table 1.1 (Continued)

Country	Population (millions), mid-1995	GNP per capita, 1995 $[a]	GNP growth (%), 1985–95[b]	PPP GNP, 1995[c]	*L.E.B at birth (yrs), 1995[d]	Adult literacy (%), 1995	HDI	GNP– HDI[e]
Brazil	159.2	3,640	-0.8	5,400	67	17	0.783	0
Czech Republic	10.3	3,870	-1.8	9,770	73	—	0.882	3
Malaysia	20.1	3,890	5.7	9,020	71	17	0.832	-13
Hungary	10.2	4,120	-1.0	6,410	70	—	0.857	5
Chile	14.2	4,160	6.1	9,520	72	5	0.891	13
Saudi Arabia	19.0	7,040	-1.9	—	70	37	0.774	-32
Argentina	34.7	8,030	1.8	8,310	73	4	0.884	10
Greece	10.5	8,210	1.3	11,710	78	—	0.923	15
High Income								
Korea	44.9	9,700	7.7	11,450	72	—	0.89	5
Israel	5.5	15,920	2.5	16,490	77	—	0.913	3
Kuwait	1.7	17,390	1.1	23,790	76	21	0.844	-47
UAE	2.5	17,400	-2.8	16,470	75	21	0.866	-17
UK	58.5	18,700	1.4	19,260	77	—	0.931	5
Italy	57.2	19,020	1.8	19,870	78	—	0.921	-4
Canada	29.6	19,380	0.4	21,130	78	—	0.96	7
Hong Kong	6.2	22,990	4.8	22,950	79	—	0.914	-17
France	58.1	24,990	1.5	21,030	78	—	0.946	13
Singapore	3.0	26,730	6.2	22,770	76	9	0.9	-15
USA	263.1	26,980	1.3	26,980	77	—	0.942	-1
Germany	81.9	27,510	—	20,070	76	—	0.924	-3
Japan	125.2	39,640	2.9	22,110	80	—	0.94	0

[a] GNP per capita = GNP/population.
[b] GNP growth is average annual growth.
[c] PPP GNP is the purchasing power parity GNP and is measured in current international $ for 1995.
[d] *L.E.B = life expectancy at birth.
[e] GNP–HDI column gives the difference between the GNP ranking of the country and the HDI rankings.

Source: All data is from the World Bank, 1997b, except for the last two columns which are from UNCP, 1997. From *World Development Report,* 1997, by World Bank, © 1997 by The International Bank for Restructuring and Development/The World Bank. Used by permission of Oxford University Press, Inc.

From *Human Development Report,* 1997, by United Nations Development Programme, © 1997 by the United Nations Development Programme. Used by permission of Oxford University Press.

Conclusion

This chapter leads us to conclude that whether we consider the broader 'development' indices or the more narrow income-centred measures of development, GDP per capita remains a major component of development. Ultimately, the ability of an economy to finance health, education, sanitation and other welfare measures must depend upon the income of its economy. In addition, the ability of individuals to purchase food, clothing and shelter as well as education and health facilities must depend upon their individual incomes. All of these are influenced by the GDP of a country, subject to the caveats mentioned above. As we have already seen, performance with respect to growth has varied across the world. Can these differences be explained? What causes growth in some economies but not in others? More importantly, can anything be done to induce an economy to grow? These questions arise naturally from our discussion in this chapter. However, before we consider them in chapter 4, we will consider structural change and industrialization as well as distributional issues in the next two chapters.

2

Structural Change, Industrialization and Economic Growth

The terms 'growth', 'industrialization' and 'development' are often used interchangeably, to the extent that developed countries are often called industrialized economies. We have already noted that structural change is a necessary component of development. In the context of growth and development, structural change usually implies a shift in the composition of production towards manufacturing. This shift, which is also often termed industrialization, is, however, only one aspect of structural change. It is usually accompanied by increasing urbanization and rural–urban migration. In addition to broad structural change, growth and development are also often accompanied by a change within the structure of industry, away from labour-intensive, raw material processing industry towards capital-intensive industry. Sustained growth and development in Britain – the first industrial nation – began with the Industrial Revolution and the attendant change in the structure of the economy towards industry.

In this chapter, we begin by considering the relationship between industrialization and growth. We conclude that though there is a definite association between growth and industrialization, the direction of this association is not clear. The second part of the chapter concentrates on industrialization strategies. The discussion here is predicated on the fact that the state makes decisions about strategy, and therefore highlights the role played by the state (and by international trade) in industrialization and growth.

Structural change: shift towards industry

The term 'industrialization' has been used so frequently that it hardly needs definition. It is used to indicate a shift towards industrial production by enterprises that use labour, capital and raw materials to add value. These units are usually mechanized and employ a number of people. In theoretical terms, the shift from agriculture to industry is often seen as occurring spontaneously as an economy grows. At very low income levels, a large proportion of income is spent on food. As incomes begin to increase, individuals will first spend more on better-quality food (and more processed foods), and will then begin to spend on manufactured consumer products (both non-durable and durable). At the same time as demand is shifting towards manufacturing, a number of changes take place on the supply side too. Productivity in the agricultural sector increases through technological improvements and capital inputs obtained from industry. This results in a growing agricultural surplus that can be used to support people not working in the sector. Since fewer people now need to be employed in this sector, there is now excess supply of labour for the manufacturing sector.[1] Growth therefore implies that the agricultural sector will decline in importance (in proportionate terms) and that the industrial sector will grow.

In reality, of course, the shift towards an industrial structure as incomes increase is never so spontaneous. It requires investment in industries and often some government involvement. In the absence of this, the labour shed from agriculture will simply form a large pool of rural and urban workers in the informal sector. What is also not clear from such analyses is the direction of causation: does growth cause a shift towards manufacturing, or does the shift towards industry cause growth? We will consider this question later on in this chapter.

Structural change towards the industrial sector can be measured by looking at changes in the composition both of output and of employment. Between 1970 and 1993 there was an increase in the share of manufacturing and services in GDP relative to the share of agriculture in most developing countries (see table 2.1). At the same time, there was stagnation or a decline in the share of manufacturing in the medium- and high-income economies, though there was an increase in the share of productive services in these economies. The composition of employment is also often seen to reflect structural change. It can, however, provide a different picture than the composition of output if production in the manufacturing sector is capital-intensive, and therefore employment growth in manufacturing is slower than output growth.

Benefits of industrialization

What are the implications of such a shift in the structure of the economy? Why does industrialization usually accompany growth? Classical economists like Smith and Ricardo first pointed to the potential for increasing returns in manufacturing[2] arising from the increased possibilities for specialization and division of labour in this sector. Such division of labour enables increased productivity in manufacturing. Since then, the potential for *dynamic* returns to scale, arising from learning by doing and technological improvements in manufacturing has been highlighted.

In addition to the returns to scale arguments, industrialization is often seen as beneficial for growth and development because industry exhibits greater externalities and longer linkages than agriculture. Externalities are effects created by individual producers (or consumers) that have repercussions on other producers or consumers but are not reflected in cost and revenue (Weiss, 1990). Thus, an increase in the production of one firm may give rise to additional profits in another firm if the latter uses the products of the former as inputs (and the former benefits from increasing returns to scale). Similarly, increased production by firms will also cause an increase in profits amongst firms supplying inputs to them.[3] Linkages, in their turn, can be defined as an inducement to activity on the part of one enterprise created by the actions of another (Weiss, 1990, p. 98). More commonly, however, they are seen simply as a series of production relationships. Hirschman (1958) first suggested ways of measuring this by taking the ratio of total value of purchases from (or sales to) other branches to the value of total production. He concluded that 'agriculture certainly stands convicted on the count of its lack of direct stimulus to the setting up of new activities through linkage effects' (Hirschman, 1958, quoted by Weiss, 1990, p. 101). Yotopoulos and Nugent (1973) estimated linkages for developed and developing countries, and found that most forms of manufacturing show greater linkage potential than other major economic activities (agriculture and services).

Linkages also imply that, sooner or later, an increase in agricultural productivity will itself require an increase in manufactured inputs like machinery and fertilizers. In addition, as we will see below, manufacturing helps to increase agricultural productivity by absorbing excess labour in agriculture and because technical progress in manufacturing trickles down to agriculture through capital goods and other inputs (another example of linkages).

Structural change: intra-sectoral shifts in composition

We have so far concentrated on inter-sectoral shifts in composition. It is clear, however, that growth and development also cause intra-sectoral shifts. Economies typically begin with production in labour-intensive, raw material processing industries like food processing. These industries develop first because they have low capital, technology and skill requirements, and therefore can be easily set up in developing countries. Demand for their output is also always likely to exist. In addition, these industries help to increase the value added of primary products by decreasing volume, increasing shelf-life (by canning, for instance) and, consequently, decreasing the costs of transport. Over time, however, growth will involve a shift towards other industries (often in the consumer goods sectors) where technology and capital requirements remain low (like soaps, textiles or toys). In the final stage, an economy will shift towards capital-intensive final and intermediate products, and then towards high-technology products like electronics. In fact, the latter (electronics) are now being produced at earlier stages of development through a simple assembly-line process whereby inputs are imported and assembled in the country, and the output is exported. Such production, which is common in Malaysia and Thailand, has been criticized as leading to 'shallow industrialization' by writers like Lall (1996). The shift from low- to high-level manufactures can be seen in a number of countries in East Asia, including Japan and South Korea, and now China. Such structural change is seen as a necessary prerequisite for development, because the diversified industrial structure that it results in is seen as necessary for long-run growth.

Once again, however, the direction of causation is moot. Does a shift towards capital-intensive production cause growth? This underlies the Socialist push for heavy industrial production in Russia and Eastern Europe, as also the emphasis on capital-intensive production in many developing countries like India, which were influenced by the Feldman–Mahalanobis model (Mahalanobis, 1953). On the other hand, it is possible that growth itself enables such a shift. Writers who subscribe to this view argue that structural shifts are best left to the market, and will occur automatically as development progresses.

Socio-cultural consequences of structural change

Structural change towards industry involves not simply a change in the structure of production, but also attendant changes in employment, the location of such employment, and therefore the spatial context in which people live. It involves a shift from a relatively rural, subsistence and often barter-based economy towards an urban, commercial, marketized economy. Industrial production is usually concentrated in regions close to raw material sources, labour pools or markets. Industries also benefit from external economies of scale. All these factors mean that industrial production goes hand in hand with urbanization. Thus, a structural shift in production towards industry is accompanied by rural–urban migration and increasing urbanization.

Such urbanization, together with the commercialization involved in industrial employment, also results in cultural change. The modernization theorists comment on this when they maintain that development (or industrialization) requires a change from sentiment towards rationality and from communitarianism towards individuality. We will consider these changes in more detail in chapter 11.

The process of structural change: the two-sector models

The shift from agriculture towards industry that was described earlier was first formalized by Lewis (1954), and later extended by Fei and Ranis (1964) and Jorgenson (1967). Lewis (1954) put forward a simple dual-economy model with two sectors – the modern exchange sector and an indigenous subsistence sector. The modern sector uses reproducible capital and pays capitalists for its use, while the subsistence sector uses non-reproducible capital. Lewis assumes that the subsistence sector has an unlimited supply of labour, so that the marginal product of labour (MPL^4) in this sector is very small, zero or at least below the subsistence wage. Since the marginal product of labour first increases and then decreases, moving people out of agriculture may actually increase labour productivity in this sector and, along with it, wages. If this is the case, then the industrial sector can grow alongside the subsistence (agricultural) sector.

In the Lewis model, the agricultural sector faces decreasing returns, because there are too many people working within it (over-employment), given the amount of land and capital available. The industrial sector, on the other hand, faces increasing marginal product of labour as it still has insufficient labour. The model relies on this distinction to conclude that a transfer of workers from agriculture to industry is mutually beneficial, and will result in increased growth overall.

The Lewis model was criticized on a number of grounds. First, it did not pay adequate attention to the seasonality of labour requirements in agriculture. Excess labour in the off-peak periods becomes inadequate labour during peak times (for example, harvests). Transferring labour to the industrial sector would leave farmers with an inadequate labour supply during peak times. If this is the case, one can no longer assume that productivity in agriculture will increase or remain unchanged when labour shifts out. Extending this criticism, a decrease in the rate of growth of agriculture could result in bottle-necks to growth overall. Secondly, the Lewis model was criticized for underestimating the impact of growing populations on the agricultural surplus. Third, if wages in industry grow fast, then there would be a decrease in profits, which may halt the absorption of labour prematurely. Fourth, industry and agriculture require labour with substantially different skills, and therefore the transfer of labour from agriculture to industry is neither easy nor costless. Finally, the model assumes that the marginal propensity to save of capitalists is close to one – that is, capitalists save all increases in income – which need not be true. Capitalists may consume their incomes or even transfer them abroad (as has happened in many Latin American countries) rather than invest at home.

Extensions of the Lewis model by Fei and Ranis (1964) tried to take some of these criticisms into account. They emphasized that the agricultural sector must grow in line with industry if the transfer mechanism is not to halt. They therefore stress balanced growth, and maintain that the rate of labour absorption needs to be greater than the rate of population growth.

Industrialization and growth

Thus, the shift of an economy from agriculture to industry has formed the basis of much development theorizing. However, in an empirical context, the extent to which this structural shift influences growth or is influenced by it remains debatable.

Table 2.1 indicates that in 1970, the relationship between the level of income and proportion of income in manufacturing (or even industry) was positive: the higher the income level, the larger the proportion of GDP contributed by manufacturing. By 1993, however, the relationship is less clear. Looking at the cross-country pattern for 1970, we note that while in the USA, 34 per cent of GDP was produced by industry, the proportion was not very different in Peru (32 per cent), Brazil (38 per cent) or China (38 per cent). This (together with the fact that the contribution of industry to GDP decreased in most of the high-income economies between 1970 and 1993) might reflect the fact that many economies in North America and Western Europe are reaching the limits of their industrialization (and are even de-industrializing[5]), while many middle-income economies in the world are still industrializing. In the former, therefore, a large proportion of employment and GDP is provided by employment in highly productive (financial and commercial) services. While services play an important role in developing countries too, service sector employment here tends to be relatively unproductive, subsistence-type employment.

While the cross-country pattern is obscured by each country being at a different stage of development, it is clear that the role of manufacturing increased between 1970 and 1993 in all the low-income economies. Thus, the proportion of GDP produced in the industrial sector increased in every low-income economy except Kenya and Zambia between 1970 and 1993. The proportion of GDP contributed by manufacturing, as opposed to industry, is lower,[6] though again, it is increasing in most of the

Table 2.1   Sectoral shift across countries

Country	Industrial output (% of GDP)		Manufacturing output (% of GDP)	
	1970	1993	1970	1993
Low income (excl. India and China)	28	35	19	25
India	22	27	15	17
Kenya	20	18	12	10
Pakistan	22	25	16	17
China	38	48	30	38
Zambia	55	36	10	23
Indonesia	19	39	10	22
Peru	32	43	20	21
Thailand	25	39	16	28
Upper-middle income	38	—	25	—
Brazil	38	37	29	20
Malaysia	25	—	12	—
Argentina	44	31	32	20
Korea	29	43	21	29
High income	38	—	28	—
UK	45	33	33	25
France	—	29	—	22
Germany	49	38	38	27
USA	34	—	25	—
Japan	47	41	36	24

Source: Data from World Bank, 1995. From *World Development Report*, 1995, by World Bank, © 1995 by The International Bank for Restructuring and Development/ The World Bank. Used by permission of Oxford University Press, Inc.

low-income economies. In the upper-middle income category, however, the experiences seem to vary, with Korea experiencing an increase in the contribution of industry, while Brazil and Argentina have experienced decreases. All the high-income economies, including Japan, have experienced a decrease in the proportion of GDP contributed by industry. Many countries in the latter category have reached the stage of de-industrialization (Singh, 1977), and their services sector is now gaining ground.

The different patterns revealed by the cross-country statistics and the time-series figures highlight the fact that while there seems to be some relationship between the proportion of GDP contributed by the industrial sector and the level of income of an economy, the causality is not very clear. Is there a relationship between industrialization and growth? If so, does industrialization lead to the growth of an economy, or does growth result in a shift towards a more industrial structure? We have already seen that a shift towards an industrial structure often seems to lead to growth, because industries have higher productivity levels, are more dynamic and more innovative, and have longer linkages than most other sectors of the economy. On the other hand, industrialization requires investment, which can be more easily financed in a growing economy. In fact, it is becoming increasingly clear that the levels of investment required for industry to be successful and efficient are unlikely to be available in poor and slow-growing economies. Growth, therefore, is becoming increasingly necessary for industrialization. A breakthrough in this cycle is likely only if external finance in the form of foreign aid, or foreign direct investment (see chapter 8) becomes available.

benefits of industr [handwritten marginal note]

It is hard to be conclusive in the face of such evidence. Whatever the causality, much of the above discussion and most development policy assumes that industrialization is a 'good' that governments would do much to achieve. Over the last three decades, however, opponents of industrialization have gained ground. Many of these writers are concerned about the over-exploitation of natural resources and the sustainability of such industrialization in the long run (see chapter 6). Other writers highlight the pollution and environmental degradation caused by industrialization. In parallel with those making these arguments are those who point to the rapid urbanization and attendant poverty and inequalities that accompany industrialization (chapter 11), and to the alienation of individuals (through the breakdown of social networks). These arguments were first put forward during the Industrial Revolution in Britain, but they are equally relevant to developing countries today.

In spite of these dissenting voices, the necessity for industrialization has been widely accepted in practice (Singh, 1979). It is accepted that the

Table 2.2   Growth rates by region

Region	Growth of GDP (% p.a.)		Growth of industry (% p.a.)		Growth of exports (% p.a.)	
	1980–90	1990–95	1980–90	1990–95	1980–90	1990–95
Sub-Saharan Africa	1.7	1.4	0.6	0.2	1.9	2.5
East Asia and the Pacific	7.6	10.3	8.9	15.0	8.8	13.9
South Asia	5.7	4.6	6.9	5.3	6.4	11.9
Europe and Central Asia	2.3	−6.5	—	—	—	—
Middle East and North Africa	0.2	2.3	1.1	—	—	—
Latin America and Caribbean	1.7	3.2	1.4	2.5	5.4	7.0

Source: Data from World Bank, 1997b. From *World Development Report*, 1997, by World Bank, © 1997 by The International Bank for Restructuring and Development/ The World Bank. Used by permission of Oxford University Press, Inc.

'success' stories in developmental terms are the countries of East Asia, which have experienced the highest rates of growth of GDP and also the fastest transformation into industrial economies. While growth rates are 15 per cent per annum in East Asia and 5.3 per cent in South Asia, they are approximately 2.5 per cent in Latin America and close to 0 per cent in sub-Saharan Africa (see table 2.2). In this context, the desirability of the East Asian growth model is rarely questioned. However, the components of this model have caused considerable disagreement, particularly over the strategies that were adopted for industrialization. Should growth be balanced or unbalanced? Should it be capital- or labour-intensive, encourage primary processing or secondary industries, capital goods or consumer goods, be import substituting or export promoting? The position taken on each of these questions depends upon the ideology of the policy-makers. Thus, structuralists are in favour of government involvement in the economy and in government planning, while neo-liberals oppose such involvement and place greater reliance on the market. We will consider these choices in a little more detail in what follows.

types of industr.. [handwritten marginal note]

Industrialization strategies

Prior to decisions regarding the strategies to be adopted for industrialization is the decision regarding whether governments should be involved in making such choices or whether all such choices and decisions are best left to the market. As mentioned earlier, this is the subject of much passionate debate in the development arena, and is considered in more detail time and again throughout this book. In this section, however, we will assume that the government makes the necessary strategic choice, as was (and to a large extent still is) the case in much of the developing world. Armstrong (1987) in his study of Canada, Australia and Argentina concluded that a successful national strategy of industrialization required 'the ability of the sovereign state, in collaboration with a powerful industrial class, to control and promote the conditions of growth' (quoted in Griffin, 1989, p. 102). Chang (2002), in a detailed study of institutions and policies adopted by the developed countries historically, concludes that the UK and the USA, which today are 'paragons of free-trade and free-market policies, were the most ardent users of such (non-free trade and free market) policies in the earlier stages of their development' (Chang, 2002, abstract). The strategic role of the state in encouraging industrialization and industrial competitiveness has also been emphasized by Sercovich et al. (1999), who provide examples from East Asia and Brazil to support their argument.

If industrialization is not a natural, spontaneous process but is to be encouraged, then the state has to make a number of strategic decisions regarding the industries in which to invest scarce resources, the types of technology and scale to encourage, the extent of balance to push for, and the extent of trade to permit or encourage. These issues have been widely reviewed in the industrialization literature, and will only be touched on here. Many governments, following in the footsteps of the centrally planned economies, attempted to do this through their regular (five- or seven-year) plans.

Chenery and Elkington (1979) classified countries on the basis of their *avowed* strategies. Thus, Algeria, Iran, Iraq and Tanzania planned to develop through primary product specialization, while Brazil, Chile, India and Mexico went in for import-substituting industrialization. Countries like Pakistan, Hong Kong and South Korea planned to specialize in industry, while Greece, Peru and South Africa went in for balanced industrialization. Of course, such classifications change over time. Many plans are not realized because circumstances change. Thus, while Malaysia may have intended to specialize in primary production in the 1960s and 1970s, it would today be classed as a country specializing in industrial production. A more detailed consideration of the issues involved in choices like these follows.

Table 2.3   The Chenery classification of development strategies[a]

Primary specialization	Balanced development/ import substitution	Other balanced	Industrial specialization
Algeria	Argentina	Costa Rica	Egypt
Bolivia	Brazil	El Salvador	Hong Kong
Dominican Republic	Chile	Greece	Israel
Indonesia	Colombia	Guatemala	Kenya
Iran	Ecuador	Ireland	Lebanon
Iraq	Ghana	Jamaica	Pakistan
Ivory Coast	India	Morocco	Portugal
Malaysia	Mexico	Peru	Singapore
Nicaragua	Turkey	Philippines	South Korea
Nigeria	Uruguay	South Africa	Taiwan
Saudi Arabia		Spain	Tunisia
Sri Lanka		Syria	Yugoslavia
Tanzania		Thailand	
Venezuela			
Zambia			

[a] This is dated information but helps us see what was expected of these countries as opposed to what has actually transpired. Thus, though Malaysia was categorized as a primary specialization country in 1979, it is one of the South-East Asian Tiger economies and as such has industrialized at a very fast rate, though there is considerable disagreement about the depth of such industrialization (Lall, 1996). *Source*: From Chenery and Elkington, 1979, pp. 30–3: 'Table 1.3, pp. 30–33', from *Structural Change and Development Policy*, edited by H. B. Cheney and H. Elkington, © 1979 by the International Bank for Reconstruction and Development. Used by permission of Oxford University Press, Inc.

Choice of industry

Countries have a choice as regards the products they wish to produce. As seen in table 2.3, they can choose to specialize in primary products, industrial production, or a combination of the two. Many developing countries have a 'comparative advantage' in producing primary products (through agriculture and mining).[7] As can be seen from table 2.3, oil-producing countries like Saudi Arabia, Iran and Iraq, as well as countries like the Ivory Coast, Tanzania and Zambia put forward policies to encourage primary product specialization. In this context, industrialization has often meant the processing of primary products, a logical step up from simply producing primary products. Even quite basic processing of food products, raw materials or minerals adds considerable value to the exports and reduces bulk and therefore transportation costs. It can usually also be done with very limited technology. However, the growth of such processing is limited by the output of the primary sector. Further growth would require broader industrialization.

An industrialization strategy based on heavy industries (capital and intermediate goods) was formalized by the Socialist planners. Beginning with a closed economy in which capital goods could not be imported, Mahalanobis built a model in which the capital goods sector was the driver of growth in the future (Mahalanobis, 1953). Such a strategy was considered to be particularly effective, because heavy goods industries have longer linkages than most other industries. They use the outputs of other industries as intermediate inputs, while their final output is used as capital goods inputs into other industries. Convinced by these arguments, Indian planners in the 1950s consciously opted for a heavy industrialization strategy (Chakravarty, 1987).[8] It is worth noting, however, that in open economies capital goods could be imported, so that the conclusion of the Mahalanobis model would be invalid. But in this case, countries may end up with a higher import bill than their export earnings could pay for. This would lead us to the Prebisch argument (see chapter 5) for industrialization.

In many developing countries, though, a heavy industrialization strategy of this kind is not feasible, because it is capital-intensive and requires large domestic markets to be successful. Even in India, the inadequacy of the domestic market for many products resulted in substantial under-utilization of capacity in many industries. In South Korea, the government took additional steps to develop heavy industry in the early 1970s, because increasing wages had decreased her competitiveness in labour-intensive products. In many countries, the heavy industrial sector was developed to help the needs of defence. Whatever the reasons for its development, the survival of these sectors often requires the export of their output, which, in turn, requires a highly efficient and competitive industry (see chapter 7).

Thus, the choice between primary goods processing and heavy industries is not straightforward. Specializing in consumer goods industries is often seen as an intermediate, more viable option. Consumer goods industries are easier to enter into, as there is latent domestic demand for the output of these industries. Additionally, the volume of investment required in these industries is smaller than in heavy industry, and the technology is simpler. Many countries in Latin America opted for consumer goods-based industrialization in the early stages of their import-substituting policies. However, many of these industries soon faced problems, because they required the import of capital goods from abroad and were constrained by the limits of the domestic market. Early Indian planners rejected this strategy, because they feared that consumer goods-based industrialization would highlight the divide between the 'haves' and the 'have-nots', leading to social and political problems.

Choice of scale and technology

Associated with decisions regarding the choice of industry are decisions regarding the scale at which to operate and the technology to employ. Should production in small units be encouraged? Or are larger units more efficient? Should a labour- or a capital-intensive technology be used? Discussion of these issues has been encapsulated in the 'small is beautiful' and the appropriate technology views. Since they are closely related, we will discuss them together in this section.

The idea of appropriate technology was comprehensively articulated by Schumacher (1973) in his book *Small is Beautiful*. Schumacher traced the idea back to Gandhi and his advocacy of hand-loom textiles in India. Appropriate technology has come to embody the ideals of self-reliance and the rejection of materialism and of the technico-economic values of developed countries. It is closely related to the notion of sustainable development today.

In practical terms, adherence to appropriate technology implies the use of labour-intensive techniques in a labour-abundant economy and the use of capital-intensive techniques in a capital-abundant, labour-scarce economy. Even though this may seem logical, many developing countries use less labour-intensive techniques than their factor endowments would permit, for a number of reasons. First, capital is often substituted for skilled labour, because the latter is harder to develop and import than the former. In many developing countries, government subsidies and the activities of trade unions increase wages above market-clearing levels. Labour costs therefore increase relative to capital, leading to a decrease in the labour intensity of production in these countries. The World Bank (1983) examined a sample of thirty-one countries to consider the extent of such distortions in six markets (foreign exchange, labour, capital, manufacturing, agriculture and public utilities). Countries like

South Korea, Thailand and Malaysia revealed a low degree of distortion; India, Brazil and Mexico a medium degree, and Pakistan, Argentina and Peru a high degree of distortion.[9] Second, the relatively low productivity of labour in many developing countries implies that even with low wage rates, wage costs per unit of output remain high. These factors lead enterprises in developing countries to employ more capital-intensive techniques of production than are warranted purely by their resource endowments. Appropriate technology, though accepted in rhetoric, has not led to the adoption of more labour-intensive modes of production.

Opponents of appropriate technology argue that the use of more capital-intensive technologies increases growth rates. Dobb (1955, p. 149) claimed, for instance, that 'the same grounds which would justify a high rate of investment . . . would justify also a high degree of capital intensity in the choice of investment forms, and vice versa!' The adoption of labour-intensive techniques involves a larger share of output being paid out as wages as compared to profits. Assuming that the marginal propensity to consume out of wages is higher than that out of profits, an increase in the share of wages in national output will decrease the volume of savings, and therefore will decrease funds available for investment. Though this argument is commonly advanced in favour of capital-intensive production, it is dependent on a number of stringent assumptions: a constant wage in the industrial sector, all profits being saved and all wages being consumed, consumption being unproductive, and the government lacking the ability to tax and subsidize labour, amongst others. Relaxing these assumptions, Thirlwall concludes that 'labour can be substituted for capital, provided co-operating factors are available, without the level of output being impaired' (Thirlwall, 1994, p. 236).

Globalization (see chapter 7) has also dampened down the arguments in favour of intermediate technologies. To begin with, a larger proportion of production is accounted for by transnational corporations (TNCs), which use similar technology in all the countries in which they produce. There is also more intra-firm trade, so that all branches of a TNC use the same inputs. Jenkins (1992a) gives the example of Ford cars. In the 1960s, the Ford Cortina was a British car, designed in Britain for the British market and produced using British components, albeit by an American firm. In the 1980s, however, the Ford Escort used parts from fourteen countries other than Britain. It was produced for the international market, at a number of different locations within Ford's global operations. Only the final assembly took place in Britain.

Secondly, with most research and development being undertaken in the capital-rich, labour-scarce Western economies, new technology is more likely to be labour-saving. International competition and the need for efficiency, together with the reliance on imported capital goods, have reinforced the tendency to use the most up-to-date technology (usually labour-saving) even in labour-rich developing countries. In general, therefore, the capital intensity of production in developed and developing countries is very similar for similar products. Capital intensity varies across countries largely because the composition of final output differs between these countries, rather than because the technology used to produce similar goods varies across countries.

Thus, while the scale and technology of production must depend upon domestic resource endowments, they are increasingly influenced by the extent to which domestic industries compete with exports and imports – that is, by the extent of outward orientation. We will therefore consider this choice next.

Choice of outward orientation

In the 1950s, many developing countries opted for import-substituting industrialization (ISI), which, as the name suggests, is industrialization that attempts to substitute domestic production for imports. Here, the domestic market is protected for domestic firms through tariffs and taxes on imports. Decisions regarding the extent of outward orientation have therefore long been at the centre of industrialization strategies, and have influenced the path adopted towards industrialization in different countries.

Table 2.3 shows that a number of countries in Latin America, as well as India, Ghana and Turkey, planned to develop through import-substituting industrialization. By the late 1960s, however, many countries were disillusioned with ISI. This was because they had either reached the limits of their domestic markets (which were small) or because, having substituted imported consumer goods with domestic production, they were unable to do the same with more technology-intensive capital and intermediate goods industries. Imports of this technology or the capital goods that embodied this technology required foreign exchange that could only be earned through exports. Many economies have therefore had to move towards export promotion or a neutral export environment through structural adjustment policies. In fact, the experience of the East Asian economies has led to a wider acceptance of the view that ISI should be used only as the first stage in a process leading towards export-led growth. The issues involved in this choice and the history behind it are discussed in more detail in chapter 7.

Choice of balance

The debate regarding balanced versus unbalanced growth was especially strong in the 1950s and 1960s. On the one hand, there were those who felt that, given the scarcity of resources, investment should be targeted towards a few narrow sectors based on priorities (Hirschman, 1958). These sectors would then become 'growth centres', or nodes. But critics argued that such unbalanced growth could give rise to bottle-necks in the economy. Thus, if industry is prioritized, then there may be food and raw materials bottle-necks in agriculture, and if capital goods industries are prioritized over intermediate or consumer goods, then there may be bottle-necks in the latter sectors, which would threaten growth. To avoid such bottle-necks, Nurkse (1953) advocated balanced growth, which involved spreading resources over a wide range of sectors. This was criticized on the grounds that spreading resources so thinly might decrease their effectiveness. This debate has never been resolved, with most countries following the dictates of their resource constraints and of political expediency to decide on the sectors that are to be supported at any point in time. Thus, we will see in chapter 10 that though China began by concentrating on heavy industry, it could not continue this strategy for long, given the large proportion of its population that was dependent on agriculture. It therefore shifted to a strategy of 'walking on two legs' – industry and agriculture – under Mao (Singh, 1979, p. 589). The Soviet Union, as well as many East European economies, on the other hand, continued their concentration on heavy industry until their breakdown in the 1980s.

Conclusion

This chapter has discussed the changes caused by growth and development in an economy. It highlights the structural shift of an economy towards industry, and within industry towards more sophisticated manufactures. However, as for many other processes in development, the precise causality between industrialization and growth is not clear. There are many reasons to argue that industrialization leads to growth. But equally, industrialization requires resources, which are more likely to be available in fast-growing economies. This is therefore only the first of many examples of circular causality in development that I mentioned in the Introduction.

The chapter also picked up on the possible role played by the state and by trade in such structural change, and therefore development. Thus, the discussion of the choices made with regard to industrialization, technology, openness to trade, and balance was predicated on the fact that the state makes these choices. Countries have varied considerably regarding the choices they have made and the paths they have chosen to follow. These choices are also being adapted in the context of increasing global interaction in the first quarter of the twenty-first century. Nevertheless, industrialization has tended to accompany growth and development in most economies. It has also resulted in many other socio-economic changes, like rural–urban migration, urbanization and industrial employment, which will be discussed in Part IV of this book.

3

Growth, Distribution and Equity

As seen in the previous chapters, early development writers expected growth to trickle down to achieve the end objective of development – an improvement in general living standards. Over time, however, it became clear that the trickle-down was very limited. This led to a shift from a 'growth first, then redistribute' strategy towards a 'redistribution with growth' strategy, and finally to a basic human needs strategy, associated with an increasing emphasis on ends rather than means. Today, it is widely accepted that economic growth is necessary, but not sufficient, for development. It is necessary because it permits an increase in incomes and living standards without encroaching on the incomes of others. But it is not sufficient because equality (or its subjective counterpart, equity) is required if households and individuals are to benefit from growth.

The relationship between growth and equity, then, is central to development. Once again, the basis for much debate in development is whether growth leads to equity or equity influences growth. In this chapter, we will consider this two-way relationship in more detail before looking at poverty. The Millennium Development Goals (MDGs) of the United Nations have brought poverty back into focus at the centre of the development agenda. We will consider them in some detail. Before we do so, however, we will consider the measurement of inequality.

Income inequality across the world

Equity implies a relatively equal distribution of income/consumption/assets across all individuals in society. But it involves a judgement regarding whether certain individuals need or deserve more or less than others. It therefore carries with it implications for a fair or just distribution of income. Equality, on the other hand, implies quantitatively equal distribution of income/consumption assets. In spite of this difference, the two concepts are often used interchangeably because of problems relating to making judgements about what is fair or just. Before we can consider equity or its relationship with growth, we therefore need to consider how it is measured.

The size distribution of income shows the proportion of income received by people at different levels of income (usually classified in terms of quartiles, quintiles or deciles). In some cases, the income distribution is inferred from the distribution of consumption because the latter, it is felt, provides a more accurate measure of income. This is because it takes subsistence production, barter, subsidies, loans etc. into account and these can be quite significant in developing countries.

These data are often presented graphically using a Lorenz Curve. A Lorenz Curve plots the proportion of income received by the poorest x per cent of individuals against x itself. Since complete equality requires that x per cent of individuals receive x per cent of income, the Lorenz Curve reflecting this would be a diagonal (45 degree line). The closer the Lorenz Curve is to the diagonal in figure 3.1, the more equal is the income distribution. It is, therefore, possible to compare two income distributions using Lorenz Curves. However, if two Lorenz Curves cross each other, then such a simple comparison is no longer possible. Another disadvantage of the Lorenz Curve is that it does not provide a summary measure of income inequality, which is often required when comparing a range of countries to each other.

The Gini coefficient (derived from the Lorenz Curve) is a convenient, summary measure of inequality. It is simply the ratio of the area A in figure 3.1 to the area A + B. The larger the area A, the higher the Gini coefficient will be. If the income distribution is absolutely equal, then the area A is 0, and the Gini coefficient is also 0. While the Gini coefficient provides us with an easy-to-use, summary measure of inequality, it is also a problematic measure if the Lorenz Curves cross. In such cases, it is possible for the same Gini coefficient to result from two very different distributions. The Gini coefficient is also insensitive to changes in the distribution, especially for low-income groups, because its reference point – perfect equality – is very limited.

Table 3.1 provides information on inequality prevailing in both high- and low-inequality countries. The measure used here is the proportion of income held by the poorest and richest quintiles. The table indicates that in the high-inequality countries, the richest 20 per cent of the population have more than 60 per cent of the total income, while the poorest 20 per cent have less than 3 per cent of the income. But in the low-inequality countries like the Czech and Slovak republics, Austria and Japan, the

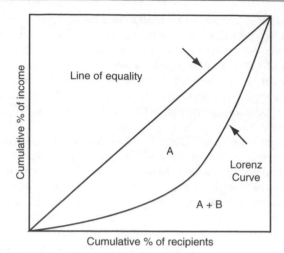

Figure 3.1   Lorenz Curve

Table 3.1   Share of income (per cent) of the poorest and richest 20 per cent of populations

High-inequality countries	Lowest 20%	Richest 20%	Gini coefficient	Low-inequality countries	Lowest 20%	Richest 20%	Gini coefficient
Honduras	1.6	61.8	53.7	Slovak Republic	11.9	31.4	19.5
Bolivia	1.9	61.8	42.0	Japan	10.6	35.7	24.9
Paraguay	1.9	60.7	59.1	Austria	10.4	33.3	23.1
Brazil	2.6	63.0	60.0	Czech Republic	10.3	35.9	25.4
Swaziland	2.7	63.4	—	Bulgaria	10.0	36.8	28.3

Source: Data from World Bank, 2001. From *World Development Report*, 2001, by World Bank, © 2001 by The International Bank for Restructuring and Development/ The World Bank. Used by permission of Oxford University Press, Inc.

income distribution is much more equitable. Here, the richest 20 per cent of the population have between 30 and 36 per cent of the income, while the poorest 20 per cent have between 10 and 12 per cent of the income. Looking at the Gini coefficients, we find that the lowest one is in the Slovak Republic, while the highest is in Brazil. The table presents a stark contrast across the world, with a large number of developing countries having very high levels of inequality. The relatively equitable income distributions in many ex-Socialist countries confirm that government policy is significant in determining income distributions.

A closer look at the world tables on inequality (World Bank, 2000/1) reveals that many developing countries suffer from very unequal distributions of income and consumption. The poor in developing countries lose out on two counts: they live in poor countries, and are poor in these countries. This distinguishes them from the poor in rich countries, and translates into differences in access to many basic needs. Thus, inequality in the UK may be socially and politically just as significant as inequality in Burkina Faso, but it is less likely to decrease people's chances of survival[1] than inequality in the latter. People's reaction to such inequality will depend upon the length of time that it takes for growth to trickle down to improved living standards. At the beginning of the growth process, the improvement in living standards of a few is likely to be greeted with some optimism by all concerned, as everyone hopes that their condition will also improve. However, if inequalities persist over time, such optimism vanishes, and can give way to considerable social and political unrest (Hirschman and Rothschild, 1973).

We have already argued that both growth and equity are required for development. The relationship between growth and equity is therefore crucial to our understanding of development, and we will look at this two-way relationship in the next section.

Growth and equity

As indicated at the beginning of this chapter, growth is of significance to development because it permits increased incomes without encroaching on the incomes of others. Equity is of significance to development because it ensures that a larger number of individuals and households benefit from these increased incomes. What is not clear, however, is the precise relationship between these two entities. Much debate within development has centred on this: does growth lead to equity, or is equity more likely to inhibit growth? In this section, we will consider the relationship between these variables.

Growth–inequality relationship

The effect of growth on inequality has received considerable attention in the literature because of its implications for improved living standards and poverty alleviation, the major objectives of development. The study of this relationship has been hamstrung, however, by the poor quality of the data. Kuznets (1955), in a seminal study analysing the changes in income distribution in the UK, Germany and the USA over a long period of time, found that the growth of per capita income is initially accompanied by increasing inequality, but is later associated with decreasing inequality. Kuznets rationalized this on the grounds that while the income distribution is relatively equal in the rural agricultural sector, it is relatively unequal in the urban, industrial sector. Over time, industrialization and growth result in a movement of individuals from the more equal agricultural sector to the less equal industrial sector. This causes an increase in inequality in the early stages of growth. It is only when the urban sector itself becomes more equitable, as the children of migrants adjust to city life, and as poorer urbanites become politically more powerful, that this pattern is reversed. Note that the inequality between the agricultural and industrial sector as well as the inequality within the industrial sector need to be taken into account. This was termed 'Kuznets's inverted-U hypothesis', and many studies since then have attempted to prove or disprove it.

some evidence

Ahluwalia (1976) analysed Kuznets's relationship for a sample of sixty countries, and found that the income share of all groups except the top 20 per cent tends to fall initially with an increase in per capita GNP, but increases beyond a certain point. The richest 20 per cent of individuals experience a reverse pattern, with income shares increasing first and then decreasing. Similarly, Chatterjee and Ravikumar (1997) found that economic growth benefits the wealthy faster than the poor, and Gaiha (1995) argued that it takes a long time for agricultural growth to trickle down to the rural poor.

But: problems e.g. availability of historical data

Most such tests of Kuznets's hypothesis, however, are problematic. The hypothesis is best tested using historical data over long periods of time, much as Kuznets did. However, for most developing countries such data are not available. Therefore, analysts resort to testing the hypothesis across countries. This makes the implicit (though questionable) assumption that because different countries are at different points of their development trajectories, they will together trace out the path that a single country would take over time. In addition, it has been found that the variance around any estimated Kuznets curve is greatest in the low- to middle-income ranges, and becomes much less in the upper-income range. This has generated much debate about the increase in inequality, and less concern about the decreases (Williamson, 1997, p. xxiii).

The significance of Kuznets's conjecture in the evolution of development theory and policy cannot be overestimated. It was provided with theoretical ballast by Lewis's surplus labour model, which was discussed in chapter 2. This model, which describes the shift in the structure of an economy towards industry, provides two reasons for an initial increase in inequality. First, as industrialization occurs, the share of income going to capitalists increases. Second, the inequality in the distribution of labour income also increases as workers move from the low-wage subsistence sector to the higher-wage industrial sector. This is because now, instead of all workers being poorly paid, some are paid well. Inequality in these terms arises as conditions improve for some individuals relative to others. This increase in inequality is finally halted when the labour surplus has been absorbed into the industrial sector and wages begin to increase in the subsistence sector too. We will see in the next section that the Lewis model emphasizes both sides of the growth–equity relationship.

More recently, however, writers like Fields (1980) have argued that part of Kuznets's relationship is caused by purely statistical factors. If growth increases the incomes of some individuals while leaving other incomes unchanged, then this will manifest itself as increased inequality. Thus, in a society of five individuals working in the agricultural sector and earning 100 units each, the income distribution is very equal. Now, if growth results in development and a transfer of one individual from agriculture to industry where she earns 200 units, then the income distribution in the first instance will be (100, 100, 100, 100, 200) – that is, there will be increased inequality. This increase in inequality will persist until everybody in agriculture has transferred to industry, and incomes in agriculture increase, giving an income distribution of (200, 200, 200, 200, 200).[2] While growth has caused increased inequality, the latter is related to improvements in living standards for some and no worsening for others. In this sense, it is a Pareto-improvement and must be distinguished from cases where some people become better off and others become much worse off. Fields (1991) also argues that inequality increases with growth in both low- and high-income countries, and that there is no tendency for inequality to increase more in the early stages of economic development than in later stages, as Kuznets suggested.

Whether the increased inequality that accompanies growth is purely statistical or is caused by growth, historical evidence also seems to suggest an inverted-U relationship between growth and inequality. Thus, in England, inequality certainly seems to have increased during the Industrial Revolution (see chapter 10). Across Europe and in the European-settled areas of the Americas and Australasia, income inequality reached a peak in the first decade of the twentieth century, and has since decreased because of a combination of increasing wages and redistributive policies.[3] Some researchers have found that if we allow for country-specific effects and move away from cross-sectional studies (which assume a similar pattern across countries), the inverted-U relationship breaks down. Thus, Ravallion (1995) finds that there is no systematic relationship between the Gini coefficient and mean income. He concludes that the 'impact (of growth) on inequality is so diverse that no systematic bivariate relationship can be detected' (p. 415).

Whatever the precise nature of the relationship, there is consensus regarding the fact that the downturn in inequality (or trickle-down) hypothesized by Kuznets, if left to itself, can take a very long time. From a practical point of view, therefore, it has long been accepted that government redistributive policies are required to encourage the spread of the benefits of growth. Fei, Ranis and Kuo (1979), in a study of Taiwan, found that it was government redistribution of land that helped improve the distribution of income, while Fishlow (1972), in his study of Brazil, found that government policies which emphasized secondary (over primary) school enrolments accounted for a large proportion of the increase in income inequality in Brazil.

Inequality in incomes and consumption also arises from inequality in a large number of other assets – human (labour and skills), land, access to infrastructure, savings and credit, as well as social assets (in the form of networks and access to contacts) (World Bank, 2000/1). The state can help to improve income distribution through taxation of incomes and redistributive policies, as well as through land reforms (see chapter 12), education (chapter 13), employment (chapter 14) and other policies. The role played by the state in determining the distribution of income (equal or unequal) in most developing countries is very significant.

One of the most important factors determining the relationship between growth and equity is the initial level of inequality in income distribution as well as the regional and sectoral composition of growth. If growth bypasses poor regions, and poor people cannot easily migrate to the growing regions, then it can cause increased inequality and poverty.

As indicated at the beginning of this chapter, the impact of growth on equity is only one aspect of this relationship. It leads us on to a number of related questions. Is an equitable distribution desirable in itself? Might it also have a beneficial effect on growth? Or is it more likely to hinder growth as was initially suggested?

Inequality–growth relationship

The Harrod–Domar model of growth (see chapter 4), and many others since, have emphasized the significance of savings in initiating growth. But savings accrue only when there are at least a few people whose incomes are greater than their consumption. In fact, in this context, some inequality has historically been seen as beneficial, because it enables the rich to save and invest. A more equal income distribution may mean that everyone has just enough income to finance consumption, resulting in fewer savings and therefore slower growth.

Early development literature, therefore, was caught in a dilemma. Should it advocate greater inequality as a way of increasing growth and incomes? The Lewis model did. In his model of economic development with unlimited supplies of labour, Lewis highlights the two-way relationship between growth and equity. Inequality is not just a result of growth in this model, as we saw in the previous subsection; it is also necessary for growth. The more income that profit-earners receive, the more they invest, and the faster the economy grows. Here, Lewis has recourse to an increase in the marginal propensity to save of the high-income groups rather than to an increase in the share of profits in total income. According to this model, attempts at premature redistribution of income will therefore stifle growth. There is some evidence (Partridge, 1997) that higher income inequality between regions within a country does result in increased growth.

More recent evidence, however, seems to suggest that this need not be the case. Taiwan and South Korea both grew very fast, but had relatively equal income distributions to begin with, in 1945, compared to other countries at similar levels of income. Intuitively, there are many reasons why greater inequality may not result in increased savings and growth. First, the rich in developing countries (often rural landlords) are much more likely to indulge in conspicuous consumption. Therefore, greater inequality in these countries will not necessarily lead to an increase in savings and investment. It is also possible that the rich may invest or transfer their savings abroad. Secondly, low income levels amongst the poor will decrease the mass demand for local produce (on the assumption that the rich are more likely than the poor to buy foreign goods), and therefore decrease growth. Thirdly, highly unequal income distributions create psychological and material disincentives to growth. Finally, and probably most importantly, low income levels will result in poor levels of health and education, which, in turn, will decrease the productivity of these groups and so lead to lower growth. Given the emphasis on the quality of human capital in new growth theories, this last factor is likely to be especially important. Redistribution, in the form of increased expenditure on health and education, will therefore improve both growth and equality.

The World Bank (2000/1) also rejects the trade-off between growth and equity on the grounds that unequal societies are more prone to difficulties in collective action, to political instability, propensity to populist redistributive policies, and greater volatility in policies – all of which can decrease growth (World Bank, 2000/1, p. 36). Also, if inequality in income coexists with imperfect credit markets, then poor people may be unable to invest in human and physical capital, which will further decrease growth in the long run, as seen above.

Testing the equity–growth relationship across countries, Alesina and Rodrik (1994) found that countries with greater income inequality experienced lower future growth. To explain this, Alesina and Perotti (1996) hypothesized that income inequality caused political instability, which, in turn, inhibited investment and therefore growth.

There is very little consensus in the empirical literature. It is clear that growth does not trickle down automatically. Governments must make attempts to decrease inequalities through redistributive policies. The new growth theories have taken the sting out of this suggestion by indicating that redistribution in the form of investment in health and education is likely to improve growth prospects rather than worsen them. Today, therefore, the debate has lost much of its urgency. It is increasingly being accepted that redistributive policies are necessary, and therefore that redistributive policies that emphasize the formation of human capital are most attractive from the point of view both of growth and of equity. In addition, much of the focus has shifted to addressing absolute poverty, and this is what we will consider in the next section.

Poverty

There is, of course, an obvious relationship between inequality and poverty. Poverty concerns people at the lower end of the inequality spectrum. Absolute poverty can be said to exist when people do not have the means with which to purchase adequate levels of food, clothing and shelter. Adequate levels, in turn, are debatable, and will differ from society to society. In addition, there is a relative dimension to poverty, whereby a person's poverty is judged relative to societal norms. Peter Townsend has defined poverty as a lack of the resources required to participate in activities and enjoy living standards that are customary in a society (Townsend, 1979, p. 31). Thus, in some societies a person may be considered poor if he or she is unable to watch television or take holidays, while in others the ability to do this may class the person as very well off. While the concept of relative poverty has been strongly attacked, it has also gained widespread acceptance in recent years. Thus, the World Bank uses a figure of US$14.40 per day (in 1985 PPP $s) as a cut-off point to calculate the numbers in poverty in industrialized countries, whereas it uses $1 per day for developing countries.

The concept of relative poverty is less appropriate for developing countries, where the numbers in absolute poverty are themselves very high. Absolute poverty is usually measured using 'poverty lines' which give a critical threshold level of income, consumption or expenditure on goods and services below which people are considered to be poor. Poverty lines are usually nutrition-based and relate to the amount of expenditure required to guarantee a minimum consumption of calories in each country.

One summary, but detailed, measure of poverty is the UNDP's Human Poverty Index (HPI), which has already been introduced in chapter 1. This index measures deprivation in the same dimensions as the human development index – longevity, knowledge and a decent standard of living. But whereas the HDI focuses on progress in the entire community, the HPI focuses on the poorest people. Longevity is measured as the proportion of people expected to die before 40 years of age, and knowledge by the proportion of adults who are illiterate. The standard of living measure is a composite of three variables – the proportion of people with access to health facilities and to safe drinking water and the proportion of children under 5 who are malnourished. According to the (1997) HPI rankings, Trinidad and Tobago, Cuba, Chile, Singapore and Costa Rica are at the top, with HPIs of less than 10 per cent; that is, human poverty has decreased in these countries to the point at which it affects less than 10 per cent of the population. At the other end of the scale are countries whose HPI exceeds 50 per cent – Niger, Sierra Leone, Burkina Faso, Ethiopia, Mali, Cambodia and Mozambique. The HPI has been calculated for both the developed and the developing countries. In the former, life expectancy below 60 years is substituted for the 40 years used for developing countries. In addition, instead of measures of health and educational achievements being part of the index, an income measure of living standards is included, together with a measure of unemployment (which allows for social exclusion).

Such summary measures of poverty, however, do not reflect the complicated ways in which poverty can manifest itself. Poverty may be temporary, for instance, and arise just before a harvest or in off-peak times in tourist areas. Or it may be chronic. A household may be above the poverty line, while some members within it may be consuming less than the minimum. Intra-household inequality must therefore be considered carefully. Women and the old tend to be discriminated against when allocating consumption within households (Kabeer, 1994).[4] Many studies also indicate a gender bias in educational and health provisions. Low female–male ratios in many Asian countries are seen to be a direct manifestation of such a bias.

Poverty indices are also only able to measure material deprivation. They are unable to measure wider notions of deprivation, including social exclusion. This has been defined as 'a process through which individuals or groups are wholly or partially excluded from full participation in the society in which they live' (European Foundation, 1995, p. 4). The notion of social exclusion is useful, because it allows for deprivation that may arise because of gender, ethnicity, caste, disability or health, rather than simply inadequacy of material endowments.

The 2000/1 *World Development Report* (*WDR*) further extends the definition of poverty to include vulnerability and exposure to risk, voicelessness and powerlessness. Thus, increased levels of vulnerability or risk because of ethnicity, gender, age or health are all included in this definition of poverty. This extends the 1990 *WDR* definition, which defined poverty as material deprivation together with low levels of achievement in education and health. It is accepted that each of these dimensions of poverty will interact with the others. Thus, improving health will improve well-being as well as income-earning potential. Similarly, improving education will improve health as well as income-earning potential (World Bank, 2000/1, p. 15). This extension takes the World Bank's definition of poverty beyond that of the UNDP.

Table 3.2 provides information on income poverty by region between 1987 and 1998. When looking at the share of population living on less than $1 a day, we note that the Middle East and North Africa perform best, with less than 2 per cent of people in this category. The worst

Table 3.2   Income poverty by region, 1987–1998

Region	% of population living on less than $1 a day				
	1987	1990	1993	1996	1998
East Asia and Pacific	26.6	27.6	25.2	14.9	15.3
Excluding China	23.9	18.5	15.9	10.0	11.3
Europe and Central Asia	0.2	1.6	4.0	5.1	5.1
Latin America and the Caribbean	15.3	16.8	15.3	15.6	15.6
Middle East and North Africa	4.3	2.4	1.9	1.8	1.9
South Asia	44.9	44.0	42.4	42.3	40.0
Sub-Saharan Africa	46.6	47.7	49.7	48.5	46.3
Total	28.3	29.0	28.1	24.5	24.0
Excluding China	28.5	28.1	27.7	27.0	26.2

Source: Data from World Bank, 2000/1, p. 23. From *World Development Report*, 2000/1, by World Bank, © 2000/1 by The International Bank for Restructuring and Development/The World Bank. Used by permission of Oxford University Press, Inc.

performer in 1998 was sub-Saharan Africa, with 46 per cent of people living on less than $1 per day, followed by South Asia with 40 per cent. The average across the world is 24 per cent. The table also indicates that while most regions have seen an improvement in this regard, Europe, Central Asia and sub-Saharan Africa saw increases over much of this period, whereas in Latin America this proportion stagnated.

With approximately 24 per cent of the world's population living on less than $1 a day, it is not surprising that poverty has returned to the centre of the development agenda. The United Nations published a set of Millennium Development Goals (MDGs) in 2000, which put forward the ambitious target of halving extreme world poverty by 2015. In addition, it suggested the following six goals (from *www.worldbank.org/data/dev/devgoals/html*):

1 *Poverty*: decrease by half the proportion of people living in extreme poverty.
2 *Mortality*: decrease by two-thirds the mortality rates of infants and children under 5 years, and by three-quarters, the mortality rates for mothers.
3 *Education*: achieve universal primary education in all countries.
4 *Health*: provide access to reproductive health services for all.
5 *Gender*: progress towards gender equality and the empowerment of women. This is to be done by eliminating gender disparities in primary and secondary education.
6 *Environment*: implement national strategies for sustainable development by 2005 to reverse the current loss of global resources by 2015.

The 1990 *World Development Report* highlights two basic actions for poverty reduction: policies to increase the productivity of labour and the provision of basic social services to the poor. In addition to this, the 2000/1 *WDR* also argues that 'attacking poverty requires promoting opportunity, facilitating empowerment and enhancing security – with actions at local, national and global levels' (World Bank, 2000/1, p. 37).

Conclusion

In this part of the book, I have argued that growth is a necessary though not sufficient condition for development. While some countries (like Sri Lanka, Costa Rica and Cuba) have better welfare provisions than their growth alone would suggest, this has arisen from a conscious redistribution of its benefits by the state. However, in most poor countries some growth is necessary if such benefits are to be financed. Given this, an understanding of what causes growth is a significant step. Theories of growth have all focused on an increase in savings and on the efficiency of capital. Improvements in the capital–output ratio require technical progress, and most new theories of growth consider this in more detail. Thus, improvements in both physical and human capital have become very significant.

Part II

Explaining Development

Part I of the book defined development, and considered the ways in which it can be measured as well as the changes required in a country as it develops. In Part II we will consider theories of development. Chapter 4 considers theories of growth. These theories concentrate on economic growth, abstracting from other dimensions of economic development – structural change and distributive equity. They emphasize the role of savings, investment and technical progress. Theories of growth have returned to centre stage since the 1980s, and the literature in this area is growing. In chapter 5, we go beyond growth to consider broader theories of development – Marxist theories and dependency and modernization theories. The 1960s saw a further interdisciplinary broadening of development theory. Writers within the sociological framework catalogued the idea that development requires a transition from a traditional to a modern state, requiring changes in attitudes (Lerner, 1964; McClelland, 1961) as well as in social and political institutions (Hoselitz, 1962; Apter, 1965; Myrdal, 1968). The Marxists, too, stressed the qualitative leaps that a society makes as internal contradictions manifest themselves. Finally, in chapter 6 we examine the disillusionment with development theorizing in the 1980s and the routes along which it has progressed. Specifically, we consider the roles of gender and the environment in development theorizing. All these theories highlight the centrality of the roles of the state and of trade in development theorizing, and we will point to this as we go along.

4

Theories of Growth

Once the first industrial nation had been born it provided the model to imitate for the rest of Europe (as well as her North American replica). Not to imitate would mean permanent dependence on the 'workshop of the world' and danger to the other nation-state projects. This basic dilemma was to be repeated more generally in the relation between the West and the decolonized world. In order to develop it was deemed necessary for the 'new nations' to imitate the Western model – it was a modernisation imperative.

Hettne, 1995

The growth, first of Britain and then of Europe (see chapter 10) gave rise to the view that growth would follow a predetermined path. Even Marxists agreed that 'the country that is more developed industrially only shows, to the less developed, the image of its own future' (Marx, 1867, preface, p. 1). The means used to achieve such growth (or development), however, could vary from country to country, though once growth became a project of the nation-state, the role of the state was clearly paramount. Thus, 'later developers' even within Europe witnessed more state intervention than Britain, while countries within the Soviet model were almost totally dominated by the state. Lucas highlights the role of the state in economic growth when he asks, 'Is there some action that a government of India could take that would lead the Indian economy to grow like Indonesia's or Egypt's?' (Lucas, 1988, p. 4). In the post-war period, industrialization, rapid capital accumulation, the mobilization of underemployed manpower, planning and an economically active state were identified as important strategic aspects of development (Sen, 1983).

Describing the components of such growth (through growth account-ing) and theorizing about the causes of growth have therefore been major preoccupations of economists, especially development economists. The-ories of growth have progressed from an emphasis on savings (Harrod–Domar (HD) model) to one on technical change (Solow) to an emphasis on activities leading to increasing returns to scale (the new growth theor-ies). On the empirical side, many studies of growth have used the so-called growth accounting framework, which attempts to decompose growth into its possible sources – land, labour, capital and technical change (which is usually seen as a residual). These empirical studies have concentrated on two main questions. First, to what extent is growth simply a result of increasing inputs, rather than improvement in the efficiency of use of these inputs (increased productivity)? Second, is it true to say that low-income economies have grown faster than high-income economies? If so, is there evidence of convergence in growth rates across the world? In this chapter, we will provide a brief introduction to the theoretical and empir-ical studies of growth before we consider broader theories of development in chapter 5.

Savings-led theories of growth

For an economy to grow, it must invest. To invest, it must save – that is, it must prevent resources from being used up in current consumption. The problem of growth is therefore a problem of how resources must be allocated over time (between present and future consumption). While consuming nothing today and investing everything for the future may maximize growth, it also defeats the purpose of growth – to maximize consumption in the long run. To an economist, therefore, the optimum growth rate is the one at which the additional sacrifice of current con-sumption is just worthwhile given the addition to future output that will be obtained by the extra investment. In such a calculation, society's preference as between present and future consumption needs to be taken into account (Beckerman, 1974, p. 19).[1]

This view of the sources of growth was first formalized by Harrod and Domar. They saw growth as a function of the ability of an economy to save and of the capital–output ratio.[2] According to their model, a high savings rate enables increased investment, and therefore leads to in-creased growth. Additionally, a low capital–output ratio implies more efficient investment, because each unit of capital is associated with more output. This seems intuitively plausible: savings generate invest-ment, and the greater the productivity of such investment, the more effective will savings be in generating growth. In this model, the capital–output (KO) ratio is determined exogenously,[3] and cannot be changed. As we will see in chapter 10, many countries (like China) have implicitly used a model of this kind to determine the level of investment they should aim for.

Rostow's (1960) model of an economy 'taking off' at a certain level of investment is based on such a theory. In his book *The Stages of Economic Growth: A Non-Communist Manifesto*, Rostow discusses development as a linear historical process consisting of five stages: traditional society, pre-conditions for take-off, take-off, drive to maturity, and the age of high mass consumption. The most significant stage, from the point of view of development, is take-off. This is interpreted as 'a period when the scale of productive economic activity reaches a critical level and produces changes which lead to a massive and progressive structural transformation in economies and societies of which they are a part, better viewed as changes in kind than merely in degree' (Rostow, 1960, p. 40). The three conditions required for take-off include:

- an increase in productive investment to more than 10 per cent of national income (this is based on the importance of investment within the Harrod–Domar model);
- development of one or more manufacturing sectors with a high rate of growth;
- the existence or quick emergence of a political, social and institutional framework that will reinforce the moves towards expansion in the modern sector.

Thus, take-off enables societies to progress from the traditional stage to a modern stage with high mass consumption. All of this can be done through the private sector and through markets. In practical terms, this approach gave rise to the notion that a massive dose of aid and foreign capital to less developed countries would enable them to get ready for take-off (chapter 9). Once this take-off occurred, aid would no longer be required.

The Rostow model provides only a summary description of a vast and diverse field of historical changes. It is uni-directional and linear – that is, a stage materializes, runs its course, and never recurs – though growth has often been seen to be cyclical. Like other models of this kind, it ignores the impact of external historical forces like colonialism and imperialism on Third World economies. It has therefore been criticized for failing to acknowledge that economic growth is as much about the *power* to control resources as it is about the *ambition* to do so. Rostow's theory has also been criticized on the grounds that though in many countries an increase in investment – to 11 per cent in the UK and 25 per cent in China, for example – has preceded growth, it is impossible to identify any unique or relatively short historical phase as the take-off period in those countries. Finally, it is often maintained that though investment may be a neces-sary condition for growth, it cannot be sufficient. Technical progress or changes in labour quantity and quality are also important.[4] The next stage in growth theorizing was Solow's growth model.

Solow's growth model[5]

Whereas the Harrod–Domar (HD) model emphasizes the role of savings, in the Solow model, savings are seen as influencing only short-run growth. Such growth tapers off, because decreasing returns to scale decrease the productivity of investment over time. The only way to maintain growth over time is for technical change to improve the efficiency of investment – that is, to shift the production function upwards, as we will see. This model held centre stage for over two decades, until the emergence of new/ endogenous growth theories.

The Solow model differs from the HD model in including a second factor of production – labour. Thus, in the Solow model, output is a function of both capital and labour. While there are constant returns to scale for both inputs together, each input on its own would face decreasing returns to scale. If both capital and labour increased by 10 per cent, then output would also increase by 10 per cent. However, if capital increased faster than labour, then before long each unit of capital would be complemented by less labour than the previous unit, and would produce less output than the previous unit. The production function therefore is upward-sloping, but flattens out after a point. This production function can be seen in figure 4.1 as $y = f(k)$, where y is output per unit of labour and k is capital per unit of labour.

The Solow model has three functions: the production function, the savings function and the depreciation function, as figure 4.1 shows. The *savings function* (sy) shows that a constant proportion of income is saved by every individual. This is assumed in the model and gives the savings function shown in the figure. The *depreciation function* (dk in the investment requirement function in figure 4.1) shows that a certain volume of investment is required to replace the capital products that are used up in production each year (i.e. depreciation). If a constant proportion of capital is depreciated every year, then this can be depicted as a straight line.

Given these assumptions, if savings = depreciation (for instance, at point C in figure 4.1), then the amount of new investment undertaken is just sufficient to replace used-up capital every year. However, if savings exceed depreciation (all points to the left of C), then net investment takes place, which increases the economy's capital stock. With a constant number of workers, we now have a higher capital–labour ratio. The economy will move to the right in the figure, and output will increase. During this period, therefore, the economy grows. However, this growth will stop when the economy reaches C, where savings = depreciation. At

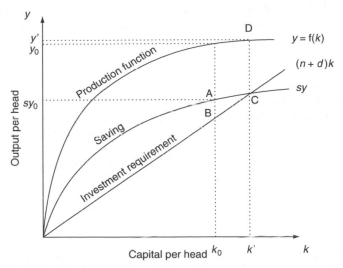

Figure 4.1   Solow growth model

this steady state, both income and capital are constant, and there will no longer be any growth.

The economy always moves towards this steady state in the Solow model. It can be perturbed from this state by a change in the savings rate or in the production function. Any growth that takes place within this model is likely to be short-run. This is because an increase in savings above depreciation will cause an increase in the capital–labour ratio, if labour inputs remain unchanged. Consequently, the returns to capital will decrease, thus stifling future growth. The Solow model requires that capital increase faster than labour for growth to occur. But when this happens, decreasing returns will decrease the marginal contribution of capital to output, and will force a decrease in the rate of growth of output.

Long-run growth within the Solow model requires that the production function shift upwards – that is, that there is technical change in the economy. Such a technical change implies that capital is now employed more productively, so that for each unit of capital, output is higher. The upward shift in the production function offsets the decreasing returns to scale within the model and results in long-term growth. There is, however, no explanation for such technical change within the Solow model. In fact, it is seen as a residual: any growth that cannot be explained by increases in labour or capital inputs is attributed to technical change. This is one of the main criticisms of the model.

Both the HD and the Solow models provide useful insights into the growth process. Empirical evidence seems to confirm the HD hypothesis that savings rates and growth are positively correlated across countries.

Theoretically, however, the Solow model provides a more realistic account of the way in which production is determined, by bringing a second factor of production, labour, into the picture. Ironically, therefore, the HD model seemed to fit the evidence better, while the Solow model captured the process of production better. Growth theory remained in this impasse until the 1980s, when a major breakthrough was made by Paul Romer (1986) and Robert Lucas (1988). Their new growth theories, unlike the Solow model, were able to explain long-run growth from within the model instead of having to rely on perturbations.

New growth theories

As seen above, the main limitation of the Solow model is its inability to explain long-term growth because of the assumption of diminishing returns to scale. In recognition of this, the new growth theories are built around an assumption of increasing returns to scale. Within these models, growth is endogenous: that is, it arises from within the model, rather than from unexplained technical progress. However, the logic for diminishing returns is very strong in economics. If a single factor increases and is not accompanied by increases in the other factors, then this factor will increase output but not by as much as before. Doing away with this assumption would imply that there are constant returns to a single factor, but increasing returns to all factors combined. The result would be that the firm that enjoyed increasing returns to scale would continue to expand until there was only one firm in the whole economy. This is not what we see around us in the real world. Why would firms which benefit from expanding not expand?

Endogenous growth theories argue that this is because some of the benefits of increased production accrue not to the firm but to agents outside the firm – that is, are external to the firm. Thus, while there may be increasing returns to the economy overall, the returns to the firm itself may be constant or even decreasing. Since the firm does not capture all the benefits of the increased production, it has no incentive to continue to expand for ever. However, the external benefits that accrue to other firms and consumers within the economy imply that the aggregate (economy-wide) production function will experience increasing returns to scale.

A production function that does not incorporate diminishing returns remains a straight-line function, as seen in figure 4.2. Such a straight-line function indicates that output per head can grow indefinitely so long as capital is increasing. In figure 4.2, the savings function ($sf(k)$) is always above depreciation ($(n + d)(k)$), and as long as this is the case, net investment is taking place, which will increase the capital–labour ratio in the economy, and will therefore lead to growth. This can continue for ever.

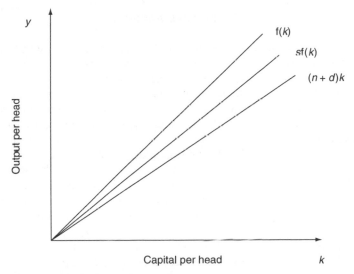

Figure 4.2   Endogenous growth model

What factors may enable a firm to grow but would have external benefits to other agents in the economy too? The new or endogenous growth theories identified two factors: investment in human capital and technological progress. Technological progress may be seen as embodied in capital (to provide better-quality machines or increased technical know-how).[6] Technical progress arises from R&D expenditure, which has a private return for the firm undertaking the investment and a positive external effect for all other firms in the economy, including those that do not undertake this investment. Therefore, though the returns to scale to each individual firm may be constant, those to the entire economy may be increasing. Such technical progress arises both from deliberate innovations which are undertaken by firms and from spill-overs from one firm to another (Ray, 1998, p. 124).

Another factor that has considerable external benefits is investment in human capital, a factor that is especially important in developing countries. Such investment directly benefits the individuals who undertake it, by increasing their earnings and quality of life (see chapter 13). However, it also benefits other individuals in society indirectly, through improved performance of the economy, a more literate, cultured society, and so on. Once again, therefore, such externalities imply that while investment in education will have decreasing returns to private individuals, it could have increasing returns to society overall. Thus, investment in education and training have been emphasized recently by new growth theories.

Empirical evidence

The above discussion indicates that theoretical work on growth has been concerned mainly with the sources of growth. Empirical studies of economic growth have been concerned largely with two main issues. The first relates to the extent to which the growth experienced by many countries has been caused by increases in inputs (especially labour and capital) rather than increases in the efficiency of use of existing inputs (through improvements in technology). The empirical growth literature uses the growth accounting framework – that is, it estimates production functions (with capital, labour and raw materials) to decompose the sources of growth. Technical change in this framework is measured as a residual (all growth that is not accounted for by increases in inputs), as was the case in the Solow model. The second issue that the empirical literature has been concerned with is the extent of 'convergence' in growth across the world. More specifically, is it true that poor countries grow faster than the rich, so that, over time, one can expect them to catch up?

Attempts to study growth and productivity go back a long way. Maddison (1970) studied twenty-two developing countries over 1950–65. He found that acceleration of investment was the most important factor causing growth in his sample. However, the results vary depending upon the weights given to labour and capital. While Maddison gave both capital and labour a weight of 0.5, Nadiri (1972) gave capital a lower weight in his analysis.[7] Surveying a number of production function studies for developing countries, he found that for Japan, Israel and Mexico, increases in labour inputs contributed more to growth than increases in capital inputs. But both studies found that capital accumulation was a much more important source of growth in developing countries than in developed countries.

A study by the World Bank (1991) for 1960–87 concluded that the major source of growth is not productivity growth but the growth of inputs themselves. Young (1995) reiterated this conclusion in his study of the growth experience of the East Asian economies. He showed that increasing participation rates, transfers of labour between agriculture and industry, changes in education levels, and the rapid pace of capital accumulation all contributed to economic growth in East Asia (see table 4.1).

Such growth cannot last for ever, because inputs cannot increase for ever. We will consider other factors that influenced the growth of the East Asian economies later in this book (chapters 9 and 10). Productivity growth[8] improves the efficiency with which inputs are used. Though the Total Factor Productivity (TFP) of countries in East Asia is higher than that for countries like Canada, Italy and the USA, it is not much higher than that for Germany (1.6), Japan (2), Brazil (1.6) and Venezuela (2.6) over different periods. Thus, Young (1995) concludes that the very high

Table 4.1 Components of growth in the East Asian economies

Component	Hong Kong (1966–91)	Singapore (1966–90)	S. Korea (1966–90)	Taiwan (1966–90)
GDP growth per capita	5.7	6.8	6.8	6.7
Total Factor Productivity (TFP)	2.3	0.2	1.7	2.6
Change in labour force participation (%)	38 → 49	27 → 51	27 → 36	28 → 37
Change in secondary or higher education (%)	27.2 → 71.4	15.8 → 66.3	26.5 → 75	25.8 → 67.6

Source: Dornbusch, Fischer and Startz, 1998, *Macroeconomics*, p. 71. © 1998 Irwin McGraw-Hill. Reproduced with permission of The McGraw-Hill Companies.

rates of growth experienced by the East Asian economies can be attributed to the traditional, extensive increases in the labour force and capital accumulation, rather than to technical progress and an increase in productivity (table 4.1).

The second issue that growth economists have been concerned with is the extent to which countries are converging to a similar level of income or growth. Simply put, convergence would imply that the poor countries are growing faster than the rich ones, so that over time they converge to a similar income level. If such convergence did occur, it would have significant implications for international inequalities and the future of developing countries. In table 1.1, we had a brief look at the growth rates of a number of developing countries. We concluded that the East Asian countries have grown fastest between 1985 and 1995. We found that countries in Africa and in Eastern Europe experienced very poor growth during this period. A look at table 4.2 confirms this finding. Thus, there is some convergence in Asia but not in Africa. The World Bank (2000/1) reports that the gap in average incomes between the richest and poorest countries is widening. 'In 1960, per capita GDP in the richest 20 countries was 18 times that in the poorest 20 countries. By 1995, this gap had widened to 37 times, a phenomenon often referred to as 'divergence' (World Bank, 2000/1, p. 51).

A simple test of convergence is to calculate the correlation between the level of productivity, or the per capita income, and the growth rate of countries. If productivity is higher in the high-income or growth countries, then the rich countries are growing faster than the poor ones, and there is divergence. Alternatively, a strong negative correlation, wherein countries with higher income levels had lower rates of growth, would be evidence of convergence. There is no clear evidence in either direction. Baumol (1986b) showed an inverse correlation between the productivity level and average growth of productivity for industrialized and middle-income countries, but not for the poorest. Parente and Prescott (1993), on the other hand, studying 102 countries between 1960 and 1985, found that the standard deviation of per capita real GDP of each country relative to that of the

Table 4.2   Growth in the developing world, 1950 and 1992

| Country | GDP (1990) per capita $ | | Cumulative growth (%) |
	1950	1992	
USA	9,573	21,558	125.2
Bangladesh	551	720	30.67
China	614	3,098	404.56
Egypt	517	1,927	272.73
India	597	1,348	125.8
Indonesia	874	2,749	214.53
Mexico	2,085	5,112	145.18
South Korea	876	10,010	1,042.69
Taiwan	922	11,590	1,157.05
Tanzania	427	604	41.45
Thailand	848	4,694	453.54
USSR	2,834	4,671	64.82
Zaire	636	407	36.01

Source: Dornbusch, Fischer and Startz, 1998, Macroeconomics, box 4.1. © 1998 Irwin McGraw-Hill. Reproduced with permission of The McGraw-Hill Companies.

USA increased, rather than decreased. Rigorous tests do not confirm convergence towards the levels of the rich. The poorest countries, it is accepted, are being left behind. However, there seems to be some evidence of catch-up, or convergence, amongst the middle-income economies.

Overall, empirical studies of growth have concluded that:

- The major source of growth is an increase in factor inputs (labour and capital), together with improvements in the quality of labour through investments in health and education.
- The growth of total factor productivity in developing countries is relatively slow compared to the developed countries.
- There is no obvious convergence between rich and poor countries.

Conclusion

As indicated earlier in this book, growth only provides the means to development. For growth to actually translate into development (even purely *economic* development), it needs to trickle down, decreasing inequalities in income distribution and reducing poverty in the first instance. In the next chapter, we will consider theories of development (rather than growth). These theories are concerned with the role played by politics (especially international links) and sociology (changes in society and culture) in development.

5

Development and the World

Prior to the emergence of capitalism, the existence of agricultural societies with feudal property relations resulted in very slow growth or even stagnation of output. The advent of industrialization, and capitalism with it, perceptibly increased the rate of growth of output. The spectacular advances made in increasing output and in the processes of production from this time on brought forward the notion of continuous progress and 'development' (see chapter 10). Classical political economy emphasized the role of trade in enabling the division and specialization of labour and in overcoming the limitations of the internal market.[1] Attempts to understand the causes of this increase in output were considered in chapter 4. In this chapter, we discuss the wider, more holistic theories of development.

These theories have highlighted different aspects of the development process – the role of trade and international links, the significance of the state, the importance of class relations, and the importance of socio-cultural factors (ethnicity, religion, etc.). We will highlight two of these issues – specifically, the roles of trade and of the state – in Part III of this book. Though these issues have been emphasized in development theories, there has been considerable disagreement regarding their precise role. Thus, while Marxist theories saw trade as beneficial, dependency theories saw trade as disadvantageous. Similarly, the role of the state has been both emphasized and criticized within these theories. Most early development theories saw development as a linear process. Both the Marxists and the modernization school accepted that development would follow a certain pattern within which a stage once passed would not recur. In reality, however, as we argued in the Introduction, development is neither linear nor so straightforward. The interlinkages between the various stages, and between the causes and consequences, are so strong that a stage theory of development is hard to accept today.

In this chapter, we will consider three main schools of development theorizing: the Marxists, the modernization theorists and the dependency school.

Marx and development theory

Marx was the first to explain change and development as an economic, social, political and institutional phenomenon. His main proposition was 'that in every historical epoch, the prevailing mode of economic production and exchange, and the social organisation necessarily following from it, form the basis upon which is built up, and from which alone can be explained, the political and intellectual history of that epoch' (Marx and Engels, 1840). As the means of production and of exchange develop, the feudal relations of property become outmoded and have to be done away with. In these periodic crises, most of the existing production and most previously created productive forces are destroyed. Thus, revolutionary change is built into this system. As the forces of production evolve (through technical progress and knowledge), so competition between the oppressed and the ruling classes becomes more intense, with the former fighting for change and the latter resisting it. This results in social revolution, which pushes the economy on to a higher level, at which change continues. Marx also maintains that 'the history of these class struggles forms a series of evolutions in which nowadays a stage has been reached where the exploited and oppressed class – the proletariat – cannot attain its emancipation from the sway of the exploiting and ruling class – the bourgeoisie – without, at the same time, and once and for all, emancipating society at large from all exploitation, oppression, class distinctions and class struggles' (Marx and Engels, 1840).

Marx accepted capitalism as the most advanced mode of production in history, and as one that was most capable of promoting the development of productive forces. Capitalism is characterized by production for the market. Within it, one class (the capitalists) owns the means of production, and another (the proletariat) sells its labour power in exchange for wages. Capitalists make profits (surplus value), which they then appropriate. In order to maintain these profits, they invest and innovate, increasing the productivity of labour and creating change and growth within the system. Over time, however, capitalist competition exerts a downward pressure on the average rate of profits. In order to avoid this, capitalists begin to export to markets abroad, trade with pre-capitalist societies, and plunder their wealth through the formation of colonies. These efforts enable the rate of profit to be propped up temporarily, but before long the internal contradictions within the system rear their heads again, and cause its eventual downfall. However, since 'no social order ever disappears before all the productive forces for which there is room in it have been developed; and new, higher relations of production never appear before the material conditions of their existence have matured in the womb of the old society' (Marx, 1859, quoted in Oman and Wignaraja, 1994, p. 200), the capitalist system of production, in spite of its brutality, was regarded as historically progressive, and even necessary for the development of backward societies. The dynamics of capitalism and its capacity for expansion, it was felt, could be reproduced in any society, but development would require progression from feudalism through bourgeois capitalism to socialism.

While Marx spoke in general terms of development and change, it was Lenin who first explicitly extended Marxist analysis to less developed countries to consider the unevenness of development on a world scale. In fact, as Palma (1978b) argues, Lenin's (1899) study, *The Development of Capitalism in Russia*, can be seen as the first study of dependent development. Lenin's views on the effect of capitalism on less developed countries were further advanced in *Imperialism: The Highest Stage of Capitalism* (Lenin, 1982). In this study, he argued that once capitalism reached its 'monopoly phase', competition amongst capitalists would result in what the neoclassicals call an 'oligopoly'. Monopoly pricing and profits in advanced countries would result in decreased output, slower growth, and a potential for instability. The surpluses would accumulate, and would then be exported to less developed countries in search of opportunities for investment. This investment abroad slows down accumulation at home, but results in development overseas; that is, imperialism has a progressive impact on the recipient economies.

Following on from Lenin, Luxemburg (1951) maintained that the 'under-consumptionist crises' in capitalist economies would force capitalists to seek new markets in pre-capitalist regions. The penetration of merchant capital into the colonies would compete with local industry and postpone (albeit temporarily) its development. However, capitalism would soon spread here, and the under-consumptionist crisis would occur here too. Luxemburg has been criticized for not emphasizing the increase in wages that would occur as capitalism developed. These increased wages would increase domestic demand, and thus delay the under-consumptionist phase.

As mentioned earlier, these theories propounded by Marx and his early followers viewed development as a sequence of stages from feudalism to capitalism to socialism, with socialism being the highest form of development. Like the modernization theories discussed below, these theories are linear ones, in which societies have to pass through each successive stage to reach the highly developed socialist stage. The Marxist view is particularly significant, because it contributes much to later theories of development, especially the dependency and neo-Marxist theories.

Before we consider these, however, we turn to the growth of modernization theories.

Modernization theories

Like Marxist theories, modernization theories are teleological, and see advanced capitalist societies as models for all developing nations. They also tend to be uni-linear – all societies go through the same stages to become developed. But, unlike Marxist theories, modernization theories specifically addressed the issue of developing countries and development. These theories reached their economic climax in Rostow's (1960) 'stages of growth' theory, which was discussed in chapter 4. They accepted the structure of relationships that emerged between rich and poor countries, and attempted to analyse ways in which the poor could become 'rich'. In this sense, modernization theories were problem-solving: how could economies progress from being traditional and poor to being modern and rich?

Modernization theories were put forward by a group of American scholars against the backdrop of the Cold War. They provided a theoretical rationale for making economic and technological aid available to the Third World, aid which would then accomplish a political objective, that of keeping these countries non-Communist. However, such aid was not expected to help development without wider social, cultural and political changes in these countries. There were calls for 'comprehensive social and economic change', and sociologists set about the task of developing a comprehensive theory of all the processes and structural changes required to transform non-industrial into industrial societies.

In constructing their account of development, modernization theorists drew on the distinction between tradition and modernity, which was first put forward by Durkheim. They argued that the transition from the limited economic relations of traditional societies to the innovative and complex economic associations of modern societies depended on a change of values, attitudes and the norms of people; in other words, development depended on 'primitive' values being replaced by modern ones. Modernization could therefore be seen as the increasing significance of economic as opposed to social, cultural, racial or religious distinctions. Parsons (1951) developed this distinction, and it was further developed by theorists like McClelland (1961), who argued that it was necessary to develop an 'achievement orientation' amongst people. Lerner (1964), too, maintained that society is defined by what it wants to become. Analysing the factors that make some societies modern, Weber (1930) argued that differences in the religious and ethical beliefs of people are the key. Calvinism, with its emphasis on frugality and hard work, was, he felt, a major influence on the development of capitalism in Western Europe.

Modernization theories faced considerable criticism in the 1960s and 1970s. They were criticized for not really defining the 'traditional' except in relation to the 'modern'. Thus, India, China, Burkina Faso and New Guinea were all considered 'traditional', simply because they were neither modern nor industrialized. Additionally, 'traditional' and 'modern' are simply ideal types, rather than systems existing in reality (Bernstein, 1971). These theories have also been criticized for being Eurocentric: that is, for seeing development as a process of change towards social, economic and political systems that have developed in the West. Thus, 'even admitting the possibility of different "routes", there is but one "destination"' (Bernstein, 1971, p. 147). As Nettl points out, 'the methodological approaches of Western social and political scientists ... often assume that developing countries are infant or deviant examples of the Western experience and can be studied in terms of a shortfall from a norm' (Nettl, 1967, p. 193). Such Eurocentrism in modernization theories is most obvious when modernization is seen as synonymous with Westernization.

However, in the 1980s there were attempts to rethink modernization theories. Nash (1984), for instance, attempted to delink modernization and Westernization, while Roxborough (1988) questioned the need for a unilinear approach within modernization. Some analysts (Apter, 1987) have argued that a careful reconstruction of the modernization and dependency approaches could result in a more coherent, comprehensive theory of development. Roxborough (1988) makes this attempt by replacing the term 'traditional' with the terms 'pre-capitalist' or 'pre-modern' societies, in an attempt to overcome objections to the traditional–modern dichotomy.

In practical terms, modernization theory saw modern values as being diffused through education and technology transfers to the 'elites' of the periphery. The shortcomings of this theory were first made apparent in Latin America, where, in spite of a long history of independence, there had been very little modernization. In fact, many critics felt that modernization theories had 'failed to grapple with the outstanding feature of the last 100 years – the emergence of a world system of social relations' (Worsley, 1965, p. 374). Thus, modernization theories were criticized for ignoring the relationship between the developed and developing countries. Dependency theorists responded to this gap in existing theories by including power relations between the core and the periphery in their theory of development. This is what we turn to next.

The centre–periphery paradigm

The first attempt to articulate the differences in achievement between the developed core and the developing periphery was undertaken by the

Economic Commission for Latin America (ECLA). Economists within the Commission noted that, in spite of having substantial industrial capacities and groups of local industrialists producing consumer goods, countries in Latin America continued to be very sensitive to cyclical and structural changes in the developed countries. This, it was felt, could only be explained by directly modelling the relationship between the developed and developing countries. This gave rise to the 'centre–periphery paradigm'.

According to the centre–periphery paradigm, the world economy is comprised of two sectors – the centre and the periphery – in which production structures are very different from each other. In the periphery, backward sectors (with low productivity and backward production techniques) coexist with modern sectors and high productivity levels. The periphery also tends to export a small range of products and to benefit from very few linkages (horizontal or vertical).[2] At the centre, on the other hand, production structures are modern throughout, and cover a wide range of capital, intermediate and consumer goods.

The differences in productivity result in an international division of labour, with the periphery producing and exporting primary products, and the core specializing in manufactures. Outward-oriented strategies favouring trade based on comparative advantage tend to reinforce these differences. In addition, economists within ECLA noted that there was a secular trend for the terms of trade to move against the less developed countries; that is, the prices of primary commodities were decreasing in the long term relative to manufactures, which were exported by the developed countries. This would lead to a transfer of income from the periphery to the centre (Prebisch, 1959; Singer, 1950). Finally, the income elasticity of demand was higher for manufactures than for primary products. Therefore, whenever the periphery grew faster than the centre, it would import more, and incur recurrent trade deficits. Protection was needed to counter this. Progress and development at the periphery could therefore occur only if it moved away from such a narrow specialization on primary products, through industrialization. However, given that industries at the periphery are less productive than those at the centre (infant industry argument), they require government protection through deliberate, government policy supported industrialization.[3] While the roles both of the state and of trade were also considered by earlier theories, it was with ECLA that they moved to centre stage in development theorizing, a position they still retain.

ECLA's proposals gained great popularity in the 1950s in Latin America, where they were formalized as the import-substituting industrialization strategy. In the 1960s, ECLA advocated attempts to increase the export of manufactures from the periphery, both to the core and to other countries on the periphery. Agrarian reform (land and tenancy reforms), as well as technical assistance, price policies and credit supports, were advocated. Emphasis was given to social policies in the form of active state support for health and education services, training, employment programmes and housing, while there was considerable debate regarding the role of the state. Planning techniques were also refined.

By the late 1960s, ECLA was being strongly criticized from both the left and the right. On the right, its critics maintained that the data used by Prebisch did not support his hypothesis. They even argued that decreases in transport costs might explain the decrease in primary product prices without implying deterioration in the incomes of producers. Secondly, it was felt that these long-term patterns were likely to be less important than short-term fluctuations in influencing investment and enterprises at the periphery. Thirdly, though revenue per unit of output might decrease, this effect would be offset by the fact that labour and capital would both become more productive over time. The increased output resulting from these improvements in productivity would offset the decrease in prices and leave aggregate incomes unchanged. The net welfare consequences of trade for primary exporters would therefore be positive in the long term. To his credit, however, Prebisch did not argue that trade led to increases in absolute poverty, but that there was a bias against the periphery in *sharing* the *gains* from trade. Finally, the cases of Australia, New Zealand and Denmark were cited as counter-examples to ECLA's rejection of agriculture-led development. On the left, criticism came from the dependency school, which was beginning to gain ground in Latin America. We will turn to consider the views of this school in the next section.

Dependency theories

The basic argument of the dependency school was that poverty and underdevelopment in Latin America were caused by exposure (economic and political) to the advanced countries. Thus, underdevelopment was seen as having been 'created as an intrinsic part of the process of Western capitalist expansion' (Bernstein, 1971, p. 152, paraphrasing Furtado, 1964). In this sense, it was an extension, albeit critical, of the centre–periphery paradigm. It also had its foundation in two aspects of classical Marxist analysis: the 'epidemic of over-production' that occurs during crises in capitalism and the consequent search for foreign markets. However, dependency theories rejected the basic Marxist thesis that capitalism is inherently progressive.

Baran (1957), noting the importance of geography in development, wrote that the advanced economies gain by obtaining cheaper raw materials, and are therefore able to extract considerable surpluses. These surpluses are largely expropriated by foreign capital, and are partly squandered by local elites, providing very little opportunity for investment in future growth. Though dependency analysis has varied from study to study, all the models agree that the main outcome of such dependency is that surpluses produced at the periphery are extracted and expropriated by the centre. Each of the models has emphasized a different mechanism for surplus extraction and appropriation. These include:

1   *Cheaper raw materials.* Firms at the centre are able to access cheap raw materials in the periphery. They are therefore able to make larger profits, which are retained at the centre.
2   *Subsistence output and low wages.* Industrial wages at the periphery can be maintained at relatively low levels, because industrial workers obtain some subsistence output from agriculture and fishing. This increases the profits that can be extracted by firms at the centre.
3   *Increased demand for imports from the centre.* When incomes increase at the periphery, people do not demand more domestic output. Instead, they demand more imports, either of final consumer goods or of the capital and technology that are used in the production of these goods. In either case, the main benefits of the increased demand accrue to the centre. The periphery itself is simply left with a balance of payments deficit.
4   *Increasing budget deficits.* The state at the periphery spends more than it earns. It borrows from abroad to finance this spending. Sunkel (1969, p. 31) identifies 'the overbearing and implacable necessity to obtain foreign financing' as summing up the situation of dependency in his view.
5   *Foreign investment.* Multinational enterprises invest in import-substituting industries at the periphery and repatriate profits to the core. Before long, therefore, capital outflows exceed inflows, resulting in a balance of payments constraint on imports.

Even though dependency theories have been strongly criticized (see next subsection), the mechanisms of dependence identified by them have relevance even today. Whether it is the inability to maintain high prices for primary produce,[4] the recurrent balance of payments deficits of many developing countries and their increasing demand for Western products, the debt crisis in Latin America, or the increasing globalization of production, dependency arguments find resonance in many problems faced by developing countries today.

Baran argued that 'economic development in underdeveloped countries is profoundly inimical to the dominant interests in the advanced capitalist countries' (Baran, 1957, p. 28). In order to stifle such development, the advanced nations will form alliances with the pre-capitalist or feudal elites in the underdeveloped countries. These elites (also called the 'comprador' elites) would ally themselves with the metropolitan centres, and help transfer the surpluses abroad. They co-operate in these alliances because they fear being displaced from their positions once capitalist development occurs. They are therefore unable or unwilling to establish more diverse economic activities in the peripheral countries. Thus, there is a 'chain of dependency' running from the centres to the satellites through which economic surpluses are passed upwards within a nation and then out internationally. Such dependence implies that countries on the periphery cannot develop independently of the centres, and that even when they do, their surpluses are always passed on to the centre. This cycle of surplus extraction cannot be broken through regional industrialization. The only way to break it is to overthrow the structures of metropolis–satellite relations through a socialist revolution. Thus, incorporation into the world capitalist system has resulted in the development of a few and the underdevelopment of many.

Many writers (e.g. Cardoso and Faletto, 1979) within the dependency paradigm, however, rejected the generalization, as well as the 'mechanico-formal' theorization of dependency. Instead, they made an attempt to concentrate on 'concrete situations of dependency'. These writers paid particular attention to differences in local conditions – the interaction between local classes and foreign elites, the organization of different state forms, and the different strategies used to cope with imperialist challenges. They did not see dependence and industrialization as contradictory. Foreign investment occurring through transnational corporations (TNCs) creates conditions for *both* dependence and industrialization. Though such development would redefine dependency, it would not eliminate it – there would be 'dependent development', as opposed to 'dependent underdevelopment'. Investment by TNCs at the periphery would increasingly be diverted towards manufacturing, and ever more towards attempts to satisfy local markets. It would generally benefit the rich and increase inequalities. Cardoso and Faletto (1979) saw the need for 'political-structural' change, and argued that, ultimately, only socialism would help to achieve development.

Critiques of dependency

Given its position at the centre of development thinking, it is not surprising that dependency analysis has faced considerable criticism. Though its central concepts have struck a chord amongst many development thinkers, it has been criticized for being vague and circular (Lall, 1975): 'dependent countries are those which lack the capacity for autonomous growth and they lack this because their structures are dependent ones' (O'Brien, 1975, p. 24). This leads to a confusion between dependency and underdevelopment. Thus, for example, Canada is dependent, but not underdeveloped. On this point, Lall (1975) critiques a number of dependency studies, arguing that the characteristics generally attributed to underdevelopment in dependent countries are not exclusive to these economies but can also be found in non-dependent economies. He found that 'Canada and Belgium are more "dependent" on foreign investments than are India or Pakistan, yet they are presumably not in the category of "dependent countries"' (Lall, 1975, p. 803). Both dominance and dependence exist at both the centre and the periphery.

More specifically, though it is generally accepted that Frank's (1966, 1969) critique of the supposedly dual structure of peripheral societies is extremely valuable, he has been criticized for using the deterministic framework of the same model (economic) that he criticizes (Palma, 1978a). From the left, Frank has been criticized for displacing class relations from his analysis of underdevelopment. His theories have also been criticized for locating exploitation in the sphere of circulation and exchange, rather than in the process of production. Thus, critics like Laclau (1971) maintain that the extraction of surpluses through trade is not a defining feature of capitalism; it happens even in feudal economies. It is more important to know how the surplus is produced. This, Frank failed to do.

The notions of 'dependent development' put forward by Cardoso and Faletto (1979) have been criticized because development in this context is dependent on the demand of high-income consumers for the products of foreign TNCs. Such consumers are in a minority in Latin America. It also depends on the ability of strong governments to curb unions. Such growth therefore does not lead to decreases in poverty or to an increase in wages (Frank, 1984). Instead of eliminating dependency, such development simply redefines it.

Dependency thinking has also been criticized by Marxists, who feel that capitalism has a progressive effect on poorer countries. They reject the conclusion drawn by dependency writers that the draining of surpluses from the Third World results in its underdevelopment. Warren (1980), like other Marxists, argues that imperialism and its policies led to industrialization and reduced dependency in the Third World. He claims that capitalist development has been taking place in these countries since World War II, and that potential obstacles to this development have been internal rather than external. The prospects for successful capitalist development were good in many developing countries, and would result in a shift of power within the capitalist world. Warren (1980) claimed that there were many less developed countries throughout the Third World that were developing rapidly: for example, Egypt, Argentina and Brazil. The experience of those countries, he claimed, proved, contrary to dependency theories, that the periphery could develop. Yet Warren himself has been strongly criticized on the grounds that both capitalists and workers in the First World enjoy the fruits of imperialism, while Third World workers are exploited.

Later developments: marginalization of the periphery

Later writers like Amin and Emmanuel saw the low wages existing at the periphery as the root cause of its dependency. These writers, together with other world systems and unequal exchange theorists, used frameworks similar to dependency models but varying in particulars. Emmanuel (1972) based his model of unequal exchange on the hypothesis that whereas profit rates are equalized between the centre and the periphery, wage rates are not. He argued that although labour struggles have increased wages at the centre, peripheral wages are still at subsistence level because labour is immobile. Amin (1976) also argues that increases in labour productivity at the periphery can only be translated into higher wages if workers are able to fight for them. Emmanuel (1972) argues that since prices are determined largely by wages, the price of products produced at the periphery will be lower than those produced at the centre, so that the terms of trade turn against the periphery.

Echoing the above argument, Wallerstein (1979, 1984) maintains that there are two levels of surplus expropriation: from workers by capitalists, and from the periphery by the centre. Wallerstein also represents a departure from other dependency theorists in arguing the case for three regions – the centre, the periphery and the semi-periphery. The semi-periphery comprises the intermediate countries that shift upwards from the periphery and act as a buffer between the core and the periphery, trading with countries from both the core and the periphery, buying high-technology products from the former and exporting semi-manufactures to them while importing raw materials from the periphery. The East Asian newly industrializing countries (NICs) were seen as part of the semi-periphery. Thus, both upward and downward mobility are possible in the world economy.

A Summary

We have discussed dependency theories in considerable detail because they were central to development literature in the 1970s. It is worth summarizing the common themes of all these models before we conclude.

1   Underdevelopment (as distinct from un-development) is a historical process, which is not due to some original state of affairs, as modernization theorists claimed, but is rather the result of the same historical processes by which the now-developed countries became developed.
2   The dominant and dependent countries together form a capitalist system (a point taken up by later world systems theories).
3   Underdevelopment is an inherent consequence of the functioning of the world system. The economic penetration of the colonies resulted in a distorted structure, which led to economic stagnation. This was

reinforced by the extraction and transfer of surpluses from the periphery to the centre by various means.

4   Many dependency theorists also agreed on the role of multinational corporations: TNCs impose a universal consumption pattern, use capital-intensive techniques, out-compete domestic capital, and attempt to transfer surpluses back to the centres. However, there is considerable disagreement, as we have seen, as to whether they can be seen as causing industrialization or preventing it – that is, on whether they result in dependent *development* or in *underdevelopment*.

Conclusion

Each of these theories either implicitly or explicitly emphasizes the roles of trade and of the state. Thus, Marxist theories are clear that trade provides an opportunity for firms that are facing the limits of their domestic market to continue to expand and earn profits (abroad). In the process, such trade helps both the developed and the developing countries. Dependency theories, on the other hand, argue that trade is never mutually beneficial. Instead, it helps the developed countries to continue to exploit the developing countries. More recent dependency writers see debt and foreign direct investment also as ways in which such dependency is reinforced. As regards the role of the state, Marxist theories see the state as being central in the final stage of development – socialism. Early centre–periphery (and to some extent later dependency) models see a well-functioning state as necessary to avoid the negative effects of free trade. Thus, the state can help subsidize domestic firms and protect them from unfair foreign competition.

The theories discussed in this chapter formed the mainstream of discussion and debate within Development Studies until the late 1970s, even though the debate surrounding them has often been virulent. All of these theories are Eurocentric. They accept the notion that all countries have one goal – economic growth – and that once Britain had set the scene or target by industrializing, all the other countries had, perforce, to follow if they were to survive as nation-states. Much of development economics and the early sociology and politics of development accepted this view. In fact, modernization theories were based on the notion that the developing world both would, and should, follow in the footsteps of the developed world. As we have seen, both Marxist and dependency models are open to this criticism, assuming as they do that all the countries of the Third World wish to grow, differing only in the reasons that they advance for their 'backwardness'. Thus, Hettne (1990, p. 34) claims that the Marxist model is Eurocentric, because it accepts the need for countries to move through capitalism towards Marxism. It accepts the need for industrialization and modernization. The dependency model is seen as a shift away from such Eurocentrism, and to some extent it was – analysing as it did the power relations between the West and the rest of the world. But it remained within the Western evolutionary framework. As Cowen and Shenton (1996) put it, it is very hard to avoid Eurocentrism in development analysis when the very aim of development is often defined by the first movers in Europe.

In addition to accusations of Eurocentrism, modernization theories and Marxist and dependency theories were all criticized for being macro theories that attempted to analyse the large issues of growth and development at the national and sometimes international levels, without considering regional, local or familial distinctions. Though some attempt was made to include class analysis into these models, most other differences – regional, local and gender – were subsumed within the overall framework.

During the 1980s, these 'grand' theories of development were increasingly being rejected within Development Studies. The later dependency theories (concrete situations of dependency) had begun to grapple with the notion of difference, but it was left to the new approaches to Development Studies – those of gender and of the environment especially – to take this further. We turn to this in the next chapter.

6

Beyond the Impasse: Development Theory in the 1990s

There are reasons to doubt whether it (development economics) will survive much longer, indeed whether it can be considered a subject at all.

Seers, 1979

[N]ew ideas are ever harder to come by and ... the field is not adequately reproducing itself.

Hirschman, 1981

[I]t is alarming how wrong we were, and how sure we were that we were right.

Chambers, 1985

The slayer of the dragon of backwardness seems to have stumbled on his own sword.

Sen, 1983

[D]iscrepancies between policies and concrete results have been so great and experiences so often disastrous that another round of thinking is called for.

Apter, 1987

In a book entitled *Beyond the Impasse: New Directions in Development Theory*, Frans Schuurman (1993) edited articles by a number of left-inclined development theorists. The notion of an impasse in development theory had been growing throughout the 1980s. There were concerted moves towards neo-liberalism and a growing feeling that developing economies were very similar to developed economies and that there was nothing new being contributed by studying them as different. As Schuurman's book and other contributions during this period (Booth, 1994) show, there were a number of strands to this disenchantment. What was common to all of them was the feeling that the radical Marxist theories that had dominated Development Studies until the mid-1980s had failed to deliver their promise. In fact, as Booth (1994) puts it, there seemed to be 'no viable middle position between the polarized paradigms of the 1970s' (p. 5).

Another critique that found considerable resonance during this period was put forward by M. Edwards (1989) in an article entitled, 'The Irrelevance of Development Studies'. Edwards's basic argument was that 'development had become a spectator sport, with a vast array of experts and others looking into the "fishbowl" of the Third World from the safety and comfort of their armchairs' (M. Edwards, 1989, p. 124). People were being seen as the objects of study rather than the subjects of their own development. There was too much distance between the researcher and the researched, and indigenous knowledge was devalued, as was the role of emotion in understanding people's problems. Edwards proposed the need to 'learn from below' and to participate in the processes of development rather than study them. 'Higher level work must grow out of and be based upon participatory research at lower levels' (M. Edwards, 1989, p. 124).

Others claimed that it was the nature of the problems facing developing countries that had changed. Hettne (1990), for instance, argued that there was a crisis in the 'Three Worlds' – in the North (of the welfare state), in the East (of the Socialist project), in the South (of survival). He claimed that 'one of the reasons why development theory is in crisis is a complete change of the development agenda from long run development issues to more immediate concerns' (Hettne, 1990, p. 21). This included the debt problems in Latin America, the food problems in Africa, and the ethnic problems in Asia. Similarly, Leys (1996, p. 29) maintained that 'the prerequisite of any new development theory that aims to be practical must surely be the analysis of the now de-regulated global market and the social forces that dominate it'.

As Leys (1996) puts it, 'the domain of "development theory" is radically changed, if not abolished' (p. 28), because market forces rather than strategic state action have become the major drivers of change. Powerful states and market actors are the main determinants of this world economy, and lesser states, social movements and communities without military or market power can at most delay or bring about minor changes in these actions (p. 29).

Overall, many agreed with Schuurman (1993) that there cannot be one 'grand and glorious metatheory' (p. 32). Partly in response to such criticisms, empirical research began to be more sensitive to the great diversity of situations in the Third World. In Development Economics, for instance, there was a shift from grand theories, which asked 'why underdeveloped countries are underdeveloped' towards disaggregated models directed to the heterogeneity of developing countries (Meier and

Rauch, 2000, p. 70). These theories allowed room for manoeuvre at the micro, meso and macro levels, without abandoning the attempt to explain broad patterns of development (Booth, 1991). We will discuss some of these approaches in what follows. Before we do so, it is worth considering the contribution of post-modern thought to development studies.

Dealing with difference: post-modernism in Development Studies

Jean-François Lyotard summarized post-modernism as 'an incredulity towards metanarratives' (Lyotard, 1984, p. xiv). It questions the belief that rational thought and technological innovation can guarantee progress and enlightenment. Post-modernism also reiterates 'the indignity of speaking on someone's behalf' (Deleuze speaking of Foucault). It therefore provided a framework for those within Development Studies who had long questioned its Eurocentrism and its 'top-down' approach towards development problems (M. Edwards, 1989) and called for a more individual-centred approach to development.

Within post-modernism, which questions the ability of Western theories or thinkers to understand the rest of the world, Eurocentric theories (discussed in chapters 4 and 5) are criticized as being 'privileged discourses' that have silenced dissidence. Within this framework therefore, a search had begun for locating difference and for previously 'silent voices'. As we have already mentioned, both the liberal and the Marxist approaches can be seen as Eurocentric – defining progress as the move towards a 'Western' mode of living and producing. They are also intrinsically linear, seeing development as a move forward from underdevelopment (which was equated with traditional institutions and values), to full development (modern/rational/industrialized societies) based on the Northern model (Marchand and Parpart, 1995). Even the later dependency theories, which originated in Latin America, continued to subscribe to development as implying industrialization and modernization. It is these arguments that have led to criticism of the term 'developing countries' to describe Third World economies. 'Developing' implies that these economies are moving towards a target deemed desirable, and is seen as value-laden and hence unacceptable.

The Eurocentric approaches were criticized on the grounds that modernity could not be defined without using the West as a reference point, and therefore it was not universal, as many development thinkers claimed it to be. Post-modernists also criticized the fact that Development Studies has exaggerated claims about Western knowledge, while it has tended to ignore or silence the voices of experience from the South. Critics, however, point out that, taken to its extreme, this search for voices from the South becomes circular. Many post-modernists argue, for instance, that women from the South who are able to partake in such debates with their

Western counterparts are themselves privileged, and therefore cannot claim to talk for their sisters (Marchand and Parpart, 1995). While this is probably true, it brings into question any voice from the South, as women who can speak for themselves can be similarly dismissed, and before long there would be no voice from the South that would be accepted as 'genuine'.

Critics of the post-modernist view maintain that the modern Western tradition is not only a source of 'meta-narratives' that prescribe what is to be known and what progress should consist of, but is also a source of such critiques as post-modernism itself (Corbridge, 1994). Corbridge, for instance, sympathizes with writers who wish to 'celebrate the voices of the rural poor' (like Chambers, 1983). He is also in sympathy with the need to insistently question and deconstruct the meaning of development, as well as the Eurocentrism of many definitions of development. However, he argues that entering into an era where no criteria of knowledge or the possibility of progress hold any meaning is self-defeating.

Thus, post-modernism touched on some of the crucial criticisms of the earlier theories of development – Eurocentrism, talking from above, and so on. At the same time, development theory found itself branching out into new, narrower areas within which it could analyse issues in more detail. Two such frameworks have become very popular in Development Studies – the gender and development and the environment and development frameworks. We will turn to them in the rest of this chapter.

Women, gender and development

As we saw in chapters 4 and 5, development theories (whether liberal or radical) have traditionally been concerned largely with issues of growth and distribution (or trickle-down to the poor). In the 1980s, however, these theories were extended to look beyond broad patterns to consider the 'differences' between nations and individuals. Instead of talking of the 'poor' (whether people or nations) as a single category, these theories attempted to consider *who* was poor. This coalesced with the rise of feminism in the West, and gave rise to the view that since women were some of the poorest citizens of the world, development literature should attempt to deal with their concerns more directly. A number of factors fell into place during this period – the crisis in the broad-based theories of development, the rise of feminist views in the West, and the designation of 1976–85 as the UN Decade for Women. All these factors together gave rise to a 'new direction' in development – the women, gender and development framework.[1]

There is considerable disagreement about the origins of the women and development movement. While some Northern feminists claim that the

UN Commission on the Status of Women and the US women's movement were leading players, Southern feminists, amongst others, challenge this. They argue that in Africa the movement was formed and shaped by pre-colonial traditions of economic and political activism and wars of liberation from colonial rule. Still others argue that Southern women's activism is linked not only to liberation struggles but also to unionism. Thus, Weiringa (1995), for instance, argues that Southern women are not interested solely in survival but also in political activism.

Third World women often argue that their role in their societies, as well as in the historical struggles for independence, made them less subordinate and more complementary to men in their societies than Western women. They maintain that Western feminists impose their own experience of sexual discrimination on the 'other' women that they are writing about. In fact, many of these women feel that the depiction of women as weak, feminine and 'victims' is a peculiarly Western, and Victorian, notion that has been imported into colonies from the West. These writers also feel that writing about Third World women as a group is too broad to be useful. Writers like Spivak (1987) maintain that many of these approaches view 'sisterhood as global' and try to smudge the differences between women. When the differences are acknowledged, many studies turn these women into a non-Western 'other', removing agency from Third World women and viewing them as passive objects and victims of barbaric practices.

Two things have caused a breakdown in this kind of theorizing. First, black women have provided a powerful counter-challenge to the 'racist and ethnocentric assumptions of White feminists' (Moraga and Anzaldua, 1983; hooks, 1984; Snyder and Tadesse, 1995; Mohanty, 1991). Second, in some cases, sexual difference came to be celebrated (Scott, 1988), and writers maintained that the problem was not the difference, but how it was constructed and dealt with (Bock and James, 1992). There are numerous differences amongst Third World women, much as there are amongst men – differences in age, class, traditions, ethnicity, nationality, religion and even generation – that would influence their approach to issues. Thus, African women, writers argue, were always more equal to men in their work and life-styles than European or Asian women. In what follows, we will look more closely at the development of this field.

Women in Development (WID)

The origin of the women, gender and development literature is often traced back to Boserup's 1970 work *Women's Role in Economic Development*. This book, for the first time, explicitly considered women's contribution to agricultural production. Boserup analysed data from three continents to show that women's agricultural production was critical in sustaining local and national economies. She also distinguished between

African shifting agriculture and Asian plough cultivation. In the former, easy access to land and low population densities, as well as less class differentiation, meant that men and women shared the work – men cleared the land and women cultivated subsistence crops on it. In Asia, high population densities, excess supply of labourers, and the use of plough technology discouraged women's involvement in agriculture and encouraged segregation of the sexes (Beneria and Sen, 1997, p. 43). Boserup documented the role played by colonialism in imposing Western values regarding the role of women in the household and in society on sub-Saharan Africa. By elevating the work done by men and by granting men land rights, the colonial administration succeeded in many countries in marginalizing women.

This analysis laid the foundation for what was later called the 'Women in Development' (WID) framework. This WID framework subscribed to the assumptions of modernization theories and was based on the idea that modernization is necessary and beneficial for all. It concluded that efforts were required to enable women to share the benefits of such modernization. Writers within this framework talk of a transition from traditional, authoritarian, male-dominated societies to modern, egalitarian, democratic societies. Though they seem to reflect sensitivity to the oppression of women (Visvanathan, 1997, p. 17), they came in for considerable criticism from more radical feminists.

Just as the definition of development went through a number of stages (see chapter 2), from an emphasis on growth to equity to poverty and, finally, efficiency via the neo-liberal consensus in the 1980s, so also, Caroline Moser (1993) argues, there are five distinct temporal approaches within WID. The first, *welfare approach* focused solely on women's reproductive role and on decreasing population growth as a way of alleviating poverty. The second, *equity approach* called for gender equality, and received considerable support from the UN during its Decade for Women. The third approach, the *anti-poverty approach*, concentrated on increasing women's incomes, and therefore concentrated on women's productive role. The *efficiency approach* considers women's reactions to the IMF structural adjustment programmes in the 1980s and their attempts to solve practical problems. Both the anti-poverty and the efficiency approaches concentrated on the practicalities of living, rather than on strategic gains. The fifth approach, *empowerment*, addresses the strategic need to transform the laws and structures in society through grassroots organization. It is often associated with Third World feminist writing.

Women and Development (WAD)

The Women and Development (WAD) paradigm approached the role of women in development from a more radical perspective than WID.

Writing within this framework, Marxist feminists, like liberal feminists, locate women's inferior status in the sphere of production. They maintain that capitalism led to a cleavage in the public and private tasks of households. Women were assigned the private tasks of reproduction and consumption, which are unpaid or poorly paid, while men assigned themselves the better-paid productive tasks. Marxist feminists therefore attach considerable importance to moving women into paid (productive) employment. Some Marxists stress the fact that the unpaid work done by women at home enables workers' wages to be suppressed below their true value, and therefore enables profits to be made. While Marxist feminists were able to reintroduce class divisions into the study of women's roles, they are criticized for paying very little attention to women's reproductive roles as well as for downplaying the role of men in oppressing women (Kabeer, 1994).

Gender and Development (GAD)

Both the WID and WAD approaches view women separately as biological or physical constructs. They do not consider the relationship between men and women or the notion of gender as a social, personal and emotional construct. The Gender and Development (GAD) school attempts to meet this criticism by considering the relationships between men and women, both in the workplace and outside it. The GAD model adopts a holistic approach, in which development is a complex process of political and socio-economic improvement. It analyses women's work in both production and reproduction, and recognizes that intra-household conflicts arise because of gender divisions (between men and women) and generational differences (between women of different generations). Thus, this school attempts to explain why women are at the forefront of feet binding in China, dowry and other problems in India, and circumcision in Africa. Why are women, as mothers and mothers-in-law, willing to reinforce such gendered activities? It is often argued within this literature that patriarchal attitudes linger because, having already experienced these problems when they were young, older women receive a pay-off in being able to dominate younger women in the family as they grow older (Kandiyoti, 1997).

This approach sees women as active agents and not passive recipients. However, they are still unable to analyse the causes of their subordination. Though this approach does not always assume that women are right and men are wrong, it does maintain that, given the different sources of their privileges, they are unlikely to ally themselves with each other. Writers within this approach consider a number of sources of power for women. Though GAD stresses the need for self-organization of women to increase their political power, it also emphasizes the role of the state, at all levels – local, regional and central – in women's emancipation. Unlike the

WID framework, GAD is not very optimistic about the role of the market in enabling women to improve their position (Young, 1997). The ability to draw on gender relations enables this approach to evaluate the distribution of household power, land and resources more carefully and completely than most other theories or approaches.

Conclusion

In practical terms, this new gender awareness has increased women's participation in 'political life' in the Third World. Women have become 'able to organise themselves to increase their own self-reliance, to assert their independent right to make choices and to control resources which will assist in challenging and eliminating their own subordination' (Keller and Mbewe, 1991, p. 76). and so empower them. In the process, many women's movements have become popular. They include trade union-like organizations (like SEWA, which helps self-employed women to get access to credit and markets in Gujarat, India); community-based popular movements focused on everyday practical problems including domestic abuse, food shortages, housing deficiencies, inadequate schooling and health care; and groups focused on environmental degradation (or ecofeminist groups). As we will see later in this chapter, women have commonly brought to these movements a 'holistic ecological perspective which stresses interrelationships and interdependencies between the various components of nature and society that are vital to overall systemic well-being and sustainability' (Agarwal, 1989, WS 60).

Writers within the broad women and development arena argue that it is not possible to see families as single entities wherein the household head makes decisions to improve joint welfare and behaves altruistically towards other family members. In fact, they argue that just as the unequal distribution of incomes across families causes poverty, so also the intra-household distribution of income and consumption disadvantages certain members, usually the women. Over time, the argument has been developed, and has moved away from the notion of women merely as victims in the process. Instead, it is argued that where women are given the power and ability to act, the outcomes are often more favourable in welfare terms, with women more likely to spend their incomes on their family's welfare than men.

Environment and development

All the theories of growth and development that we considered in chapters 4 and 5 have taken the desirability of growth as a given. This was publicly challenged in the 1970s at two events. The first was a report written for the Club of Rome (Meadows, 1972) entitled *The Limits to*

Growth. This report called into question the sustainability of high rates of growth into the future, on the grounds that the known reserves of many key minerals were likely to be exhausted if current rates of consumption were maintained. The second was the Stockholm Conference on the Human Environment in 1972. In this forum, fears for the environment if unlimited growth were pursued were first voiced.

The *Limits to Growth* report was a landmark in environmental discussions. It was the first high-profile study that called the sustainability and desirability (on environmental and socio-political grounds) of continued economic growth into question. It spoke of an apocalyptic end to growth and life if consumption were not curtailed. This report was criticized on a number of grounds. Critics maintained that as a resource becomes scarce, its price will increase, and this will automatically decrease the demand for the resource. Thus scarcity of the kind envisaged in the report was unlikely. Critics also maintained that as prices increase, it becomes more profitable to explore previously marginal reserves; techniques are improved to minimize the use of the resource, and new substitutes are found. These critiques have been reinforced by the fact that the predictions of the report have not been confirmed by experience in the three decades since it was published.

In 1982, the UN Conference on Environment and Development (UNCED), the so-called Earth Summit held at Rio de Janeiro, called upon all industrialized countries to support huge investments in developing countries in health, sanitation, conservation, education and technical assistance (Agenda 21, UNCED). In return, it was hoped that the South would co-operate in decreasing carbon dioxide emissions and preserving biodiversity and the earth's forests. The resulting development, it was hoped, would be sustainable. Each of these events reinforced the notion that development had to take into account the costs to the environment if it was to be sustainable.

While the idea of sustainable development seems simple, there is considerable uncertainty regarding the exact definition of this term. The World Commission on Environment and Development defined it as 'development that meets the needs of the present without compromising the ability of future generations to meet their own needs' (WCED, 1987, p. 43). Though intuitively reasonable, it is hard to pin down the details of such a definition. A more practical but limited definition maintains that a sustainable growth policy would try to maintain an 'acceptable' rate of growth without depleting the national capital or environmental stock (Turner, 1988, p. 12). There has been considerable debate regarding what would be included in the national capital and environmental stock (Pearce and Turner, 1990; Dasgupta and Maler, 1991). In addition, using such stock without depleting it would require that the rates of utilization of resources must be commensurate with their rates of replacement. Also, the rates of emission of effluents must not be greater than the capacity of the ecosystems into which they are released to assimilate them. In this context, the ecosystems are also part of the natural capital of the world, and the rates of recovery and regeneration must ensure that its quality is not depleted. If they are not maintained, then natural capital is being consumed, and the situation is not sustainable (Guimaraes, 1992, p. 52). The environmental stock can be extended to include the stock of all living organisms, large and small, and its maintenance would require the preservation of biodiversity. Extending the preservation of biodiversity to include the preservation of cultural diversity, some authors have argued that true sustainable development requires the preservation of the cultural diversity of the world (a laudable objective so long as it does not fossilize cultures and refuse them the possibility of progress). In the final analysis, therefore, there are those who define sustainable development as 'indistinguishable from the total development of society' (Barbier, 1987, p. 103).

A narrow, technical definition of sustainable development, which focuses on the ability of ecosystems to maintain levels of production, encourages 'environmental managerialism'. This results in attempts to find solutions to environmental problems on a piecemeal basis rather than within a broader framework. As a reaction to such narrowness, the political ecology approach was developed, which focuses on resource users and the social relations in which they are connected, links local relations to the broader socio-economic and geographical context, and uses historical analysis to understand the contemporary situation. It therefore sees environmental issues as political and redistributive, and requires democratic participation and popular empowerment to achieve sustainable development.

Eco-development calls for specific solutions in each ecoregion; solutions that are approached in the light of cultural and ecological data as well as immediate and long term needs. Thus, the most important aspect of this approach is to develop strategies appropriate to the ecological and cultural contexts of each country/region rather than looking for quick-fixes or solutions developed elsewhere.

In recent years, the inability of the earth's atmosphere to absorb the carbon dioxide being released into it has become a significant measure of the sustainability of current levels and types of development. The earth's temperature is controlled by greenhouse gases which radiate solar radiation back into the atmosphere. This keeps the earth cooler than it would otherwise be. Scientists have found, however, that in the last 100 years, the earth's temperature has increased by 0.5°C. This warming has been attributed to the carbon dioxide that is emitted when fossil fuels like coal, gas and oil are burnt, as well as to the release of CFCs (or chlorofluorocarbons) used in refrigeration and other compressor equipment. Some estimates suggest that the earth's temperature could increase by 3°C in the first few decades of the twenty-first century. This would melt the ice-caps, increase evaporation from the seas, and therefore increase precipitation.

The resulting increase in sea-levels, it is argued, could drown some of the low-lying regions of the world, like parts of Bangladesh.

What can be done to prevent this? Equally important, what will be the costs of such preventive measures? Writers like Beckerman (1992) claim that even if the global warming figures are accepted, the economic costs of preventing such warming will be much greater than the consequences of just letting it happen. Should parts of Bangladesh be flooded, the world could compensate Bangladesh for this flooding, and would still be better off in *economic* terms. This, of course, is the operative point. While economic compensation may be possible, it is impossible to evaluate the human and socio-cultural costs of such flooding or other consequences of global warming. In addition, the effects are too uncertain for us to be able to set values on them.

The discussion of global environmental issues has focused on allocating responsibility for pollution to different nations and thus partitioning the costs of prevention across them. Many studies have indicated that the USA bears responsibility for the largest volume of greenhouse gas emission, though they disagree considerably on the exact proportions. The countries of Eastern Europe and the Commonwealth of Independent States come next. Amongst the developing countries, India, China and Brazil make the largest contribution. On the Polluter Pays Principle (PPP), the responsibility for preventing pollution or minimizing environmental damage should rest with the polluter. However, this has created considerable controversy in recent years. Vandana Shiva (1994a), for instance, argues that the responsibility and cost of preventing global warming have been passed on to the millions of future users of refrigerators and air-conditioners in India and China, rather than the small number of transnational corporations like du Pont which are responsible for the production of CFCs.

While global warming is a problem that has occupied the minds of many analysts, there are those who argue that not all environmental problems arise from too much progress. In fact, say these writers, echoing Mrs Gandhi, 'poverty is the greatest polluter'. Many significant environmental problems arise from poverty. In addition, poverty also makes it harder to deal with these problems. Environmental problems arising from backwardness, unemployment and stagnant technology include problems of urbanization (see chapter 11) as well as land degradation (box 6.1) and loss of forest cover. In Bangladesh, the attempt to provide rural areas with clean drinking water led to the sinking of millions of tube-wells in the 1970s. However, the pumping of water from these tube-wells has led to fluctuations in the water-level, which, in turn, seem to be contributing to the release of arsenic that occurs naturally in the alluvial soil. This can be detected only by individual tests at the pumps, which will take considerable time and cost a lot of money, which Bangladesh can ill afford.

Box 6.1   Unsustainable development: land degradation in Africa

That certain types of development are unsustainable can be seen from the experience of land management in the Sahel. The traditional system of cultivation in the Sahel depended upon the conservation of the topsoil and moisture (through the use of cattle dung and crop residue) as well as on the recycling of nutrients. To ensure this, cropping systems in this region were mixed, consisting of millet, sorghum, ground-nuts and cotton. The traditional pastoral system also relied on the movement of herds and pastoralists from region to region in search of pasture. Such measures helped to sustain a small population over long periods of time, though they were unable to provide high incomes or growth (Shanmugaratnam, 1989).

Over time, however, the increasing pressure of population and attempts to increase incomes (especially foreign exchange) led to the spread of cash cropping (ground-nuts and cotton) and commercial ranching in place of the traditional pastoral system. The new systems have resulted in a depletion and degradation of the soil. Peanut cultivation left no crop residue, and the outward migration of the pastoralists meant that organic manures were no longer available. There was no system of fallowing or rotation of land use. Once the peanuts were harvested, land was left bare until the following season, and this allowed the topsoil to be eroded. The result has been the intense vulnerability of these regions to drought (which is common in this area) and the famines that have accompanied it. These have left most cash crop producers destitute, as they had no incomes to tide them over crop failures. Thus, attempts to increase incomes and standards of living through changes in agricultural systems have resulted in a complete breakdown of livelihood systems, and have proved unsustainable.

Similarly, the urbanization associated with development has led to a number of environmental problems (see chapter 11). The intense pressure of population in small areas has led to water, air and noise pollution, as well as congestion. It has resulted in a lack of clean water and sanitation, and therefore in diseases from faecal and chemical contamination. The shanty towns in which most people live in these cities are also more likely to be affected by natural disasters like floods and earthquakes. Some of these disasters could be avoided, or their effects mitigated, through the use of early warning systems, as well as insurance and compensation for those affected. However, this would require considerable funds. As Karshenas (1994) indicates, time-series evidence suggests that environmental management in developed countries has improved, as has the rate of environmental resource depletion per unit of GDP in the industrialized countries. The poor countries are worse off, because they cannot prevent environmental problems, correct them, or live healthily with them.

Thus, the environment and development literature is wide-ranging and diverse. It studies the problems of global warming and environmental sustainability as well as issues relating to who (nationally and internationally) should pay for the problems created. Of course, the environment enters into all aspects of economic growth and development – industrialization, agricultural change, irrigation, waste disposal and even leisure activities. Awareness regarding the costs of progress to the environment has certainly increased in recent years. However, the extent to which this translates into action has still to be seen.

Women, Environment and Development (WED)

The Women, Environment and Development (WED) framework pulls together these two new strands, gender studies and sustainable development. In the 1970s, Northern feminists drew parallels between male control of women and of nature. These ecofeminists trace the decline of the ecological health of the planet to the dominance of patriarchal and Western scientific authority in development planning. Writers such as Mies (1986) and Shiva (1989) therefore call for a move back to subsistence agriculture, a solution that is often dismissed as romantic.

Braidotti et al. (1997, p. 55) trace this school back to the Chipko movement in India, which involved local initiatives to protect forests (see box. 6.2). This inspired other local initiatives in the South, and at

---

Box 6.2   Environmental movements and popular empowerment

Third World environmental movements tend to operate from 'the bottom up'. This broadly participatory approach is common to them all, though they also have quite a diverse membership and ideological orientation. The Chipko movement in India brought to a head the conflict between commercial logging interests and the interests of the tribals who relied on the trees for subsistence (fuel, timber and fodder). In 1973, the villagers stopped the felling of trees by hugging (chipko) them. The movement soon caught the popular imagination in India and abroad.

More recently, environmental interest in India has turned towards the building of dams. Dams provide water for irrigation and industrial and household uses. They also provide electricity, which is in short supply in most developing countries. More importantly, this electricity is based on hydro-(water) power and is therefore cheaper, less polluting and more renewable in the long run than coal. The problem is that the dams which are built displace large numbers of people living and farming in the region. Additionally, there is a wedge between those who pay for the dam (through displacement) and those who gain from it.

A good example of such a distinction between those who pay and those who gain arises from the Sardar Sarovar Dam project in India. This dam is to be built in the state of Madhya Pradesh, while its benefits in the form of increased water resources as well as electricity are due to accrue to the state of Gujarat lying downstream on the Narmada River. In most cases, of course, the distinction between those who pay and those who gain is not made 'explicit' through geographical boundaries. In general, it is the urban, industrial groups that benefit and the population of the submerged villages who lose out.

In the early years after Independence, dam building in India was represented as dynamic and progressive. Those who lost out in the process were convinced to co-operate on the grounds of the greater public good and of the trickle-down of benefits to them. After 50 years during which the fruits of progress have not filtered down, it has become increasingly hard to convince people of the desirability of such projects when they have to forgo their homes and means of livelihood, and compensation is often inadequate.

The project in the Narmada Valley is a case in point. It is expected to involve the building of 30 major dams, 135 medium and 3000 minor dams (Gadgil and Guha, 1994). The Sardar Sarovar itself is expected to displace 100,000 people. The environmental consequences of such dams in submerging forests and the species living within them are also very serious. The protests against the dam began in 1977, but the movement really gained momentum in 1980. The protest is still going on, with a number of activist groups involved, foremost amongst which is the Narmada Bachao Andolan. It has been successful in publicizing the costs of such dam-building activity and in garnering considerable support against it both in India and abroad.

What remains uncertain, however, is how the increasing needs of the population for electricity and water are to be met if all such projects are rejected. While many suggestions have been made, few have been really convincing.

the 1985 Nairobi Forum, women were portrayed as environmental managers. Once environmental issues emerged as the centre-piece for sustainable development, the role women played in the environment became more important.

The WED perspective encompasses many streams. On the one hand, there are those within it who accept the need for economic development but stress the role of women as 'environmental managers' who can minimize the negative effects of such development. On the other, there are writers who maintain that the whole development project is flawed and Western in conception.

Why are women seen as 'environmental managers'? Economists would claim that this is because the sexual division of labour has assigned to women the lower-value, reproductive roles, which require a woman to be in constant contact with her environment. Others maintain that women are naturally privileged in this field because their close interaction with nature has enabled them to accumulate specific knowledge about natural processes and to maintain a reciprocal, symbiotic and harmonious relationship with nature. Shiva (1989) constructs the practical relationship which rural Indian women have with nature as the embodiment of the feminine principle (*prakriti*). According to Shiva, this relationship needs to be recovered for sustainable models of development. Mies (1986) sees women as nature because they give birth to and nurture their children. Both Mies and Shiva wish for a move away from the current, male-dominated, Western model of development towards a more indigenous alternative.

The WED framework has been critiqued and extended by a number of writers. Northern feminists argue that since culture is seen as more powerful than nature, equating women with nature reinforces women's subordination to men. Others, like Agarwal (1991), claim that women have a 'special relationship' with nature not because of their biological make-up but because their marginality (and poverty) have forced them to maintain this link for survival. This link is socially and culturally constructed.

Conclusion

Thus, the study of growth and development began with the simple notion that growth was development. It could therefore be maximized through an increase in savings (chapter 4). It has, however, evolved into one where development is today seen as requiring the broadest welfare of individuals (economic, social, political and cultural). The lack of development in countries of the Third World has been explained by referring to the dependence of these countries on those of the developed world or to the lack of modernization and inadequacy of human and physical capital. While early theories attempted to explain broad patterns of poverty and underdevelopment, there have been refinements in these theories that attempt to consider the specific groups that are underprivileged. The Gender and Development and the Environment and Development strands indicate ways in which the knowledge accumulated by the early theories can be further extended. While the gender frameworks are concerned with improvements in distributing the benefits of growth, the Environment and Development strand calls into question the desirability of growth itself.

In Part III, we will consider development strategies in more detail. In this context, we will consider both the role of the state (chapter 9) and the role of international links (chapters 7 and 8).

Part III

Development Strategy: The State and the International Economy

Parts I and II helped us to define development and explain it. In Part III, we will consider the strategies that can, and have been, employed in the search for development. These relate mainly to the role played by the state and by international links in the development process, both of which have been affected by the shift towards a neo-liberal and increasingly global world system. The role of the state has been undermined, while the role of international linkages has been emphasized.

The '*dirigisme* versus free markets' and the 'protection versus free trade' debates have occupied development theorists and policy-makers since the Industrial Revolution in Britain. While modernization theorists advocated minimum state intervention and maximum trade, dependency theorists explained underdevelopment by pointing to excessively free trade and international investment. These international links are seen as the conduits through which rents appropriated from the periphery reach the core. Dependency theories saw the state as encouraging such expropriation. More recently, neoclassical models (like the modernization theories of old) have advocated minimum state intervention and maximum trade, while Keynesian-type models have opted for greater state involvement and less trade or greater autarchy. Thus, the early 'grand' theories of development defined development strategy in terms of the position taken with respect to the roles of the state and of trade in the process of development.

Development literature has also tended to lump the free trade and free market issues into a single approach to development strategy. This has led to the implicit assumption that countries that have free markets will also have free trade. Consequently, much of the debate has revolved around polarized positions, though in practice, neither extreme is very likely. While theoretically it may be true that free markets must involve free trade too, in reality, any combination of these policies is possible. In most countries, therefore, there was some government intervention, but also some role for the market. There was some protection, but also much free trade. Thus, there is an entire spectrum of positions from highly interventionist, autarchic Socialist states to countries like India, which have mixed policies with regard to both trade and state intervention, to relatively free market and free trade countries like the UK, the USA and, in the developing world, Hong Kong.

The polarization of the debate on development strategies reached its peak in the 1980s when the World Bank published its report on the East Asian miracle (World Bank, 1983). This report characterized the East Asian growth performance as a consequence of free trade and free market policies. Over the 1980s and 1990s, there was much virulent debate over this characterization. In recent years, the free trade and free market hypotheses have been delinked. It is now increasingly being accepted that while the East Asian miracle has resulted from export-led growth (though not free trade), it has also been characterized by significant strategic state intervention in the economy.

The major development in the last two decades that has had an impact on development strategies is an increase in the speed and intensity of globalization. While globalization is generally accepted as being a long-term historical phenomenon, the term was not coined until the last quarter of the twentieth century. It has contributed significantly to the debate surrounding development strategies during this period. Its role in undermining state power and influence will be touched upon in chapters 7 and 9, though I argue that, in spite of this, the state has played, and continues to play, a significant (though possibly decreasing) role in development in most countries. Of course, globalization has increased the impact of international links in development, because most countries are now more open than they were in the 1960s and 1970s. Their trade strategies will therefore have a significant impact on the economic performance of these economies (see chapters 7 and 8).

In this part of the book, we consider these development strategies in greater detail. In chapter 7, we consider the issue of globalization broadly and the role of international trade in particular, while in chapter 8, we concentrate on international financial links – commercial debt, aid and foreign direct investment. Chapter 9 deals with the role played by the state in development, and in chapter 10, we draw together threads from the earlier chapters to discuss three cases – Great Britain, South Korea and China – in terms of their development experiences as well as the development strategies (if any) that they employed.

7

Globalization, Trade and Development

In Part I of this book, we saw that most theories of growth and development implicitly acknowledged the role played by external factors, though it was not until the dependency models arrived on the scene that this role was explicitly recognized. Thus, modernization theories, which were concerned with significant increases in levels of investment (for take-off) and in changing cultural conditions, did accept that in the context of developing countries, foreign aid would play an important role in providing funds for take-off. Marxist theories, despite their absorption in class matters, still recognized that external markets (which could be tapped through trade or foreign direct investment) were important in providing breathing-space to entrepreneurs facing declining profits in the home market.

It was not until the 'onset' of dependency theories, however, that trade and foreign links became central. As we saw in chapter 5, dependency theories saw trade and foreign direct investment (FDI) as a means of extracting surplus rents from developing countries and as providing a channel for these rents to flow into the 'core' countries. Trade and other financial flows between the centre and the periphery then formed the basis of development in the centre and underdevelopment at the periphery. Thus, these theories diagnosed that Europe could not have developed as it did in the absence of its colonies. Analogously, the Third World would not have been left so far behind in the developmental stakes had it not been for their role in the international division of labour. Since then, international links have occupied centre stage in development studies.

Since the most dramatic developments on the international front in the later part of the twentieth century can be subsumed under the heading of globalization, we will begin this chapter by considering globalization briefly in abstract terms. We will then turn to consider the position of the developing world in world trade. Any analysis of globalization or of international links must consider the arguments in favour of, and against, free trade. These arguments have been developed over many decades of debate, and I will summarize them in this chapter before considering other international links in chapter 8.

Globalization

The most talked-about development on the international front over the last few decades has been the increasing globalization of the world economy. However, there is considerable debate over the definition of globalization, as well as over the nature and extent of global interaction. World trade as a proportion of world income is not very different today from levels early this century (Balasubramaniam, 1998), though it is growing faster than it was in the 1970s and 1980s. More significantly, the rate of growth of world exports is higher than the rate of growth of world income. This growth in exports has been facilitated by improvements in transport and communications (especially the Internet), dismantling of trade barriers under GATT/WTO, liberalization of economies under structural adjustment programmes, the birth and growth of regional groupings and many legal instruments attempting to ease trade flows (Balasubramaniam, 1998, p. 3). Another aspect of globalization is an increase in the volume of FDI that has been taking place in recent years. The rate of growth of FDI, at approximately 12 per cent per annum, is higher than that of exports, at 7 per cent per annum (Balasubramaniam, 1998). Can globalization be defined largely in relation to trade and other international links? If not, what more do we need to include in its definition? We will consider these questions in the rest of this section.

Globalization is often seen simply in terms of economic liberalization, Westernization, Americanization or the Internet revolution. Some see globalization as the ascendancy of capitalism, while others see it simply as a replacement term for imperialism and modernization (Kellner n.d.). Globalization is also seen to involve a process of standardization in which global media reinforce sameness and homogeneity. These, of course, are populist interpretations, which, while having some relevance, do not engage with the processes underlying these developments. In an attempt to add precision to definitions of globalization, social theorists argue that globalization refers to fundamental changes in the spatial and temporal contours of social existence, so that time-space distance is annihilated. Time-space distantiation, a term first coined by Giddens (1990), refers to the degree to which the friction of space has been overcome to accommodate social interaction. Technological progress, for instance, has compressed the time-space equation through decreasing the time taken to travel anywhere, while telecommunications have virtually annihilated it by making such interaction almost instantaneous. In this context, Held et al. (1999) describe globalization as the 'widening, deepening and speeding up of worldwide interconnectedness in all aspects of contemporary social life, from the cultural, the financial, to the spiritual' (Held et al., 1999, p. 2). McGrew (2000, p. 347), in turn, points out that globalization involves much more than simply interconnectedness or a shrinking world, for it captures a sense that world-wide connectivity is a permanent or 'institutionalised feature of modern existence'. It signifies a deepening enmeshment of societies in a web of flows of capital, labour, ideas, images, weapons, criminal activity and pollution. It is therefore not merely economic, but also political, legal, cultural, military and ecological. In a similar vein, Robertson (1992) identifies two aspects of globalization: world compression and the intensification of global consciousness.[1] World compression implies that the way we live our lives has immediate implications for people on the other side of the globe, while global consciousness is highlighted when we speak in terms of world order, international recessions and global biodiversity.

In this context, Reich (1991) argues that globalization is occurring at such a pace that 'there will be no national products, no national corporations, no national industries' in the twenty-first century. The example of Ford production in the UK in the 1960s and 1980s, discussed in chapter 2, supports this view. Similarly, the production of washing machines by the Japanese company Matsushita also reflects this trend. Matsushita has a joint venture with a local firm in Malaysia 'producing washing machines for the local market, re-exports to Japan and exports to third countries. The outer case, control unit and drive shafts are made in Japan, the motor comes from Matsushita's subsidiary in Taiwan, the condenser from the firm's subsidiary in Thailand and the valve magnet from South Korea, with other components supplied by local suppliers in Malaysia' (Jenkins, 1992a, pp. 24–5). This, of course, is not the end of the story, because most of these components are, in turn, made from parts in different countries.

Others, however, disagree with this interpretation. Writers like Sachs (1998) see globalization simply as an international division of labour and location of economic activity based on comparative advantage. Wood (1994) takes this argument further by showing that increased trade with developing countries has decreased the demand for unskilled workers in developed countries. Helliwell (1998), examining trade linkages among Canadian provinces, shows that these linkages are many times more extensive among the provinces than between these provinces and the American states that are equally close. While this may be true today, these latter linkages may well be increasing over time.

In spite of such disagreement regarding the true extent of globalization, there is consensus about certain aspects:

1   De-territorialization [refers to the fact that] a growing variety of activities today take place irrespective of geographical location. This is facilitated by telecommunication media like teleconferencing, mobile phones and the Internet, so that many jobs can be done anywhere.
2   Increasing social interconnectedness implies that distant events and forces influence local and regional actions and events. In this context, globalization refers to 'processes of change which underpin a trans-formation in the organisation of human affairs by linking together and expanding human activity across continents and regions' (Held et al., 1999, p. 15).
3   Globalization increases the speed or velocity of social activity.
4   Most analysts agree that globalization is a long-term phenomenon, though many also argue that contemporary globalization is of a distinct nature from that in other periods, because it is more intense.
5   Globalization is a multi-pronged process because the de-territorializa-tion, social interconnectedness and increased speed affect economic, political, social, military and cultural arenas.

Globalization: a long-run phenomenon?

Though the term 'globalization' has been used only recently (in the last three decades of the twentieth century), the concept has been recognized throughout history. Marx, for instance, saw the imperatives of capitalist production as driving the bourgeoisie to 'nestle everywhere, settle every-where and establish connections everywhere' (Marx and Engels, 1848, ch. 1). Most writers today accept that globalization is a long-term, histor-ical phenomenon wherein the world has become smaller and more inte-grated over centuries. However, this compression has occurred at different speeds and in different ways at different points in time. As modes of transport and telecommunication infrastructure have improved, so the pace of globalization has increased.

Global movements on the military, religious and trade fronts existed even in pre-modern times, as did the migratory movements of individuals. In the early modern era (1500–1850), a period which was characterized by the 'rise of the West' and the emergence and development of European institutions and empires, the agents of globalization were the demo-graphic, environmental and epidemiological flows between Europe and the New World.

These flows, however, picked up speed in early modern and modern times, during which financial globalization became important, with funds flowing into many colonies for investment in infrastructure. Between 1850 and 1945 (termed the 'modern' era), Europe began to acquire industrial capital, advanced militaries and powerful state institutions (see chapter 10). Globalization during this period was achieved through economic flows, particularly of trade and investment, especially with the colonies. The slave trade and later the movement of indentured labourers also helped the process of globalization, as did new technologies for transport and communications, especially railways and the telegraph. In contemporary times (post-1945), globalization on the trade, financial, international business, cultural and environmental fronts has become very significant. This period saw the establishment of the Bretton Woods monetary system, and with it, many of the international institutions that today are at the forefront of globalization. Since the end of the Cold War, globalization has resulted from financial and trade liberalization across the world, under the aegis of the International Monetary Fund (IMF), the World Bank and the World Trade Organization (WTO). This has been reinforced by the breakdown of the Soviet Union and the transition of her constituent republics towards a market economy. At a technical level, it has been made possible by the development of communication technologies and systems, especially of the Internet.

Nation-states in a global system

The nature of contemporary globalization has called into question the role of nation-states (see chapter 9). Many writers argue that nation-states are decreasing in importance, and that important decisions are increasingly being made in a global context. Nation-states are no longer (if they ever were) self-sufficient entities, and even the most powerful and privileged political units are now subject to increasingly de-territorialized activity over which they have limited control (Scheuerman, 2002). Dewey, writing in 1954, observed that increasingly dense networks of social ties across borders left local forms of self-government ineffective. Dewey was therefore concerned with how a public can be organized when it does not stay in place, and how citizenship can be sustained in such a mobile, interconnected world (Dewey, 1954). Rodrik (2002) calls this the political trilemma of the global economy, and argues that 'the nation-state system, democratic politics and full economic integration, are mutually incompatible'. If the nation-state system and democratic politics exist, then full economic integration is not possible; for full economic integration undermines the nation-state system and democratic politics. In this latter context, the role played by international institutions – NATO, OECD, IMF, World Bank – becomes more important than the role of national democratic institutions.

Given that globalization has such a significant impact on national boundaries and national social and economic performance, as well as on international institutions, it is not surprising that it has both advocates and critics. Proponents of globalization (generally the neo-liberals and those who subscribe to the Washington Consensus) see globalization as a positive force leading to larger markets and general prosperity for all. They rely on neoclassical arguments relating to comparative advantage to make the case in favour of such globalization. The IMF, World Bank, and WTO are the most high-profile and influential of these advocates.

Critics of globalization, on the other hand, see it as reflecting the West's efforts to maintain its hegemony over the world economy. They include a large number of diffuse and often conflicting groups – environmentalists, a large number of NGOs (in the First and Third Worlds), as well as individuals and groups who do not subscribe to the Washington Consensus. These groups oppose globalization because of a fear of Westernization, a recognition that economic liberalization and globalization have caused enormous problems in many developing countries and have not really delivered on their promises (Weisbrot et al., 2001), and because of the fear that many developing countries and nation-states are losing their voice and position in the global arena in the face of the power of the large international institutions, which are themselves undemocratic and controlled by Washington. In the West, some groups oppose globalization because of concerns that competition from abroad will drive down domestic wages, that financial crises like the East Asian crisis of 1997 or the earlier debt crisis in Latin America might affect the stability of the Western financial system, or fear that environmental pollution and other problems (like SARS) from elsewhere will adversely affect people in the West.

Rodrik (1997) argues that there are three possible problems that may arise from increasing globalization. First, globalization increases substitutability of certain types of labour across national boundaries, and has thus undermined the post-war social bargain (increasing wages and job security in return for peaceful labour relations) in the West. In this context, those who are flexible and have skills that are valued in the global market gain, while others lose out. Second, globalization creates strains, both within and among countries, because domestic norms and social institutions vary across countries. These tensions come to the fore when labour standards or public health standards vary across countries (witness the differences between the USA and Europe over trade in beef). Third, Rodrik argues that since trade can generate benefits only by restructuring economies, this restructuring will mean that some will gain and others lose. However, since contemporary globalization is occurring in the context of decreasing government, then it also implies that those who lose may not be covered by social insurance, thereby creating further tensions.

Thus, for good or bad, the world is becoming much more closely integrated than it has ever been before (except possibly in the 1920s).

Trade and financial links have become increasingly significant. A number of changes have accompanied this development. To begin with, late twentieth-century globalization seems to have decreased the pessimism regarding exports that was common in the 1960s and 1970s. At the same time, however, the characteristics of this globalization, as well as the way in which it is linked with neo-liberalism, have resulted in other causes for concern. The fear that some countries and some groups in all countries will be left behind in this increasing internationalization has grown. We will consider this and many other arguments for and against greater integration in the rest of this chapter.

Changing patterns of world trade

Developing countries were traditionally seen as exporting primary products (usually raw material and food products) which suffer from low income elasticities and decreasing prices. In the 1960s, therefore, pessimism regarding the prospects for exports from developing countries was rife. In recent years, however, both the proportion of manufactures in developing country exports and the proportion of medium- and high-technology exports from developing countries have been increasing (Lall, 1999). In the rest of this section, we look at these two changes in more detail.

1° product exports – now also others [handwritten marginal note]

Proportion of manufactures in developing country exports

Table 7.1 shows the proportion of manufactures exported by a random selection of developing countries. We see that this share has increased for every country in the table, though often from very low levels (from 0 to 4 per cent in Ethiopia and from 2 to 53 per cent in Indonesia between 1980 and 1993). In India and China the growth has been from higher levels (from 59 to 75 per cent in India and from 48 to 81 per cent in China).[2]

While world manufactured exports grew by 8.1 per cent, developing country manufactured exports grew by 14 per cent (Lall, 1999). This caused an increase in the share of developing countries in manufactured exports from 9.8 per cent in 1980 to 23 per cent in 1996. A more detailed analysis of the composition of exports from developing countries in 1995 (see table 7.2) indicates that 66 per cent of total exports from developing countries originate in East Asia. While East Asia leads on every front, its advantage is much greater in clothing, in which it contributes 83 per cent of developing country exports, chemicals (67 per cent), machinery and transport equipment (83 per cent), and iron and steel (56 per cent). Latin America has a relative advantage in food, beverages and tobacco. The

Table 7.1   Structure of exports from developing countries

Country	Manufactures as a % of total exports		Major exports
	1980	1993	
Ethiopia	0	4	Coffee, tea, hides and skins
India	59	75	Textile yarn and fabrics, industrial extractives, precious and semi-precious stones
China	48	81	Footwear, textiles, toys and metal manufactures
Indonesia	2	53	Crude petroleum, natural gas, veneers and plywood
Guatemala	24	30	Coffee, sugar, honey, fruits and nuts, pharmaceutical products
Thailand	28	73	Rice, transistors, valves, office machines, clothing and accessories
Brazil	39	60	Meat and preparations, metalliferous ores, coffee
South Korea	90	93	Footwear, synthetic fabrics, transistors and valves, ships and boats

Sources: Based on World Bank, 1997b, p. 243, and Ray, 1998

Table 7.2   Regional structure of manufacturing exports, 1995

Product	All LDCs ($ billion)	Of which (%s)			
		Latin America	East Asia	China	India
Total exports	1184.7	16.1	65.8	12.6	2.2
Food, beverages and tobacco	107.8	36.9	46.0	10.5	3.6
Textiles	81.5	5.4	35.0	18.2	4.8
Clothing	93.0	4.7	83.4	25.9	4.0
Chemicals	59.5	16.6	66.9	15.0	3.5
Machinery and transport equipment	331.5	14.0	83.2	9.4	0.6
Iron and steel	24.3	28.4	55.6	22.6	3.2

Source: Balasubramaniam, 1998, table 4

rest of the developing world is not performing very well, with their manufactured exports growing at only 7.4 per cent (less than the rate of growth of world manufactured exports) (Lall, 1999).

Proportion of high-technology exports originating in developing countries

Equally significant are the changes in the technological patterns of developing country trade. Analysing trade patterns with respect to their technological composition, Lall (1999) divided exports into raw material-based (RM), low- (LT), medium- (MT) and high-technology (HT) exports. He found that while world RM exports grew at 5.7 per cent, high-technology exports grew at 11.6 per cent between 1980 and 1996 (table 7.3).

Lall points out that developing countries have higher growth rates in each category, and that their lead increases with increasing technological complexity. Thus, while RM exports from the developing countries grew at 2.2 per cent, MT exports grew at 10.2 per cent and HT exports at 11.3 per cent. While the faster growth of HT exports may seem surprising, Lall argues that it relates to the nature of the technology. MT products tend to be technologically demanding (with respect to scale, skill and linkage intensity), and include products like automobiles, machinery and chemicals. They are generally more difficult to relocate as they have long lead times. Only a few newly industrializing countries (NICs) have the industrial base required to produce these products. On the other hand, in HT industries like electronics, some production processes and design are complex, but the final assembly is not very skill-intensive. It is therefore easy to relocate in the context of decreasing transport costs. Many East Asian economies have become assembly centres for these products. This accounts for the significant presence of developing countries in HT exports (LDC share in 1996 was 30 per cent in HT exports and only 11.5 per cent in MT exports).

This shift towards exports (and HT exports) has been relatively recent. In fact, it is only since the growth of the East Asian economies that export

Table 7.3 Technological structure of world exports

Region	Growth rates of exports (1980–1996)			
	Raw material	Low-tech	Medium-tech	High-tech
World	5.7	6.9	7.8	11.6
Developed countries	5.2	5.9	7.2	9.8
Less developed countries	7.4	12.6	17.4	21.1
Developing (less industrialized) countries	2.2	6.7	10.2	11.3

Source: Lall, 1999, table 4, p. 1775. Reprinted from *World Development*, 27(10), S. Lall, India's Manufactured Exports: Comparative Structure and Prospects, pp. 1769–1986, © 1999, with permission from Elsevier.

exports

↑
↓

ISI

promotion has been seen as a serious option for many developing countries. Is such export-led growth feasible for all developing countries? What are the advantages of a free trade strategy? What are its disadvantages? We will consider some of these issues in the next few sections.

Trade strategy: free trade or protection?

As we saw in chapter 5, the centre–periphery paradigm gave rise to a concrete policy recommendation to break the 'bonds of dependency' – the protection of domestic industry or import-substituting industrialization (ISI). The ISI model, when it was first articulated, went against the grain of the then dominant free trade rhetoric (which was underpinned by the classical theories of comparative advantage and specialization). This was not to say that this rhetoric found applicability in practice. Protection has always been a weapon used by the more powerful to maintain their advantage. Many colonizers used it against their colonies, for instance. Thus, Britain protected its firms until it gained dominance in world manufacturing (see chapter 10). America too protected its firms until it became predominant in manufacturing. In a careful historical analysis of trade strategies in a number of countries, Chang (2002) argues that the dominant players only espoused the free trade cause once they achieved dominance. This strategy, he calls 'kicking away the ladder'. It is also reflected in the re-emergence of the neo-liberal paradigm in the 1980s, which has increased the emphasis on free trade policies. Since it has been the dominant trade ideology in the last decade, we will rehearse this case in the next section before moving on to consider the case in favour of protection.

The gains from trade

The traditional view is that trade is universally beneficial to all those who engage in it. According to this view, every country has a comparative advantage in producing some good. If two countries produce the same two goods, then even though one country may be more efficient in absolute terms in producing both goods, its advantage in producing one of them must be larger than that in producing the other. Thus, it must be relatively more efficient in producing one of them. This country would then concentrate on producing the good in which its efficiency (relative to that of the other country) is larger. Welfare is maximized when each country produces the good it is more efficient in producing and trades it, rather than when both countries attempt to produce both goods.

Comparative advantage may arise from a number of factors. If one country has more (or better) technology, then it may be able to produce some products more cheaply than the other country. Similarly, some countries may have more land or may have a type of soil or weather that is particularly well suited to the production of certain agricultural products. Third, preferences for domestic consumption are likely to influence both production and the tradable surplus. If a country has a stronger preference for cars than textiles, for instance, then it is more likely to import cars and export textiles. Finally, the presence of economies of scale is a major source of comparative advantage. Economies of scale imply that the costs of producing a good will decrease as the volume produced increases. When both countries produce both goods, then they will not be able to realize all these economies of scale. Free trade theories therefore maintain that production according to comparative advantage will decrease costs, because it allows countries to produce goods that they are most efficient at producing. Consumers benefit because they now have greater choice.

In addition to these static benefits, trade helps countries by widening the total market for their products. This has been called the 'vent for surplus' argument, which is especially important in the case of perishable natural resources like fish and mineral resources. International markets are also useful if economies of scale require a certain volume to be produced and this cannot be absorbed within the country. In this case, the total gains from trade will exceed the static gains from a more efficient allocation of resources. Other dynamic gains from trade include the stimulus to competition, acquisition of knowledge and new ideas, together with the dissemination of information, the possibility of accompanying capital flows, and increased specialization leading to more roundabout methods of production and changes in attitudes and institutions. These advantages led proponents of free trade to go beyond static efficiency arguments towards dynamic growth-related arguments in which trade features as an engine of growth. We will consider this in the next section before we move on to arguments against free trade.

Trade as an engine of growth

Britain exported cotton textiles in the nineteenth century, while the USA, Australia and Argentina exported primary products. In all these cases, international trade provided an impetus to growth. Several studies have demonstrated that exports contribute more to GDP growth than simply the change in their own volumes (Balassa, 1978; Michaely, 1977). Studying the effect of exports on growth, Feder (1983) concludes that export orientation improves growth rates because it brings the economy closer to an optimal allocation of resources. Balassa (1978) confirms this positive relationship when he concludes that 'the increase in Korea's GNP would have been 37% smaller if its export growth rate equalled the average for the countries concerned' (pp. 186-7). Michaely (1977) maintained, however, that 'the positive association of the economy's growth with the growth of the export share appears to be particularly strong among the more developed countries', so growth is affected by export performance 'only once countries achieve some minimum level of development' (p. 52).

Why might exports be expected to increase overall growth rates? Production for export markets allows capacity to be more fully utilized and technological improvements to be undertaken. Foreign trade multipliers are generally quite high, and for efficient economies can lead to almost indefinite growth. Export activities also have higher factor productivities than non-export activities, because competition encourages innovativeness, adaptability and efficient management. In addition, there are 'the indirect effects of exports operating through changes in incomes and costs' – that is, the spill-over effects (Balassa, 1978). These occur through the development of efficient and internationally competitive management, the introduction of improved techniques, the training of higher-quality labour, a steadier flow of inputs, and so on. Finally, if the exporting sector is a major intermediate input into other industrial and commercial activities, then its improved efficiency also benefits the domestic economy. Both the spill-over and the efficiency effects are maximized when the linkages between the exporting sector and the home economy are relatively strong, as we will see. The exporting sector helps economies by providing much-needed foreign exchange, as well as by improving the trade balance. These factors further reinforce the push towards growth.

Many studies (Bhagwati, 1988a; Grossman and Helpman, 1991) argue that there is a positive feedback effect from exports to growth and back to exports. Thus, increased trade leads to higher growth, and this in turn facilitates more trade – a virtuous circle. Recent studies have attempted to test this two-way causality empirically. Marin (1992), studying the relationship between exports and productivity in Germany, Japan, the UK and the USA, finds that an outward-looking regime favours productivity growth. Kunst and Marin (1989) test the two-way causality on Austrian trade data, and find that there is no causal link from exports to productivity, but that there is a link from productivity to exports, implying that only efficient and productive firms can succeed in export markets. Ribeiro Ramos (2001) also finds a two-way causation between exports and growth in Portugal, with the feedback effect from growth to exports dominating the export-led growth effect. He argues that this may relate to the smallness and openness of the Portuguese economy.

If exports and growth form a virtuous circle, how can exports be encouraged in the first place? This problem occupied development economists throughout the second half of the twentieth century, when there was considerable export pessimism amongst them (Nurkse, 1961; Lewis, 1980). The main concern during this period was the decreasing demand for primary product exports from developing countries. In his 1979 Nobel lecture, Lewis analysed the consequences of a slow-down of developing country trade because of a slow-down in the growth of developed countries. Lewis looked to South–South trade as an alternative to North–

South trade. He maintained that 'the growth rate of world trade in primary products over the period 1873 to 1913 was 0.87 times the growth rate of industrial production in the developed countries' (Lewis, 1980, p. 556). This relationship was seen as a mechanical one. Underlying it was the assumption that the products produced by developing countries are used as inputs into, or are complementary to, production in developed countries. If this is not true, then there is no reason why the growth of industrialized countries would increase demand for primary goods. Thus, each group of countries is seen to specialize in a completely different set of products, and the products produced by developing countries (primary products) are demanded (both as intermediate inputs and for consumption) by developed countries.

The Lewis relationship, if it exists today, is more complicated than the simple mechanistic relationship that Lewis suggested. First, as developing country exports become more similar to those from developed countries, the simple demand–supply relationship no longer exists. It remains true, however, that though developing country exports are now manufactures, they are still relatively low-level manufactures. Also, developing countries that export 'non-traditional' products like flowers (Zimbabwe), wine (Chile) and horticultural products (Chile and Costa Rica) depend upon good economic conditions in Europe and North America for their trade (Brohman, 1996). The precise relationship will differ from country to country, and even across products. Riedel (1984) therefore argued that the relationship was not stable.

In this context, the operative question is not whether exports lead to growth, because the experience of the East Asian economies, as well as the results of many empirical studies, indicates that they can. The key questions relate to whether exports are necessary or sufficient for growth, and whether manufactured exports from developing countries can continue to expand. This concern was articulated in a well-known paper by Cline (1982) which asked whether the East Asian miracle can be generalized. There are two sources of concern. First, if all developing countries shift towards export promotion, would there be sufficient demand to absorb the increased output? Second, would Western markets remain open to such imports?

In answer to the first question, many writers maintained that not all developing countries would produce the same goods, and that there are many niches still to be occupied. Thus, Pomfret (1997, p. 95) maintains that in the late 1960s, false eyelashes and wigs were amongst Hong Kong's leading exports, and provided her with a niche from which she picked up skills, which could be applied to marketing other fashion products. Secondly, not all developing countries are at the same stage of development. Therefore, they will be producing different goods at different stages, and need not compete directly with each other. Thus, South Korea moved out of light manufactures, and the second tier of Asian

Tigers took them up. Now, these countries are moving out of them, and a new set of countries will take them up. Third, even though developing country manufactured exports have increased, import-penetration rates into high-income markets for individual products remain below 15–20 per cent (Pomfret, 1997, p. 102), so there is a long way to go before markets become saturated. Finally, South–South trade may help to fill the gap in demand for products originating from developing countries.

In response to the second question, the fear of protection in the West has been articulated by many writers. Bello (1992) cites a number of examples to illustrate the 'demise of free trade' in the USA when competition from the Far East became threatening. First, in 1989, the USA revoked the tariff-free entry of selected NIC imports under the Generalized System of Preferences and placed quantitative restrictions on South Korean textile and steel imports. It forced an appreciation of the South Korean won and the Taiwanese dollar and aggressively drove for lower tariff barriers and other restraints on US products in the South Korean market. Washington and the US corporations have also made unauthorized technological transfer to the NICs very difficult.[3] In spite of measures like this, Bhagwati (1988a) argues that US protectionism has not been really disastrous, because many American companies invest abroad and expect to import their output back into the USA. Thus, when the US semiconductor producers gathered to discuss anti-dumping arrangements against Japanese producers, Motorola Inc. and Texas Instruments Inc. did not join the discussions. They were producing in Japan and exporting to the US market! (Bhagwati, 1988a, p. 44).

As already indicated, the export-led growth strategy gained ground in the 1980s through liberalization and structural adjustment programmes world-wide (see box 7.1). However, though accompanied by considerable enthusiasm to begin with, these strategies are increasingly being criticized for not promoting 'balanced and equitable growth' (Black, 1991, p. 85) or for producing a truncated, severely circumscribed type of development that has excluded the majority (Frobel, Heinrichs and Kreye, 1980). Saha (1991) finds that in Africa, liberalization and structural adjustment programmes have deepened underdevelopment in many sectors and have hastened de-industrialization in many cases. The export-oriented growth strategy has also been critiqued on the grounds that it lacks a concern for the broader developmental goals of improving the living standards of the majority and promoting balanced growth. It simply assumes that exports lead to growth, which in turn will trickle down to the majority. As we saw in chapter 1, this need not be the case. More significantly for this particular strategy, in the absence of well-developed linkages between export sectors and the rest of the economy, any development that does take place will be limited both spatially and sectorally.

It is clear that there are many advantages to be obtained from trade. Does trade have to be 'free' to obtain these advantages? What are the

---

Box 7.1   Export-led growth in East Asia

As indicated above, many countries in East Asia shifted very rapidly from ISI policies towards export promotion. South Korea, for instance, followed a carrot-and-stick policy of giving selected domestic companies (chaebols) considerable benefits if they met export targets. However, failure to meet these targets resulted in the withdrawal of these benefits. This allowed firms to have the advantages of size (only one or two firms in each industry were thus encouraged) while at the same time forcing them to be competitive. South Korea's success, together with encouragement from the IMF and the World Bank led to the liberalization of trade regimes in a number of developing countries in the 1980s.[1]

More recently, the South-East Asian economies have followed a similar strategy, shifting from ISI to export promotion. While they were relatively successful prior to the crisis in 1998, many writers argue that these economies have specialized in the export of manufactured goods without actually having industrialized (Lall, 1996). There has been no industrial deepening. Instead, multinationals locate their subsidiaries here to take advantage of cheap labour and to avoid tariffs. Much of the production is the simple assembly of imported inputs in export-promotion enclaves. High-value-added operations like training, design and R&D continue to be undertaken abroad.

[1]Chang (2002) notes that policies similar to these were used by both Britain and the USA in the early stages of their development. Thus, the 1721 legislation in Britain imposed duties on raw materials, allowed duty drawbacks on inputs into exported manufactures and increased duties on manufactured imports.

---

possible disadvantages of 'free trade' on the basis of comparative advantage? What are the arguments in favour of protection? We will consider these questions in the next section.

Export pessimism and the rise of import substitution

In a recent study of development strategy, Chang (2002) maintains that most countries, including Britain, have protected their industries in the early stages. Thus, Britain 'continued its policy of industrial promotion until the mid-19th century, by which time its technological supremacy was overwhelming' (Chang, 2002, p. 22). In fact, argues Chang, Britain reintroduced tariffs on a large scale in 1932 when it finally acknowledged that it had lost its manufacturing eminence. Chang (2002) goes on to implicate Germany, France, Sweden and a number of smaller European countries in such infant industry policies. He also quotes Bairoch, agreeing that the USA was 'the mother country and bastion of protectionism'

(Chang, 2002, p. 24). Given that most developed countries have used protectionism at some point in their development, Chang argues that current attempts to advocate free trade through the WTO to developing countries look suspiciously like 'kicking away the ladder' once countries have reached the top.

Analysing the trade orientation of forty-one countries between 1963 and 1985, the World Bank (1987) sees only three countries – Hong Kong, Singapore and South Korea – as strongly outward-orientated. Of these, Hong Kong and Singapore are more in the nature of city-states, and South Korea had just emerged from a period of inward orientation (see table 7.4). Fourteen of the countries were strongly inward-oriented between 1973 and 1985. They included Argentina, India and Ghana. In addition, during this period, Chile, Pakistan, Sri Lanka, Turkey and Uruguay shifted towards less inward-oriented regimes. Since then, a very large number of countries have liberalized their regimes.

> Of the 109 developing countries and economies in transition that have launched major market-oriented reform programmes since the 1980s, 75 have done so since 1989. At the same time, 107 of the 134 members of the WTO are developing countries and economies in transition, while another 28, including China, the Russian Federation and Taiwan Province, are actively negotiating their entry under special conditions. (Sercovich et al., 1999, p. 11)

Initially, the arguments against trade were the arguments against comparative advantage. Later, the debate became one of degree (how much trade) rather than of kind (trade or not). Trade, according to comparative advantage, would result in a situation where developing countries were exporting primary products and the developed countries exported manufactures. Free trade would not allow any changes in this pattern. Development theorists argued that such a division of labour would create considerable problems for the developing countries. To begin with, the detractors of free trade maintained that although overall welfare may be maximized through free trade, theory says very little about the distribution of this welfare across countries. More specifically, will all countries gain equally from trade? The division of the benefits of trade depends largely upon the types of products being produced by the countries. If the income elasticity of demand for some commodities (say manufactures) is higher than for others (say primary products), then the demand for manufactures will grow faster as world incomes increase. Countries producing these goods will benefit more from trade in the long run than countries producing lower-income-elastic primary products. Comparative advantage could also lead to excessive specialization in a narrow range of products and therefore leave the economy susceptible to outside influences.

Arguments in favour of free trade also tend to overlook the fact that some activities are subject to increasing returns to scale and others to

Table 7.4   Classification of forty-one countries by trade orientation

Period	Strongly outward-oriented	Moderately outward-oriented	Moderately inward-oriented	Strongly inward-oriented
1963–73	Hong Kong Singapore South Korea	Brazil Cameroon Colombia Costa Rica Côte d'Ivoire Guatemala Indonesia Israel Malaysia Thailand	Bolivia El Salvador Honduras Kenya Madagascar Mexico Nicaragua Nigeria Philippines Senegal Tunisia Yugoslavia	Argentina Bangladesh Burundi Chile Dominican Republic Ethiopia Ghana India Pakistan Peru Sri Lanka Sudan Tanzania Turkey Uruguay Zambia
1973–85	Hong Kong Singapore South Korea	Brazil Chile Israel Malaysia Thailand Tunisia Turkey Uruguay	Cameroon Colombia Costa Rica Côte d'Ivoire El Salvador Guatemala Honduras Indonesia Kenya Mexico Nicaragua Pakistan Philippines Senegal Sri Lanka Yugoslavia	Argentina Bangladesh Bolivia Burundi Dominican Republic Ethiopia Ghana India Madagascar Nigeria Peru Sudan Tanzania Zambia

decreasing returns. Activities in the former category will lead to decreases in costs as output increases, while in the latter category, any attempt to expand production will only result in an increase in costs. The commodities most subject to decreasing returns are primary products.

In addition to the above theoretical arguments against specialization on primary products, economists like Prebisch (1959) and Singer (1950) argued that primary product prices decrease relative to the prices of manufactured goods in the long run. There was some evidence in the 1950s and 1960s that primary product prices were decreasing from their high points during the Korean War. This relates to the argument (Emmanuel, 1972) that while increased productivity in agriculture resulted in a reduction in product prices, increased productivity in manufacturing resulted in increased wages. However, these price trends are still being debated. They are very sensitive to the commodities and time periods chosen for analysis. Though recent studies seem to show that in the very long run (since 1900), primary product prices have declined slightly relative to those of manufactures, it is felt that the trends might look different if the improved quality of manufactures is taken into account. More recently, since the oil price boom of the 1970s, the inclusion of oil prices in primary products has changed the picture completely. Apart from the long-term decline in prices, primary product prices are seen to fluctuate considerably in the short run, depending upon supply conditions. This results in unstable incomes for those dependent on primary product exports.

In addition to the decreasing prices of primary products, pessimism regarding primary product exports also related to stagnating demand for these products. Given their low income elasticities of demand, the demand for these products has stagnated even though world incomes have increased. Such a dependence on raw material exports to Western markets also leaves countries exposed to economic conditions in the West. Thus, flower exports from Zimbabwe to Europe or horticultural exports from Chile and Cuba to North America must depend upon conditions in these markets. Also, as prices increase, raw materials are used more efficiently, and more synthetic substitutes are used in place of natural raw materials. Finally, the increasing protection of agriculture in the West as well as the slow-down in population growth there have further decreased the demand for primary product exports.

In response to such arguments, many development economists maintained that manufacturing provided the way ahead for developing countries. In conjunction with the domestic advantages of manufacturing (see chapter 2), the arguments against primary product exports were seen to provide a clear case for developing countries to ignore the dictates of comparative advantage. The case against free trade became the case for industrialization and therefore protection: comparative advantage in manufacturing is not inherent. It is created through investment (in plant, machinery and infrastructure). Firms (and industries) therefore require protection while the investment becomes operational and begins to function efficiently and competitively. It was clear from the beginning that, given the early start enjoyed by firms in developed countries in most industries, attempting to industrialize in an open economy would not be feasible. The advanced and efficient firms of the First World would out-compete the late starters in the Third World. Protection of infant industry therefore became important. Protectionist barriers would enable industry to tap the domestic market, and in industries with economies of scale this would help decrease costs. It would allow local firms to compete more effectively in world markets at a later stage.

The first example of such a state-led industrialization strategy was that of Japan in the inter-war period. The Japanese MITI (the Ministry of International Trade and Industry) refused to accept static comparative advantage arguments, and strategized to move Japan into manufacturing and later into high-technology industries, and the rest is history. Had Japan stuck to its pre-war comparative advantage in light manufactures, its economic history would have been very different. Throughout the 1950s and 1960s, country after country began to explicitly adopt import-substituting industrialization policies. These countries all decided to ignore the implications of comparative advantage theory and attempted to create a comparative advantage in manufacturing through investment.

In spite of many arguments in favour of protectionism, it is quite generally acknowledged that such protectionism cannot, and indeed should not, continue for ever. In fact, problems with ISI began to surface very quickly in many developing countries in the 1960s. Countries found the first stage (entry into consumer goods industries) relatively easy, because of the latent demand for these products and the relatively simple technology involved in making them. However, once the domestic market for these products was saturated, they found it hard to move on to the next phase – the production of intermediate and capital goods or the export of consumer products. The former was difficult because in their attempt to protect local industries, most governments allowed capital imports free of tariffs. Thus, in many countries, ISI strategies often implied encouragement for capital-intensive consumer goods industries like automobiles and domestic appliances for which capital inputs were imported. Such a concentration on capital-intensive industries was in-appropriate for most developing countries, and led commentators like Scitovsky (1984, p. 953) to state that 'import substituting industrialisation seems to have meant concentrating on activities in which the LDCs had a comparative disadvantage'. In the face of low-priced imports, domestic capital goods industries were unlikely to develop. On the other hand, it was difficult to export consumer products because blanket protection, which benefits both genuine cases and inefficient firms, often implies that high levels of inefficiency persist, and domestic firms become uncompeti-tive relative to international firms.[4] Secondly, if domestic markets are too small for economies of scale, then protection will hinder rather than help firms to decrease costs. Thus, these countries cannot rely on consumer goods exports either. Many countries have found that the benefits of protection often go to foreign firms who set up within their borders. In spite of these problems, however, withdrawing protection becomes difficult because of the interest groups that develop to fight for it.

The ISI strategy faced its real crisis when it became clear that its success depended on an expansion of the domestic market, which in its turn depended upon a more equitable distribution of income and wealth. The latter was required if domestic markets were to grow, for in their absence, demand was restricted to a few rich individuals. Given the inability to achieve such equitable growth (or resistance to achieving it), opposition to ISI began to surface. ISI soon began to be criticized from both left and right. The right maintained that it involved excessive state interference, which prevented countries from exploiting outward-oriented growth. On the left, dependency theorists maintained that ISI strategies required changes in the pattern of consumption and ownership, and that, in the absence of such changes, ISI strategies would be very limited.

Experience, however, seems to indicate that most developing countries cannot rely exclusively on one strategy; they have to combine both (see box 7.1). The pertinent issue then seems to be how far to go towards ISI and when to change. Should governments encourage export promotion? Or should they leave it to the market? How are countries to push their firms to become sufficiently efficient to compete in international markets? In general, it seems fair to conclude that ISI is likely to be more successful in large economies where raw materials need not be imported and markets are sufficiently large to take advantage of economies of scale. Experience in East Asia (see chapter 10) has also revealed that ISI is likely to prove more successful if it is used only for a short period when countries first begin to industrialize. As they mature, the withdrawal of protection will force firms to become more efficient, and will also increase the size of the markets that they can tap. Writing in 1984, Singer says:

> With the benefit of hindsight, the possibilities of export-substitution were underrated, partly because of the failure to anticipate the vigorous global growth of 1950–1973. ISI should have been proposed as a temporary and transitional strategy only; more attention should have been paid to the time sequences and linkages binding the growth of the domestic market with the development of exports; product cycles in manufacturing goods should have been more closely studied; and the economic history of the latecomer, such as the United States of America and Germany in the 19th century, should have been more carefully studied from this angle. But, none of this invalidates the appropriateness of ISI. (Singer, 1984, p. 83)

Conclusion

Trade is of major significance to most developing countries. Whether a country is import-substituting or export-promoting, its approach to trade determines its policies towards industry, agriculture and other domestic sectors. Developing countries have shifted from strongly inward-oriented policies in the 1960s and 1970s towards greater outward orientation in the 1980s and 1990s. These changes contributed significantly to increasing globalization, and were in turn reinforced by other moves in this direction, including the growth of information and communication technology, the increase of foreign direct investment, the signing of the Uruguay Round declaration and the break-up of the Soviet bloc and the subsequent marketization of these economies. In some countries, the shift towards greater openness has been driven by debt, and in others by the need to attract foreign investment. We turn to consider these international financial flows in greater detail in the next chapter.

8

International Financial Flows

It is often argued, on both economic and ethical grounds, that funds should flow from developed to developing countries.[1] Economists argue that because developing countries are capital-scarce economies, they will yield higher rates of return on investment and are therefore likely to attract funds, all else being equal. The problem is, of course, that all else is not equal. As we will see in this chapter, funds rarely flow to the countries that need them most; and when they do, they rarely contribute as much to development as they are expected to. The flow of funds across the world has increased significantly in recent years with the removal of capital regulations and liberalization across the world. The 1970s and 1980s saw much flow in the form of commercial debt from the West to the developing world. In the late 1980s and early 1990s such commercial debt has been replaced by flows of FDI. Aid flows have generally been relatively small. In spite of globalization and the increasing volumes of such flows, however, funds tend to flow towards a small group of countries. More specifically, Africa (most in need of such funds) obtains the smallest percentage of funds from both debt and FDI. Technological progress has increased the levels of investment required for take-off (chapter 2). Some writers have seen international financial flows as providing a possible solution to the developmental problems of developing countries. While modernization theories emphasized the role of aid flows (from the developed to the developing world) in financing development, dependency (and Marxist) theories were concerned with the role played by foreign direct investment in the appropriation of profits from the developing to the developed world.

For many countries in other parts of the world, however, international financial flows help plug the savings and foreign exchange gaps that most developing countries suffer from. We saw in chapter 4 that growth requires investment, which, in turn, requires savings. This is true whether we are concerned with the Harrod–Domar model of growth, the Solow model, or even the new growth theories. Since developing countries generally have low GDP per capita (almost by definition), most of their incomes are consumed, and therefore they have relatively low savings. This implies that they could suffer from a chronic lack of funds for investment. Similarly, most modern economies are tied into the international economy. This implies that they can import raw materials and technology from abroad. However, these imports require foreign exchange, which in turn requires these countries to export. Most developing countries are unable to export the quantities required (except the oil-exporting economies), and therefore suffer from a lack of foreign exchange. International financial flows make funds available for investment and, significantly, these funds are in the form of foreign exchange.

In this chapter, we will consider three ways of plugging savings and foreign exchange gaps. First, funds may be borrowed by developing countries from private commercial banks and international organizations. Such borrowing reached a height in the 1970s and erupted in the debt crisis of 1982. Second, aid funds flow from developed countries to the developing world. Aid flows helped Germany to rebuild her economy after World War II, and contributed to South Korean development. Finally, foreign direct investment brings funds for investment as well as complementary resources (human capital and managerial resources) into developing countries.

Commercial debt and the 1980s debt crisis

Developing countries have always borrowed abroad. In the nineteenth century, Britain invested funds in building the railways in Latin America and in India. Until early this century, returns from Britain's investment in her colonies helped her to sustain her balance of payments position. Though countries have, from time to time, defaulted on these loans, the lending has for the most part continued unabated. After World War II, however, development funds were largely provided by official sources: the international financial institutions – the IMF, the World Bank, the European Bank for Reconstruction and Development (EBRD), the International Finance Corporation (IFC) – and national governments.

In the 1970s, a conjunction of factors increased the significance of this kind of source. The oil price increases of the early 1970s resulted in the accumulation of large current account surpluses in the oil-exporting countries. These surpluses were deposited in Western banks, creating a stock of petrodollars. Western banks, in their turn, were unable to find profitable investment opportunities at home because their own economies were growing very slowly. They therefore turned to developing countries, especially in Latin America, which had been growing very fast and consequently provided profitable investment opportunities. These countries, in their turn, found official financing insufficient for their needs, and turned to commercial banks. Perceiving these loans as being guaranteed by governments, the banks saw them as providing all the advantages of high rates of return and low risk.[2] By 1979, over 77 per cent of total external debt to developing countries was on commercial terms, as compared to 40 per cent in 1971. These loans were at higher rates of interest and at shorter maturities than official loans.

Until 1979, the situation was manageable. Increasing inflation worldwide caused by the 1973 oil price hikes decreased the real price of oil, and resulted in very low real interest rates. In addition, developing countries were able to increase their export revenues, and therefore also keep paying interest on their loans. Between 1973 and 1980, the debt–export ratios for non-oil developing countries decreased, encouraging them to continue borrowing until 1979. From 1979 onwards, two problems surfaced. First, the 1979 oil price increases worsened the balance of payments of many oil-importing countries. Secondly, in the developed world, many countries began to pursue stabilization policies to restrict inflation. This decreased their rates of both growth and inflation. The former decreased the demand for primary products produced by developing countries, and the latter increased the *real* interest rates being paid by these countries on their loans. The situation came to a head when Mexico declared its inability to service its debt in August 1982. Most banks did not foresee the crisis until it actually happened. Even in early 1982, funds continued to flow into Latin America, and most analysts were talking of the problems as temporary.

A number of factors contributed to the crisis. Chief amongst them was the use made of these borrowed funds. Borrowed funds need to be productively invested if they are to be repaid. In fact, as seen above, if they help to plug the savings and investment gaps in a country, they can increase the rate of growth of the economy, and this then helps to repay the loans in the future. Using the funds to increase export revenues is also likely to be very useful. South Korea, for instance, had the largest debt per capita in 1981, but never suffered a debt crisis because its loans were used to finance projects which generated sufficient exports to cover interest payments. By the mid-1980s, South Korea began to pay back principal, and its external debt decreased from $47 bn to $29 bn in 1985. Taiwan, the ninth biggest debtor in 1981, paid off its debts in a few years, and became a net creditor after 1987 (Pomfret, 1997).

Problems arise, however, when loans are not invested productively, as was the case in many developing countries, where the funds were used to finance consumption, rather than investment. To begin with, the oil price increases had hit the oil-importing countries hard, and in the face of increased import costs of oil, many countries used their loans to maintain their consumption levels. In some extreme cases, like the Philippines under Marcos, Nicaragua under Somoza, and Zaire under Mobutu, the debt was used for luxury consumption, extravagant military expenditure or was even embezzled. Another common problem was that these loans were often invested in projects that had long gestation periods and would yield low rates of financial return. While this in itself is not bad, it does place the loans at risk, should interest rates increase, as happened in the 1980s. In addition, even oil-exporting developing countries like Mexico and Nigeria borrowed funds because they were cheap. Given their own oil surpluses, these funds were often invested in marginally profitable projects, which became loss-making as soon as interest rates rose marginally.

Between 1971 and 1983, total external debt increased from $90 bn to $817 bn, an increase of more than 900 per cent. Debt servicing[3] increased by more than 1,000 per cent. By 1982, twenty-four countries had renegotiated payments on debts valued at $71 bn, of which Mexico's debt itself stood at $44 bn. It is not surprising, therefore, that dependency theorists saw the debt crisis as an intensification of the financial dependence of Third World countries on the countries of the West (Sweezy and Magdoff, 1984; Pool and Stamos, 1985).

However, the crisis was not limited to Latin America. Countries in sub-Saharan Africa had also borrowed large sums of money, creating a crisis of quite different dimensions. These countries had smaller volumes of debt (approximately one-tenth of total developing country debt), which were unlikely to destabilize the world financial system. However, given their already low standards of living, decreasing consumption to repay debts was likely to prove disastrous in humanitarian terms. As George (1993, p. 61) puts it, Africa's debt is 'so modest as to be a threat to no one except Africans themselves'. The obvious solution, given their relatively small debts in any case, would have been to write them off. But since the crisis in sub-Saharan Africa occurred at the same time as that elsewhere in the world, Western banks were reluctant to send the wrong signals to other sovereign debtors. There were fears that if some countries' debts were written off, all the others would expect the same treatment. There were also fears that other developing countries not facing problems would be encouraged to declare bankruptcy as a way of avoiding their debt-servicing obligations. Efforts were therefore made to renegotiate debt, reschedule it, and provide short-term loans to developing countries to prevent them from repudiating their debt (see box 8.1).

Despite the fact that developing countries paid back $700 bn between 1982 and 1987, total long-term debt increased from $568 bn to approximately $1,000 bn during this period. Table 8.1. reflects this increase, showing that debt figures increased in every region between 1990 and 1998 (a decade after the initial crisis).

Box 8.1   Attempts made to resolve the crisis

The Baker Plan, put forward by the US Treasury Secretary James Baker, sought to soften the terms of rescheduling for the top fifteen debtors by lengthening maturities and decreasing spreads on rescheduled debt. Commercial banks were asked to extend $20 bn of new loans over a three-year period to fifteen of the most indebted nations. The multilateral development banks were also asked to make similar amounts available. The Plan expected developing countries to restructure their economies, liberalize trade, and decrease public sector involvement. Funds were made available to ease such restructuring. It was followed by the Brady Plan, put forward by Nicholas Brady in 1989. This plan aimed to decrease the volume of debt rather than offer better terms for repayment. It maintained that the IMF and World Bank should make funds available to developing countries who were prepared to adopt and sustain structural adjustment and reform policies. To avoid delays caused by commercial banks which were unwilling to enter into the scheme, the plan provided these banks with the option of selling their debts back to the developing countries at a discount. Mexico, Costa Rica and the Philippines agreed terms under the Brady Plan in 1989, and Venezuela and Uruguay in 1990.

In spite of such plans, commercial banks provided relatively little credit during the crisis. Instead, they wrote off debt slowly, and increased their provisions against developing country debt. By 1987, regulators in the USA and the UK judged that the banking system was no longer at risk (BEQB, 1991).

The average of the debt–GNP ratio in all developing countries in 1994 was 38 per cent, but in the least developed countries, it was 106 per cent of GNP (UNDP, 1997). The number of reschedulings also remained high: twelve in 1986, nineteen in 1987, and ten in 1988 (Gibson and Tsakalatos, 1992). Thus, we can see from table 8.2. that debt–GNP ratios in Latin America continued to remain high, at 52 per cent in Argentina, at 50 per cent in Chile, and 29 per cent in Brazil. However, they were extremely high in the smaller countries of Africa, being 280 per cent in the Congo Republic and 135 per cent of GNP in Ethiopia and 148 per cent in Mauritania.

Much of the adjustment has taken place under the aegis of the World Bank and the IMF. These two organizations have provided funds on strict conditionality, requiring borrowers to stabilize their economies through fiscal and monetary policies. They also required the microeconomic deregulation of borrowing economies and trade liberalization. These conditions have affected debtors quite considerably. In most cases, consumption had to decrease – a decrease that had been pending since the oil price increases in the 1970s. However, investment also decreased, and this decreased growth rates in these economies. In addition, the fears that

Table 8.1   External debt in 1998

	External debt ($ mn)	
Group/Region	1990	1998
Low income	418,922	579,545
Middle income	1,041,421	1,956,501
Low and middle income	1,460,343	2,536,046
East Asia and Pacific	274,071	667,522
Europe and Central Asia	220,428	480,539
Latin America and Caribbean	475,867	786,019
Middle East and North Africa	183,205	208,059
South Asia	129,899	163,775
Sub-Saharan Africa	176,873	230,132

Source: Data from World Bank, 2000/1, pp. 314–15. From *World Development Report*, 2000/1, by World Bank, © 2000/1 by The International Bank for Restructuring and Development/The World Bank. Used by permission of Oxford University Press, Inc.

Table 8.2   Debt–GNP ratios in selected countries, 1998

Country	External debt/GNP (%, 1998)
Argentina	52
Brazil	29
Bulgaria	78
Burundi	72
Cameroon	98
Chile	50
China	15
Congo, Democratic Republic	196
Congo Republic	280
Côte d'Ivoire	122
Ethiopia	135
Indonesia	169
Mauritania	148
Nicaragua	262
Sierra Leone	126
Zambia	181
Zimbabwe	69

Source: Data from World Bank, 2000/1, pp. 314–15. From *World Development Report*, 2000/1, by World Bank, © 2000/1 by The International Bank for Restructuring and Development/The World Bank. Used by permission of Oxford University Press, Inc.

government would not be able to support their currencies led to capital flight, which further exacerbated the problem. The 1980s were judged to be the 'lost decade' in Latin America, because per capita incomes decreased by 20 per cent after 1981, bringing them back to the levels of the early 1970s. The drop in incomes was especially large in Peru, Bolivia and Ecuador, but also in Venezuela and Argentina. The adjustment in sub-Saharan Africa was also problematic, and caused enormous changes in consumption and increases in poverty levels.

Foreign aid

Foreign aid has long been seen as one way in which developing countries can obtain funds for investment and growth. In reality, though, aid tends to be sporadic and reactive (in response to crises), rather than regular and proactive (which would be necessary if an economy were to rely on aid funds for growth). In addition, the amounts involved are relatively small, and are mainly likely to affect the economies of small countries. The average across all developing countries is approximately 1.5 per cent of total GNP – small, but not negligible. These average figures, however, obscure considerable variations across donors and also recipients. Thus, although India and China get very large absolute quantities, aid per head of India's population (or as a percentage of GNP) is very low indeed, as it is in the case of China. For most large countries, like Brazil or India, the funds involved are very small (less than $1 per capita in 1999). For smaller countries, the figures are more substantial, though here factors other than

Table 8.3   Aid inflows across the world, 1998

Group/Region	Official development assistance ($ per capita)	ODA/GNP (%)
Low income	7	1.3
Middle income	12	0.4
Low and middle income	8	0.7
East Asia and Pacific	4	0.5
Europe and Central Asia	14	0.6
Latin America and Caribbean	9	0.2
Middle East and North Africa	18	1.0
South Asia	4	0.9
Sub-Saharan Africa	21	4.1

Source: Data from World Bank, 2000/1, pp. 314–15. From *World Development Report*, 2000/1, by World Bank, © 2000/1 by The International Bank for Restructuring and Development/The World Bank. Used by permission of Oxford University Press, Inc.

need play a role. Thus, in Bosnia-Hercegovina, aid per capita was $274 in 1999, while in Israel it was $199 per capita. In some countries, especially in Africa, aid is more than 20 per cent of GNP. Official development assistance (ODA) was 63 per cent of GNP in Zambia, 34 per cent in Malawi, 50 per cent in Guinea-Bissau, and 90 per cent in Mozambique (UNDP, 1997).

In naming the 1970s the 'Development Decade', the UN established an aid target of 0.7 per cent of donor countries' GNP. But very few countries meet this target. In fact, the average for all Development Assistance Committee (DAC) members in 1995 was between 0.30 and 0.36 per cent of their average GNP, while that of the USA was even lower, at 0.1 per cent of GNP.

Aid can come in many shapes and forms. The Development Assistance Committee of the OECD defines development assistance as resources transferred on concessional financial terms with the promotion of economic development and the welfare of developing countries as the main declared objective. This includes humanitarian assistance and emergency relief. Nevertheless, there are a number of problems with actually measuring the volume of aid given. Sometimes funds are transferred on concessional terms (loans or grants), but the donor ties them to its own exports, which are more expensive. In this case, the concessional terms on finance may be offset by the increased costs on inputs. Similarly, countries often claim to provide easy trading conditions for developing countries, though they provide no direct financial assistance. How are these benefits to be valued? Another problem relates to how one would define military aid, which is concessional but not developmental. Finally, what about aid received from the International Financial Corporation (IFC)? This is usually on market terms, and given to private companies (with no more than 50 per cent public ownership). However, the IFC itself is a non-profit-making body.

These questions highlight the fact that there are many different types (instruments) of aid. To begin with, there are loans and grants. Loans require repayment at some point in the future, and are often provided at concessional rates of interest, sometimes even at 0 per cent. They are generally preferred by donors, because they are less costly and also because it is felt that the recipients will be much more careful about the way in which funds are used (Japan tends to give a lot of its aid as loans). Grants, on the other hand, represent a transfer of resources that do not need repayment and are generally free. They may be conditional, in so far as the recipient may also be expected to contribute to the project. Grants, as might be expected, are generally preferred by recipients. They have a larger component of aid, and are preferred for projects which involve investment in intangibles like governance structures and social infrastructure. This is because returns on such investment will be hard to measure in purely monetary terms.

Aid can be bilateral or multilateral. Bilateral aid is given by one donor country to a recipient. It is sometimes seen as problematic, because it can be influenced by politics and implies a power relationship between donor and recipient which can be used for the donor's self-interest. Tied aid, for instance, which requires the recipient to purchase the donor's exports, is more common in bilateral aid relationships. Aid flows of this kind can be erratic. Thus, Pakistan's accession to the Central Treaty Organisation and to the South-East Asian Treaty Organisation in 1955 led to an increase in its receipt of US aid for nearly a decade. This fell sharply after Pakistan's civil war with east Pakistan. However, with the Soviet invasion of Afghanistan and Khomeini's seizure of power in Iran, Pakistan became strategically important again, and US aid commitments to Pakistan increased between 1982 and 1987.

Multilateral aid, on the other hand, is organized through multilateral institutions like the World Bank, IMF, IFC, regional banks (EBRD, ADB) and other UN agencies like the UNDP, FAO, WHO and UNHCR. Multilateralism is often seen as preferable, because it symbolizes a commitment to aid as a shared international response. Additionally, multilateral agencies are constitutionally obliged to pursue developmental or humanitarian ends and do not get involved in military assistance. They are also less affected by the donor's political or economic interests. Another source of aid for developing countries is the network of non-governmental organizations (NGOs) like Oxfam, Christian Aid, the Red Cross and the Red Crescent. NGOs are seen to directly target those who need help, have smaller administrative costs, think small and are therefore more flexible. There is considerable debate regarding how effective they really are, but they are clearly seen to have some advantages that the vast multilateral agencies and government departments lack.

In addition to the above distinctions between the sources of aid, there is also a distinction on the basis of the purpose for which aid is given. Thus, there is programme and project aid; food, military and development aid. Until the late 1970s, official development assistance was given mainly to specific projects. Donors preferred this, because they were a more tangible sign of their activities and were also easier to monitor. Aid of this kind could often bypass recipient governments and be given directly to certain projects, so that people gained most. But this meant that developing countries were unable to invest in social overhead capital (especially intangibles like social institution building or the reform of bureaucracy). Programme loans were given only for short-term balance of payments support. Since the 1980s, however, general policy-based assistance has been made available to developing countries in the form of structural adjustment loans. As mentioned earlier, there is strict conditionality attached to such loans, to ensure that they really achieve their objectives. In recent years, this conditionality has been largely economic – decreasing the role of the state in the economy.

Aid is sometimes provided in kind – food, military inputs and technology, for example. Food aid is a special case. It is often (although not exclusively) provided in times of famines, droughts and wars, and in this sense is also emergency or humanitarian aid. But outside such emergency conditions, food aid is highly contentious. Critics maintain that it may create disincentives for domestic food production by decreasing prices and may encourage dependence on food imports. Since food aid goes into consumption, rather than investment, it is not seen to contribute to development objectives. Yet, given its fungibility, the financing of consumption through food aid implies that other funds may now be available for investment. The funds generated by food aid in Asia (Lele and Nabi, 1991b) helped to bring about technological change in agriculture, as did the unpredictability of such aid, which increased India's resolve to achieve self-sufficiency in food production (Lele and Agarwal, 1991). In Africa, however, food aid has not played such a positive role though it has provided critical foreign exchange.

What motivates aid?

The simplest answer is the one provided by the Pearson Commission: 'the moral one: that it is only right for those who have to share with those who have not' (Burnell, 1997, p. 47). The moral argument arises from a belief that everyone has a right to life (and therefore a right to a means of life or to the means of subsistence), or that humanity has an obligation to relieve suffering. The changing interpretation of this moral argument can be seen from Pierre-Joseph Proudhon's observation that to perform an act of benevolence towards one's neighbour is called 'to do justice' in Hebrew, to take compassion or pity in Greek, to perform an act of love or charity in Latin, and to give alms in French. He therefore argued that we can trace the degradation of benevolence through these various expressions: the first signifies duty, the second only sympathy, the third simply affection (a matter for choice, not obligation) and the fourth caprice (Burnell, 1997, p. 62). Zinkin (1978, p. 227) maintains that 'aid is charity. If it is not charity, it is not aid. It may be enlightened self-interest; mutual defence; a boost for the export trade; a sop to a troublesome ally; it cannot be aid.' There are those who believe in Bentham's utilitarian principle that society should aim for the greatest happiness of the greatest number, and that this is achievable by redistributing funds from the rich to the poor.[4] Others look to Rawls (1972), who maintained that rights, liberties, power, opportunities, income and wealth should all be equally distributed, unless the unequal distribution was to the advantage of all, including the less well-off. According to this theory, any global inequalities would require some redistribution.

Another moral argument – one that is thrown up by history – is the entitlement of the Third World to redress for the injuries done to it in the past. The argument here is that countries which were colonized in the past are entitled to be repaid today, because such colonization resulted in permanent differences in the power and wealth of nations. Of course, there are those, including the Marxists, who argue that the colonies gained from being colonized (see chapter 5). In any case, how far back do we have to go to judge the case? As Burnell (1997) asks, should France pay reparation to Britain for the Norman Conquest in 1066? Or should Russia recompense Central and Eastern Europe for the Soviet regimes' imposition of puppet regimes in these countries? Or should we confine ourselves to the latest bout of colonization (since the Industrial Revolution in Britain)?

The moral arguments for aid are so implicitly accepted, and at the same time so problematic in political terms, that most writers have turned to the argument of mutual advantage or development objectives. Though charity has always been done at home, and most Western governments accept the need for redistribution, as does their electorate, the case is less clear when international redistribution is being considered. Selling the idea to their electorate therefore often requires governments to appeal to domestic self-interest – increasing exports or employment, for instance.

Sengupta (1993) cites three traditional arguments for mutuality of interests: trade and supply of commodities, expanding the market for manufactures, and widening the scope of profitable investments. While mutuality of interest has been put forward as an argument for aid since the 1950s, it was the Brandt Commission Report (Brandt, 1983) that gave it new life. This report maintained that if developed countries helped developing countries to withstand commodity price shocks and income instability, then this would help increase the demand for exports from the former. In addition, if foreign aid were used in developing countries to help develop infrastructure, then this would increase the productivity of investment and would, in its turn, help to attract foreign private investments with a high rate of return. It is often felt that the redistribution of global wealth through aid would increase international stability.

Countries giving aid have always attached conditions to the transfers. These conditions have been both economic and political. In the Cold War period, the political conditionality was often very clear-cut.[5] Aid went to governments that either supported the donor or where the recipient was in a strategic location and the donor required support. Thus, US aid has gone overwhelmingly to Israel and Egypt, South Korea and Pakistan, all of which have been important to the USA in strategic terms. The USSR, on the other hand, concentrated much of its aid on Cuba, North Korea and Vietnam, countries that were strategically important to it.

In recent years, though, such straightforward political conditionality has become less important. Instead, there has been increasing emphasis on good governance and the development of civil society. In June 1990,

Britain's Foreign Secretary called for good government and political pluralism in Africa, as did France's President Mitterrand. A strong link was made between democracy and development (see chapter 9), and the former was therefore included in the political conditions attached to aid. Donors gave much assistance to political reform, including multi-partyism, free and fair elections, human rights and the rule of law. The UK and Germany have also placed market economics on the agenda. Official donors are professing support for civil society (the largely au-tonomous public realm between family and household and the state, where citizens join together in pursuit of shared goals). Ideally, it means a plurality of diverse and law-abiding civic associations and NGOs, internally accountable and willing to co-operate.

This has been derided as another form of imperialism in the Third World – an imperialism of ideas and ideologies. Thus, Tandon (quoted in Sogge et al., 1996, p. 182) sees private aid agencies not as radical but as the 'advance guard of a new era of Africa's recolonisation'. Even if we abstract from such an interpretation, political conditionality can result in the emergence of democrats for convenience and the introduction of minimum institutional reforms, formal acknowledgement of the right to form opposition parties, and an electoral timetable to remain eligible for aid. Donors' enthusiasm for democracy may also be relatively limited, rarely going towards encouraging truly participatory governments. Of course, some innovative projects assist with elections, supplying ballot boxes and election monitors and giving advice on legal frameworks.

More common nowadays is economic conditionality. This is especially true of structural adjustment loans and the new programme loans pro-vided by the World Bank and the IMF. Economic conditionality requires a reduction in the role of the state in the economy and a decrease in budget deficits, together with increased private sector participation in the economy.

Does aid work?

Judging the effectiveness of aid is very difficult. To a large extent, it can only be judged against its objectives. If the underlying objectives are political, even though the ostensible objective may be developmental, then it would be no surprise if aid failed to be effective in developmental terms. There has been considerable debate surrounding the effectiveness of aid. In their book *Does Aid Work?* Cassen et al. (1994) conclude that it does – not always and not on every count but 'the great majority of aid succeeds in its developmental objectives' (Cassen et al., 1994, p. 9). Some failures are inevitable, but the successes do outweigh the failures. The World Bank (1998) observes that aid has, at times, been a spectacular success. Cassen et al. (1994) claim that the greatest success of aid has been in increasing the consumption of the poor by assisting with the growth of food production and by increasing welfare services. Poverty-oriented projects show a high rate of return. Though overall poverty in the recipient countries does not seem to be decreasing, this seems to be related to the fact that not all projects include concern for income distribution.

A micro–macro paradox in the effect of aid has also been commented upon. While evidence at the micro (individual project) level indicates that aid has been very successful, there seems to have been little effect at the macro (growth, poverty-alleviation) level. Thus, while many aid projects are very successful, the overall effect on the economy's growth is insignificant (Mosley, 1987). This might reflect the fact that aid accounts for varying proportions of growth, and there are sizeable differences between countries. In countries where aid is only $1 per capita (Brazil and India, for instance), this is not surprising. Even across all developing countries, aid contributes less than 1.5 per cent of GNP, so that while individual projects may be spectacularly successful, the overall impact may still not be significant. In sub-Saharan Africa, however, aid accounts for 50 per cent of investment and 40 per cent of imports.

Hansen and Tarp (1999) surveyed a number of studies to try and explain the micro–macro paradox, and they concluded that a positive aid-growth link is a robust result from three generations of work. They studied the effect of aid on savings, investment and growth and found that it increases all three variables in developing countries. H. White (1992a), on the other hand, concluded that there is no real link between aid and growth.

So far, we have considered two sources of finance for development in the Third World: commercial loans and aid. Both these sources finance largely indigenous projects in the countries to which they are made available. A third, and increasingly significant, source of funds is private investment from abroad.

All three sources together reflect the increase in the initial flow of funds and the growing strengths of linkages between countries. They therefore both contribute to globalization and are, in their turn, reinforced by it. Private investment from abroad may take two forms: portfolio investment and foreign direct investment. Portfolio investment is the purchase of stocks and bonds by foreigners. It does not result in a controlling interest. Foreign direct investment (FDI) is the creation or acquisition of capital assets that are fully owned or majority-controlled. This has largely been undertaken by transnational corporations (TNCs) and is also more controversial. We will consider it in more detail in the next section.

Transnational corporations and development

[The TNC] fiddles its accounts. It avoids or evades taxes. It rigs its intra-company transfer prices. It is run by foreigners from decision centres thousands of miles away. It imports foreign labour practices. It doesn't import foreign labour practices. It overpays. It underpays. It competes unfairly with local firms. It exports jobs from rich countries. It is an instrument of rich countries' imperialism. The technologies it brings to the third world are old fashioned. No, they are too modern. It meddles, it bribes. Nobody can control it. It wrecks balance of payments. It overturns economic policies. It plays off governments against each other to get the biggest investment incentives. Won't it please come and invest? Let it bloody well go home. (*Economist*, 21 January, 1976)

This quotation from the *Economist* captures the contradictory, but very real, concerns in the developing world regarding foreign direct investment. Popular concern regarding TNCs relates to the transmission of a 'Coca Cola' culture to the rest of the world. Do TNCs create, through their brand names and advertising, a demand for wholly inappropriate products in developing countries? Does the spread of Coke, hamburgers, instant coffee and powdered baby milk (see box 8.2) signal the homogenization of world tastes? If so, is this a bad thing?

A more significant concern arises when firms export 'unsafe' products that cannot be sold in their home markets. The UN, for instance, singled out Parke-Davis's Chloramphenicol, which is banned in the USA because it can cause blood disease, but is sold over the counter in many developing countries. The export of such products from the USA has, from time to time, been restricted. In fact, when the UN General Assembly voted 146 to 1 to impose stricter controls on such exports in December 1982, the only 'No' vote was cast by the USA.

The effect of TNCs on development spawned a very large literature in the 1970s. In the 1960s and 1970s, there were fears in the USA regarding the volume of funds that TNCs were investing in Europe (Servan Schrieber, 1968). There were similar concerns within developing countries

---

Box 8.2   The case of Nestlé

Nestlé became notorious when it exported powdered milk to the Third World, and used advertising to persuade mothers there to switch to this milk. This caused concern, because there is little clean water in the Third World, not enough gas to boil this water properly, and mothers often try to economize by putting in less powder. The result is that such powdered milk is less nutritious and less safe than breast milk. Additionally, it is now widely accepted that bottled milk provides less immunity for babies. This is especially important where diseases are rife. Today, Nestlé sells its milk powder with a warning that says 'breast milk is best'. New concerns relate to the safety of breast milk in the light of findings that AIDS can be transmitted through breast-feeding (see chapter 13).

Table 8.4   FDI flows to developing countries, 1980–1994

Region	% of total FDI flows to LDCs		
	1980	1988	1994
South-East Asia and Pacific Rim	15.3	39.4	56.4
South Asia	2.2	17.1	1.1
Latin America and Caribbean	71.9	41.2	24.9
Middle East and North Africa	—	—	—
Sub-Saharan Africa	0.4	5.9	3.0
Eastern Europe and Central Asia	0.1	0.2	9.3

Source: de Mello, 1997, pp. 1–34. By permission of Frank Cass Publishers.

regarding the growing influence of these firms on their economies. Much of the debate centred around trying to control these TNCs. In the 1980s, investment within the USA (from Europe and Japan) began to increase. In developing countries too, the debt crisis increased the attractiveness of FDI as a source of foreign exchange. In addition, the success of the East Asian economies, many of which had relied on FDI, did much to allay fears in developing countries.

As we can see from table 8.4, FDI is geographically concentrated, with South-East Asia and Latin America attracting the largest volumes. Though Eastern Europe's share has increased since the transition, sub-Saharan Africa still gets very little FDI.[6] Given that developing countries in general get a very small share, most countries get hardly any FDI at all. In fact, most FDI goes to countries like Brazil, Singapore, South Africa and Malaysia.

The largest number of TNCs are based in the USA, with Britain second and Japan third. Apart from similarity in culture and economic levels, TNCs also tend to invest in countries that are geographically close. Thus, US companies have tended to invest most in Canada and Western Europe, European companies in the USA and the rest of Europe. Japan has tended to concentrate on East and South-East Asia, though Japanese investment in the USA and Northern Europe has also increased. In addition, companies from Britain and France often tend to invest in their ex-colonies.

Amongst the TNCs themselves, the levels of concentration are very high. Though there are approximately 10,000 TNCs world-wide, most of the FDI is undertaken by about 400 of these TNCs. Some of these firms are very large, often larger than the countries they operate in. Thus, three oil-based TNCs (Exxon, Royal Dutch/Shell and Mobil) had a gross sales value greater than the GNP of all but seven developing countries in 1980. Their size provides these TNCs with market power within the industry as well as political power over the countries they have invested in.

Advantages and disadvantages

TNCs are seen to provide the host country with many benefits. They create an inflow of funds in the form of foreign exchange, helping to plug both the savings and the foreign exchange gaps. They are expected to create employment, increase exports, bring in new technology, managerial and marketing skills, and improve competition in relatively lethargic markets. However, they have been criticized on all these grounds and more.

To begin with, FDI is seen to be attractive to developing countries because it is expected to provide long-term capital inflows, which bring in foreign exchange and help fund the balance of payments deficit on the current account. In the medium to long run, FDI is also expected to help earn foreign exchange through exports. Critics maintain, however, that though TNCs do bring in funds, the net inflow is much smaller than is suggested by the figures, because TNCs often borrow within their host countries. A UN study of Latin America suggested that during 1957–65, US TNCs financed 83 per cent of total investment from local sources. Jenkins (1987, p. 96) found that about one-third of all funds came from capital raised locally in the host country and that about half was made up of reinvested profits of the subsidiaries. In addition to crowding out domestic investment projects, such borrowing is controversial, because the profits accruing from this investment are repatriated.

The medium- to long term contribution of FDI to export earnings also seems to be relatively small (see table 8.5). Even in the South-East Asian export-oriented economies, FDI contributed only 10.2 per cent of total exports in 1994. It was much smaller in South Asia and sub-Saharan Africa, at 1.4 per cent and 2.7 per cent respectively. This is because TNCs often set up in developing countries to take advantage of domestic markets rather than to export. These contributions are further minimized because FDI requires large volumes of imported capital and technology inputs. In

Table 8.5 Contribution of FDI to developing country exports, 1980–1994

Region	Share of FDI in exports of LDCs		
	1980	1990	1994
All LDCs	0.7	2.8	6.7
S.E. Asia and Pacific Rim	1.3	4.4	10.2
S. Asia	0.8	1.4	1.4
Latin America and Caribbean	4.8	4.4	8.5
Middle East and North Africa	−1.5	1.0	1.5
Sub-Saharan Africa	0	1.0	2.7
E. Europe and C. Asia	0	0.2	7.4

Source: de Mello, 1997, pp. 1–34. By permission of Frank Cass Publishers.

extreme cases, as in the assembly of electronic equipment in Malaysia, all inputs are imported, assembled and then exported. So, the value added locally is very low, and the net addition to trade figures is very low too. Finally, the repatriation of TNC profits in the long run also implies that developing country trade figures (on the capital account) could worsen.

TNCs have often been criticized for exerting considerable monopolistic power, especially in countries where domestic firms are weak. In 1963–4, twenty-two firms in Chile in the automobile industry produced or assembled fewer than 8,000 vehicles in total – that is, approximately 400 cars per plant. Firms entered the market to occupy niches and to prevent new entry through 'the use of scale economies, product differentiation and brand loyalty. The end result was that costs were higher than in home economies. Many TNCs also use restrictive export licenses (for instance, they do not allow their subsidiaries to export worldwide because they have branches elsewhere) to minimise competition. Others have argued that while competition may not exist in the sense of a level playing field, there is considerable competition between the oligopolistic market leaders' (Kiely, 1998, p. 71).

Many developing countries have welcomed TNCs in the hope that they will create linkages to the rest of the domestic economy through the purchase of local inputs, employment of local labour, and so on. But critics argue that TNCs minimize the use of local inputs in order to remain 'footloose'. However, this experience varies from industry to industry, and from country to country. Japanese companies, in the Mexican maquiladoras, for instance, have encouraged their suppliers to move with them, rather than simply import supplies as was common amongst US companies (Sklair, 1993, p. 237). Another argument put forward against TNCs is that while they create unskilled, low-value-added employment, they do not employ local management staff. Therefore, though TNCs help by bringing in managerial and technical skills, they increase the outflow of funds through salaries and are criticized for slowing down the development of local managerial talent.

TNCs also benefit from tax breaks and are accused of using transfer pricing to minimize the taxes they pay.[7] Though transfer pricing is very hard to prove, there is considerable anecdotal evidence about it. Thus, the UK affiliate of Hoffman-la-Roche was found to be purchasing drugs from the rest of the group at £370 and £922 per kg, whereas the same drugs could be purchased on the open market for £9 and £20 per kg respectively. Attempts have been made to regulate such activity by stipulating that for intra-firm transfer of products, arms-length (market prices) plus a percentage may be imputed.

Though many of these criticisms are no doubt valid, it is also true that TNCs can provide valuable resources for the host country. What is required is a strong and focused host government that is able to counter the power of the TNC itself. Soon and Stoever (1996) set up a framework that helps analyse the policies of developing countries towards FDI. In stage 1, countries are too small or too poor to attract FDI. This is true of many countries in sub-Saharan Africa today. In stage 2, a country begins to attract FDI by offering incentives through low wages or through the growth of its domestic market (for instance, India and China). Thus, Malaysia at one time was a centre for the assembly of electronic products, because its low wages made this potentially profitable. In stage 3, the country becomes sufficiently attractive to FDI that it can begin to impose conditions or seek added benefits like higher capital or technological content, or attempt to steer investment into certain sectors restricting profit repatriation. Finally, in stage 4, the developing country's economy is so strong and so diversified that it is able to rely on market signals to attract FDI, rather than on government policy.

In their attempts to control TNCs, developing country governments often declare whole industries off limits to FDI. Telecommunications and infrastructure are nationalized in many developing countries because they are strategic sectors. Many governments place maximum limits on equity ownership to control the TNCs. Until the 1991 reforms, the Indian government, for instance, restricted foreign equity to 49 per cent. In fact, of the US TNCs in 1977, only 44 per cent of those established in the mid-1970s were wholly owned. Similarly, governments may place maximum limits on profit repatriation.

As indicated earlier, however, the shift towards neo-liberal policies and structural adjustment reforms in the developing world has led to greater openness to TNCs. In South-East Asia, for instance, there is increasing acceptance of FDI, which comes largely from countries in East Asia – Japan, Korea and Hong Kong. China, too, has made attempts to attract FDI through a new joint venture law. The main benefits hoped for from such FDI were technological imports and market information, rather than investment funds or management skills (see chapter 10).

Conclusion

Given the savings and foreign exchange limitations faced by most developing countries, and given the findings of early growth theories that an increase in investment is a prerequisite for growth, attempts to increase the inflow of funds to these economies could be very significant for development. Funds from abroad become especially significant in view of the fact that foreign exchange is necessary to pay for up-to-date technology and capital equipment that have become essential for growth. In this chapter, we have considered three possible means of international financial inflows: commercial loans, official aid and foreign direct investment. Each has its advantages and its disadvantages, as we have seen. None matches up to the expectations held out for it, but each serves a useful purpose.

9

The State, Growth and Development

The state is often seen as necessary to 'accomplish the economical development of the nation and to prepare it for admission into the universal society of the future' (List, 1885, p. 175). List went on to argue that 'a perfectly developed manufacturing industry, an important mercantile marine, and foreign trade on a really large scale, can only be attained by means of the interposition of the power of the state' (List, 1885, p. 178). The state's involvement in the economy has ranged from production in public enterprises and investment in infrastructure to regulation of the private sector, welfare provisions and taxes, as well as the strategic planning of resource utilization in an economy. The state influences the economy, polity and society of a country, and as development occurs, this influence seems, if anything, to increase. The state self-evidently has a political role, and is the explicit expression of the formal politics of a country – authoritarian or democratic (single and multi-party). The state is therefore an all-pervasive aspect of modern life, and has become an integral part of the process of development. Its significance has, however, been undermined by the increasing importance of international organizations (both governmental and non-governmental) as well as of international businesses. We will consider the impact that such global organizations have on the role played by the state later in this chapter.

What do we mean by the state? Is the state to be defined in terms of the institutions comprising it, or in terms of the functions it performs? Is the state an independent actor able to do as it (or its main components) wishes? Or is it instrumental, in that it has to do what society wishes? According to Pye, the 'authoritarian structures of government' (Pye, 1965, p. 7) are a set of arrangements which consist of political institutions and recognized procedures for resolving political conflicts and interpreting political demands. The procedures would include statutes, laws and regulations. Pye therefore integrates both the functional and the institutional definitions. Leftwich (1990), on the other hand, defines the core of the state apparatus as comprising 'a distinct ensemble of institutions and organisations whose socially accepted function is to define and enforce collectively binding decisions on the members of a society in the name of their common interest or general will' (Leftwich, 1990, p. 45). Weber sees the state as 'a compulsory association claiming control over territories and the people within them. Administrative, legal, extractive and coercive organisations are the core of any state' (quoted in Skocpol, 1985, p. 7).

The functions of the state are carried out by a set of institutions that can command a legitimate use of force, rule over an area, and seek to maintain sovereignty, maintain control and the rule of law and oversee economic development (Haynes, 1996, p. 27). More specifically, there are three bodies: the legislature (which makes the laws, rules and regulations), the executive (which implements these rules and decisions) and the judiciary (which interprets them and undertakes to see justice carried out). The nature of each of these bodies will vary from country to country and across different types of state. Thus, in a democracy, the legislature is usually the houses of parliament or the chambers of the elected representatives of people. In an authoritarian state, however, the legislature may simply be the head of state together with a few close or trusted aides. In most developing countries, the bureaucracy (or the executive) is wide-ranging and influential, a fact that is highlighted in the developmental states model. Finally, the attempt to keep the judiciary independent of the other two wings of government is one of the major differences between democracies and dictatorships. Very few democracies (especially in developing countries) succeed, and few authoritarian governments even try. Thus, there are many permutations and combinations of institutions and functions that make up states, which can then range broadly from representative democracies to military dictatorships.

The state is often discussed as if it were a homogenous entity with a common purpose. But this is rarely ever the case in reality. The extent of power a state has depends upon its internal rifts and divisions. This is particularly true in developing countries, where state formation has preceded nation building (Haynes, 1996, p. 28) so that there are a number of social, ethnic and cultural groups who do not perceive their primary loyalty to be to the state, but rather to their own ethnic grouping.

Many contemporary ideologies distinguish between different spheres of state intervention. On the one hand, the state is seen to have a role in providing a legal framework, ensuring law and order, protecting the nation from external aggression, and upholding moral values. On the other, it is seen to have an economic role – regulating and managing production, providing public goods, and so on. While writers on the 'right' wish to increase state intervention in the first sphere and decrease it in the second, those on the 'left' wish to increase it in the second and decrease it in the first (Dunleavy and O'Leary, 1987, p. 7).

The state, however defined, has come in for criticism from left and right alike. Marxists attack the state variously as a kind of parasite (which extracts resources to sustain a privileged, bureaucratic elite); as an instrument of class domination (which at different stages of history will be controlled by the dominant classes for their own benefit); as a factor of cohesion (regulating struggles between the various classes while maintaining the dominance of the most powerful classes and preserving a capitalist system); as an institution that stays aloof even from the dominant classes and attempts only to preserve the social and economic system (Smith, 1996, p. 176). Criticism from the right has hinged on the increasing role of the state in all aspects of modern life. It is seen to give rise to nepotism, corruption, rent seeking, and other unproductive or negatively productive activities. This led, in the 1980s, to a policy shift in favour of curtailing the powers of the state across the world, which has been reinforced by the fact that the nation-state is increasingly having to share power with multinational enterprises (chapter 8), international NGOs (chapter 7), international government organizations (like the World Bank, the IMF and the WTO) and, of course, the international hegemon – the USA.

In this chapter, we will not dwell on definitional issues. Instead, we will concentrate on the effect of the state on development and the type of state organization that is 'best' for development. Much of this discussion has been encapsulated within the democracy and development literature and the developmental states literature. We will begin, in the next section, with centrally planned economies, before we move on to consider the case of the market-oriented but strategically planned economies of East Asia. Finally, we will consider the effect that the type of state structure – democratic or authoritarian – has on development.

The state and the economy

The state has played a significant role in the economy since the Industrial Revolution. This role was reinforced by two phenomena in the early twentieth century: the Russian Revolution and the establishment of Socialist states in Eastern Europe and China, as well as the 'Keynesian revolution' and the rise of the 'welfare state' in the West. Whereas the former saw the state as controlling the economy and undertaking all economic activities, the latter saw it as regulating the economy and being the primary redistributive force within it. Development economists, being motivated by the need for developing countries to catch up with the West, have found their policy prescriptions greatly informed by the Russian and Keynesian revolutions. This has resulted in an increasing emphasis on state intervention in developing countries in the Fifties, Sixties and Seventies. This intervention ranged from periodic or regular plans to allocate resources, to direct production through public enterprises in a number of strategic (economically and politically) industries, to the regulation of the economy by the state.

In the 1980s, the increasing popularity of liberal politics in the West and the breakdown of the Soviet bloc led many developing countries (often under pressure from the World Bank and the IMF) to rethink their attitude to state involvement in the economy. This has resulted in a spate of liberalizations across the world, which has included countries like India and China that have long been state-centred (though to different degrees). On the other hand, the experience of the East Asian NICs, which have relied on the market but have strategically planned their growth, has highlighted the significant strategic or managerial role that a state can play. We will discuss them in the next section. But before we do so, we will briefly consider planning and the problems faced by centrally planned economies in Eastern Europe and Central Asia.

Planning

In mixed and centrally planned economies, state intervention can occur at many different levels. First, the government may simply correct for market failures through taxes, subsidies and regulations. Secondly, it may go one step further and allow for dynamic progress (i.e. plan for growth and technical progress). This involves government intervention at the overall resource planning stage. In both these cases, the market still plays an important role, because it sets prices in the system. In the third case, by contrast, the government may direct the economy so closely that there is little or no role for the market to play.

Centrally planned economies fall into this third category. Within these economies, prices are set by the state, because it is assumed that there are too many market failures for market-determined prices to be 'correct'. The state also determines resource allocation at the national, regional, local, sectoral and enterprise level. Free market resource allocation occurs only on the supply side of the labour market – that is, workers are free to choose where they work – and on the demand side of the product market – that is, consumers are free to choose what they spend their money on. In all other markets, resource allocation is quantitatively centrally determined. Thus, the state determines production, capacity, inputs and outputs at firm level (see section on China in chapter 10 and box 9.1). This requires an enormous institutional infrastructure, and involves the state in all aspects of the economy, including the setting of prices.

Box 9.1 describes the mechanics of planning in a centrally planned economy. Detailed planning of this kind creates a number of problems. The attempt to cut enterprises off from market discipline and the inability

---

Box 9.1   China: the logistics of planning

China has an entire hierarchy of planning bodies with the central party at the top. Many of its institutions and processes are currently undergoing change, but its planning machinery still includes the state planning commissions, state economic commissions, the state council, and the bureau for material allocation (BMA). There are similar bodies at the provincial level which directly control the enterprises and the companies. The plans are both long-term (5–10 years) and short-term ones, and provide targets for the growth rates of major economic aggregates like national income, consumption, investment and foreign trade, amongst others. Guidelines are then sent to the ministries, which formulate draft plans, to be submitted to the state planning councils. The BMA prepares the assignment plans, indicating the needs and supplies of various materials and products, broken down by branch and province. Many materials are allocated locally.

Each enterprise receives eight targets: volume of output, quality, product mix, consumption of raw materials and fuel, costs of production, wage bill, profits, and the permitted amount of working capital. The state statistical bureau and the People's Bank have the main responsibility for monitoring economic activity. So the system is a very complicated one, and is further complicated by the lack of a reliable price system, which means that most plans and allocations have to be made in quantitative terms.

---

to monitor all their decisions meant that they often attempted to fulfil targets by roundabout means. Tractors in China, for example, were heavier than elsewhere, because it was easier to fulfil volume targets with heavier output. In addition, persistent over-investment, long construction periods, and inadequate controls over costs all led to inefficiency. Distortions in the price system also created problems because prices could not be used to set targets. The emphasis on non-material incentives decreased people's incentive to work and invest. Finally, implementational problems, deficiencies in the plans and their implementation, and insufficient and unreliable data all created problems for planned economies. Planning is only as good as the data on which it is based. Unanticipated external and internal shocks – war, drought, oil price increases, institutional problems, as well as corruption, bureaucracy, inefficiency, rent seeking of civil servants, and lack of political will – all decrease the efficiency of the planned system. Since changes in the system also have to be planned and are not automatic, the system is not very flexible in responding to changes in costs, demand or international conditions. This lack of flexibility is further reinforced by the centralized nature of decision making in most planned economies.

Free markets are strongly advantaged by their efficiency in the use of information. Since no central body sets prices, there is no need for the central collection of information. There is greater flexibility regarding prices and quantities, because decisions are decentralized to firm and individual level. The costs of price setting within such a system are minimal, and fewer problems arise from inefficient bureaucracies and interest groups. Finally, the emphasis of most planned economies on specific strategies like heavy industrialization, though initially successful, creates a number of distortions in the system in the long run. These include the scarcity of consumer products, which manifests itself in queues, shortages and price increases.

In the face of these and other problems, most centrally planned economies in Eastern Europe and Central Asia began marketizing their economies in the 1980s. The breakdown of the Soviet bloc and the breakup of the USSR into the CIS countries (see box 9.2) have reinforced the arguments against central planning. Even China, which is still essentially centrally planned, has been increasing the role of the market.

Box 9.2   Breakup of the centrally planned economies

The late 1980s and early 1990s have seen the transition of most centrally planned economies (CPEs) towards the free market system. This began relatively slowly, with attempts at *perestroika* and *glasnost* in the USSR, but gained momentum when these attempts at gradual reforms failed. By the early 1990s, the system had broken down in most of Eastern Europe and Central Asia. This was accompanied by political change too, with the breakup of the Soviet Union into a number of independent states and the move towards democracy and freer political regimes elsewhere. The transition has, of course, involved changes across these economies, and in most cases has required new institutional frameworks. Thus, the moves towards resource allocation through markets has required new price systems, new tax systems to be set up, new legal frameworks to be put in place (for corporate law, property rights and competition policy, for instance), new accounting conventions to be laid down, and so on. All this takes time, and the initial question during the reform was whether the changes should be introduced quickly (as shock therapy or big bang), or whether there should be gradual and organic reform of the system. This question has become largely academic in the light of changes that have since taken place, at different speeds in different countries. The main factor determining the success of the reforms has been, not so much the speed at which they were introduced, but the focus and single-mindedness of the governments that introduced them. Countries that have vacillated and in which commitment to the reforms has been uncertain are ones in which the reforms have taken longer to be successful.

Overall, a number of measures have been undertaken as part of this transition:

1 *Price liberalization*: reform of the pricing system so that prices are now determined by the market rather than by the state. Resource allocation is therefore also market-determined.
2 *Macro-economic stabilization*: strict monetary and fiscal policies, which are used to control any inflation that the price liberalization may have caused.
3 *Privatization*: the sale of state-owned manufacturing firms to the private sector. The exact process followed for this can, and has, varied:
   - voucher privatization in Czechoslovakia
   - sale of assets in East Germany through the *Treuhandanstalt*
   - sales to foreign investors in Hungary
   - internal privatization in Russia.
4 *Trade liberalization*: decreasing or removing the barriers to trade and freeing up exchange rates.
5 *Financial liberalization*: reform of the banking and financial system so that interest rates are market-determined and investment decisions reflect market criteria.
6 *Institutional reforms*: including tax, accounting reforms, legal reforms, and setting up a welfare infrastructure.

Different countries have taken different paths to the transition, but it is true to say that, for good or bad, most European countries and many in Central Asia have now transited to the free market system.

In the next subsection, we will consider the experience of countries that have used more selective state intervention. This is best represented by the East Asian economies, and has given rise to the 'developmental states' model, which we will discuss below.

Developmental states

The East Asian region has provided the most successful examples of transition from developing to developed country status in the twentieth century. After much debate on their strategies in the last two decades, it is increasingly being accepted that although they are certainly less interventionist than the Socialist economies considered above, they are certainly more interventionist than early writers (World Bank, 1983) had suggested. More importantly, state intervention in these economies is highly selective and strategic, and is therefore much more effective than it has been in most other economies. This experience has been modelled in the developmental states literature. In their introduction to a special issue of the *IDS Bulletin* on developmental states in East Asia, White and Wade argue that the East Asian states carry 'the historical legacy of a strong and economically active state' (White and Wade, 1984, p. 3).

In this context, Leftwich (1995), who traces the idea of a developmental state back to List (1885), defines developmental states as 'states whose politics have concentrated sufficient power, autonomy and capacity at the centre to shape, pursue and encourage the achievement of explicit developmental objectives' (p. 401). More specifically, he cites a number of components of a developmental state. First, a determined developmental elite, including a core of developmentally determined senior politicians or bureaucrats, who have more influence over policy making than the political and legislative elites. These developmental elites are not fixed, but represent shifting coalitions of interests. Secondly, being relatively autonomous from special interests (class, regional and sectoral), these states can work in the 'national interest' (Jenkins, 1992b; Johnson, 1985). In the case of South Korea, this autonomy has been strengthened by the inflow of substantial amounts of foreign aid, which has decreased the government's dependence on locally generated revenue.

Thirdly, in developmental states, economic co-ordination and development are managed by the economic bureaucracy. While it exists in many developing countries, in a developmental state, this economic bureaucracy is very powerful, and all economic decision making is concentrated within it. It has the authority, technical competence and insulation to make its strategies effective. In South Korea, for instance, the Economic Planning Board (EPB) was responsible for planning, budgeting, price controls, foreign aid, loans and investment, transfers of technology, and collection of statistics. In most other countries, by contrast, two or more such bodies would be responsible for policy. In Brazil, for instance, trade policy is dictated by the Ministry of Finance with influence from Planning and Foreign Affairs; export policies and fiscal incentives by Finance and Planning together with the Ministry of Industry, Commerce and Tourism and the Ministry of Foreign Affairs. The investment regime was under the Ministry of Planning and the National Development Bank, while R&D was under the Ministry of Science and Technology. Thus, the direction of policy oscillated, depending on which ministry was in control (Sercovich et al., 1999, p. 231).

Fourth, many developmental states have survived by controlling and weakening civil society, especially the media and labour organizations. In this context, it has often been claimed (Jenkins, 1992b, and Chowdhury and Islam, 1993) that East Asia has more politically quiescent labour movements than Latin America. Fifth, developmental states consolidated their power and autonomy before national and foreign capital became influential. Thus, these states differ from those, as in Latin America, where landlord and foreign capitalist interests were too deeply entrenched to allow the emergence of state economic power.

While the notion of developmental states has been very influential in attempts to explain the East Asian miracle, some have criticized this concept as being of limited relevance. In his attempt to answer why 'some developing country states end up successfully transforming their economies, whereas others end up as "rent seekers" preying on their own society's scarce resources', Kohli (1994, pp. 1286–7) sees the need to go beyond the idea of developmental states. He argues that the notion of developmental states focuses more on a state's capacity to implement goals and less on the origins of these goals. In this context, he highlights Japanese priorities (in the colonial period) as influencing South Korea's policy goals in the later period. Jenkins (1992b) also argues that the high degree of autonomy of the state and of the bureaucracy in East Asia arose from a conjunction of historical factors which resulted in a large volume of industrial capital falling into the hands of the South Korean state when the Japanese withdrew. The state then had considerable funds that it could distribute at will. It could therefore always subordinate the industrialists to its own will (though this broke down in the 1990s and has contributed to the Asian crisis in the late 1990s – see box 10.1).[1]

We have so far considered the role of the state in the economy. In the next section, we will consider the explicit interplay of politics and economics when we consider the impact that the type of institutional arrangements has on the performance of the economy. This has been an area of active debate in development, and is largely encapsulated in the democracy and development literature. We will review it in the next section.

Democracy and development

The relationship between democracy and development has long been a matter of debate. In recent years, the marketization of the formerly centrally planned economies, together with their attempts at political reform, has reinvigorated this debate. The UN Agenda for Development put forward in 1994 by Boutros Boutros-Ghali explicitly links the two concepts:

> Democracy and development are linked in fundamental ways. They are linked because democracy provides the only long-term basis for managing competing ethnic, religious and cultural interests in a way that minimises the risk of violent internal conflict. They are linked because democracy is inherently attached to the question of [good] governance, which has an impact on all aspects of development efforts. They are linked because democracy is a fundamental human right,[2] the advancement of which is itself an important measure of development. They are linked because people's participation in the decision-making processes which affect their lives is a basic tenet of development. (Quoted in Forsythe, 1989, p. 337)

Thus, those appealing to wider notions of development (political, economic and social) see democracy as an integral part of development. On the other hand, there are those who maintain that most countries that have developed have done so under authoritarian rule of one kind or the other (East Asia being a case in point). Of course, the relationship between the two can also be seen as a sequential one, whereby authoritarianism is required in the initial stages of development. As development progresses, however, it both enables and requires democracy. Thus, attempts at increasing union activity and scope in South Korea or the earlier attempts at *glasnost* and *perestroika* in the USSR can be seen as examples of such a shift.

The issue of definition

To some extent, these differences of opinion regarding the relationship between democracy and development relate to the breadth of the definitions used. At one extreme, democracy can be seen simply as a political concept – a government chosen by the people for themselves from among competing political parties – within which a change of government is possible without overturning the whole regime. Even with this very limited definition, there are many complications: there may be countries where the press is more or less free; there may be *de facto* single-party rule, transgressions of human rights, or the regime may change from being democratic in one period to being dictatorial in the next. At the other extreme, democracy can be defined as developmental democracy (Sen, 1985, 1987) within which people's well-being is defined in terms of their ability and freedom to realize their capabilities. Such broad definitions include democracy in society, and in the economy, in their scope. They allow for the fact that an egalitarian economic and social structure within which people's basic needs are met and within which they are all equal may in a real sense be more democratic than a society that has parliamentary elections but no such equality (Bagchi, 1995). Of course, parliamentary democracy may be the ultimate manifestation of such freedom and equality, but having the former does not guarantee the latter (witness India).

As we saw in chapter 1, development also encompasses a similarly wide range of definitions. This dooms any attempt to pin down the relationship between the two. At the same time however, the relationship between these variables is particularly interesting because it brings into focus economics and politics and the extremely involved nature of their interaction in development. If development is defined to include political freedoms and the right to express oneself and influence one's own future, then democracy becomes necessary for development, and may even be interpreted as part of development. However, such broad definitions lead to a convergence in the meaning of these entities and therefore make the search for a relationship between them redundant.

Relationship between democracy and development

To begin with, therefore, we will define democracy narrowly as a form of government, and development as economic growth and welfare. Using these narrow definitions, we will explore why one might expect the two to be related. To do this, we need to go back to our analysis of growth in chapter 4. Growth requires investment, and investment requires savings. As already noted, these savings imply a reduction in consumption, which is unlikely to be popular. A government that depends upon popular approval for its survival, as democracy does, is unlikely to push for growth under these circumstances, and will instead push for 'too much' welfare. Thus, 'under a system in which lawmakers ... seek the approval of the electorate, the politician cannot afford ... to follow any policies which will not produce tangible benefits for the electorate by the time the next election comes around' (Nehru, 1979, p. 57). This view acquired widespread acceptance when Samuel Huntington (1968) first articulated it. According to it, democracy generates an explosion of demands for current consumption. These demands threaten profitability (by increasing wages), and therefore decrease investment and growth. However, this dichotomy between investment for growth and expenditure on welfare is too simplistic. As already indicated in chapter 4, new growth theories predict that if the state undertakes investment in health and education, then it helps simultaneously to increase labour productivity, growth and welfare. Such expenditure is also likely to be popular amongst the electorate (see chapter 13 for further analysis of this relationship).

In addition to succumbing to pressures from consumers, the democratic state is more open to pressures from competing groups like large firms and unions. Such lobbying activity is sometimes seen as involving considerable wasteful expenditure and as resulting in transfers of income between interest groups that may be inefficient. This, together with frequent changes in policy, can make democracy inefficient from the point of view of development. In fact, the existence of interest groups can result in disorder and instability, especially when there are numerous religious, ethnic, regional and class divisions in society. Such disorder and instability prevent development.

Finally, there is the argument put forward by Roemer (1995) that dictatorships are likely to involve less uncertainty than democracies. Specifically, Roemer builds a model in which investors face a choice between a stable dictatorship and a stable democracy. In the latter, investors face considerable uncertainty, because there are several political parties with different interests, any one of which may form the government. Investors are likely to prefer a stable dictatorship, says Roemer, because they are faced with less uncertainty in such a regime. However, dictatorships usually do not have popular support, and thus are built on less stable foundations than democracies. Under these circumstances, change, when it occurs, is likely to take the form of *coups* and rebellions, which cause much more upheaval than changes of regime in a democracy. In this case, democracy can be viewed as less risky, though less certain, than dictatorship. If both (risk and uncertainty) are factored into investment decisions, Barbera (1995) argues that it is quite likely that democracy may be preferred.

Other arguments in favour of democracy claim that civil and political liberties increase people's sense of security and enable them to pursue economic goals. Some writers emphasize that the state is always ready to prey on society (North, 1990), and that only democratic institutions can prevent this.

Empirical results

Many attempts have been made to analyse the relationship between democracy and development at a cross-sectional level. Surveying the results of eighteen studies over the period 1966–92, Przeworski and Limongi (1995) conclude that there is no consensus on the relationship. All eighteen studies were cross-sectional, using a sample of countries (ranging from ten developing countries in Kohli, 1986, to 124 countries in Weede, 1983). Of the twenty-one results surveyed in Przeworski and Limongi's study, eight found in favour of democracy, eight in favour of dictatorship, and five found no difference. King (1981), studying six Asian countries, and Dick (1974), studying seventy-two countries between 1959 and 1968 concluded that democratic-type regimes seem to perform better with respect to growth. Minier (1998) also finds that democracy is positively significant in determining growth, and that in cases where there is a change in regime towards democracy, the country grows faster than a priori similar countries that did not experience democratization. However, Marsh (1979), in his study of ninety-eight countries between 1955 and 1970, concluded that democracy was a 'luxury' because it retarded growth. Berg-Schlosser (1984) also found that authoritarian regimes have a positive effect on GNP growth.

Barro (1997) found a non-linear effect of democracy on growth. Growth initially increases with electoral rights, but once a moderate amount of rights has been attained, the relationship turns negative. He interprets this as meaning that in a dictatorship an increase in democracy stimulates growth, but that for countries with a moderate amount of democracy, any further increase impairs growth because it increases redistributive programmes. Sen (1983) approaches the relationship from a different perspective. He argues that while China suffered from a major famine in 1959–61, India, with a lower availability of food per capita, has avoided such disasters (see chapter 12). This, says Sen, is because India's democracy with its free press and opposition parties is quicker at averting sporadic threats but less efficient at dealing with chronic problems like hunger and malnutrition. Thus, democracy helps certain aspects of development (avoidance of major disasters), but non-democratic regimes often fare better at the organizational effort involved in some developmental activities like eradicating mass illiteracy or malnutrition.

From development to democracy

In addition to the influence that democracy has on the level of development of a country, the latter, in its turn, may also influence democracy. Lipset (1960) was the first to argue that with economic development, income distribution becomes more egalitarian, and therefore class politics become less polarized. Lipset's argument was inspired by modernization theories in which society, polity and economy are systematically interrelated and integrated by a value consensus. Many of the early studies found a positive impact of growth on democracy, and argued that growth led to the spread of communication, education and the middle classes, which increased political interest and tolerance, and laid the foundation for democratic governance.

Ruschmeyer, Stephens and Stephens (1992) confirm that cross-sectional studies have found evidence in favour of this relationship. They claim, however, that economic development affects political democracy because 'capitalist development transforms the class structure, enlarging the working and middle classes and facilitating their self-organization, thus making it more difficult for elites to exclude them politically' (Ruschmeyer et al., 1992, p. 83).

Helliwell (1994) allows for a dual relationship. He finds that democracy has a negative impact on growth, but notes that this effect is offset by the fact that democracy leads to increased expenditure on investment and education, which in turn will increase growth. Similarly, development generates educational and communication networks, both of which are necessary to sustain democracy. Barro (1999) confirms the Lipset hypothesis that increases in the standard of living lead to increases in democracy. He concludes that democracies that arise without economic development tend not to last.

Conclusion

Thus, we see that even with a narrow definition of development and democracy, the relationship is far from straightforward. Development without political freedom is incomplete, and real democracy is meaningless without some measure of economic freedom and equality. However, as we widen the definition of these two concepts, the relationship becomes less clear, and they seem to merge into one. Thus, development can be defined in its broadest sense as 'the necessary conditions for a universally accepted aim, the realisation of the potential of the human personality' (Seers, 1979b). Democracy, in its turn, can be defined as a system in which people are able to make choices regarding their lives in such a way as to realize their potential.

Though these definitions may be too broad and diffuse to facilitate realistic analysis, keeping them at the back of our minds does indicate that, in the last analysis, a narrow debate on the effect of *political* democracy on *economic* development is incomplete.

State type and development: a categorization[3]

A problem with most of the above studies is that they concentrate on a binary distinction between democratic and authoritarian regimes. This, of course, does not exhaust the range of state types that exist in the world. Is their relative level of democracy the only axis along which these states differ? If success in achieving development requires both the ability and the willingness to work for it, then while democracies may lack the *ability*, authoritarian states may lack the *willingness* to attain development. As Sorensen (1993) argues, there is no reason to assume that authoritarian systems are likely to be more future- or welfare-oriented than democratic systems. There are benevolent dictators and selfish ones, just as there are developmental democracies and short-sighted ones. While Salazar in Portugal attempted to restrict expenditure and growth, Franco in Spain and Lee Kwan Yew in Singapore attempted to increase expenditure and consciously foster economic development (Sorensen, 1993).

Sorensen's (1993) classification of regimes on the basis of their attitude to democracy and development is a useful analytical tool. Restricting himself to defining development as growth and welfare, and democracy as a parliamentary form of government, he distinguished between five regime types – three authoritarian and two democratic – based on their attitudes to development. The authoritarian regimes are classified as developmental, growth-orientated and elite-enrichment regimes, while the democratic ones are classified as elite-dominated and mass-dominated ones.

Authoritarian developmentalist regimes are capable of promoting both growth and welfare. In such regimes the government is welfare-oriented and is relatively independent of vested interests. Its bureaucracy has the organizational capacity to promote development, and the state elite too is committed to this objective. Such states may follow free market policies (Taiwan, South Korea and Singapore) or be centrally planned (China, Cuba and North Korea). The acceptability of such a regime will depend upon the weights people attach to economic, social and political equality and freedoms.

Authoritarian growth regimes promote growth but not welfare. Such regimes tend to promote growth which respects certain vested interests, and in this sense are elite-oriented regimes. Sorensen gives the example of Brazil, where the alliance was between local private capital, state enterprises and transnational corporations. There was very little attempt to benefit the poor through redistributive and welfare policies. Countries like Uruguay, Argentina and Chile in the early and mid-1970s fall into this category. Many of these countries expected that growth would lead to increased welfare through automatic trickle-down. However, this has not happened in most of them.

Authoritarian state elite-enrichment regimes promote neither growth nor development (however narrowly defined). They are exclusively concerned with the enrichment of the elite that controls the state. Mobutu in Zaire, Idi Amin in Uganda, Papa and Baby Doc in Haiti, and Somoza in Nicaragua are cited by Sorensen (1993) as falling into these categories.

Elite-dominated democracies, like that in India, aim to benefit certain elites. Though everybody has a vote in India, most government policies, in application, if not in rhetoric, are aimed at benefiting the urban professionals, the Indian business community, and the rural land-owning elite. However, in Costa Rica, also classified as an elite-dominated democracy, the dominant coalitions – involved in export agriculture and industry and the state bureaucracy – have supported substantial welfare programmes. This has led to considerable trickle-down and has propelled Costa Rica into a high Human Development Index country (see also table 1.1).

Mass-dominated democracies push for reforms from below, often leading to confrontation with the traditional ruling classes, who continue to resist the changes. Thus, as Marx put it, democracy inevitably 'unchains the class struggle' (Marx, 1952, p. 2). 'The poor use democracy to expropriate riches, the rich are threatened and subvert democracy, typically by "abdicating" political power to the armed forces' (Przeworski and Limongi, 1995, p. 4). Chile under Allende is cited as an example of this kind of regime.

It must be noted, though, that even if we accept the above categorization to begin with, regimes may change over time. It is possible that countries may begin with authoritarian rule, which may be relaxed once some development has been achieved. Thus, development may lead to democracy. Secondly, countries may shift from elite-dominated democratic systems (which most European countries were to begin with) to mass-dominated democracies. Sorensen himself argues that democracies also have 'transformational capacities', and can move towards mass-dominated versions as development occurs.

We have so far accepted the significant role played by the state in development. In Part IV of this book, we will consider the different measures undertaken by states in the last few decades in the push for development. In the next section, however, we will consider an issue that is being debated and which we have already touched upon in chapter 7. This is the undermining of state influence in the new global order within which multinational enterprises, international NGOs and international government organizations (IGOs) are all playing an increasingly important role.

Postscript: rethinking the role of the state in the twenty-first century

Two questions emerge as significant in what we have considered so far. First, has the state really been important in influencing the performance of economies (especially in East Asia)? Second, can the state continue to be important in the light of changes that have been occurring across the world, specifically the globalization of the world system and the spread of neo-liberal ideology, both of which undermine the significance of the nation-state in policy making? We will consider these issues in turn in this section.

The neo-liberal stance of the World Bank, which argued in a series of reports (World Bank, 1983, 1987) that liberal, market-friendly economic policies had led to the success of the East Asian economies, as well as the emergence of Prime Minister Thatcher in the UK and of President Reagan in the USA, signalled a shift towards rolling back the influence of the state in the 1980s. This was reinforced, as we have seen, by the breakdown of the planned economic systems of the Socialist economies and a hardening of the neo-liberal consensus in development policies the world over. The debt crisis and the need for structural adjustment loans in many developing countries provided the context in which such market-centred policies could be pushed. Many developing countries had to borrow funds from the IMF and the World Bank in response to temporary or long-term financial problems (see chapter 8). Receipt of these funds was conditional on a number of policy changes, including economic stabilization (through restrictive fiscal and monetary policies). Governments in receipt of such loans also had to undertake structural adjustment of their economies through a reduction in government involvement. As part of this, they had to throw their economies open to foreign competition and investment. UN Secretary-General Kofi Annan argues that 'the state is no longer the creator of wealth, but is instead a facilitator and catalyst of development' (Cheema, 1998).

In this context, it is also clear that attempts to decrease trade barriers under the aegis of GATT (and more recently the WTO) have constrained the freedom of action of individual governments. However, these attempts have also been based upon broad reciprocity between governments. In this sense, they require the preservation of national diversity as well as national responsibility in order to be successful (Ostry, 1998, p. 7). However, once financial flows were liberalized, domestic fiscal and monetary policy was no longer independent, and with the ICT revolution and the increase in financial flows (long and especially short term), the independence of nation-states in determining domestic stabilization and development policies has been further circumscribed.

In addition to the above developments, the increasing importance of multinational enterprises (MNEs) and of international NGOs has further constrained the role of the state. Liberalization of trade in many developing countries has meant that MNEs no longer find market access being restricted by border barriers, trade restrictions or regulations. The barriers that MNEs face relate to differences amongst countries in cultures, laws and policies. But nation-states find it hard to control footloose global capital, and this, together with the drive towards a single global market, places considerable pressure on governments (especially of host economies) to create a welcoming environment for the MNEs by decreasing taxes and easing regulations (see chapter 8). Of course, this is not the only constraint facing nation-states. The increasing significance of international NGOs has also affected the independence of governments in domestic policy. International organizations began to play a significant formal role in international issues in 1994, when the UNCED formally endorsed their role in international policy making. The growth of ICT has made these NGOs extremely powerful and able to influence government policy making considerably. The foremost amongst these organizations are the Greens, human rights activists, and the women's rights movements.

In this context, Jessop (1999) argues that globalization is changing the role of the state on three fronts. First, there is a trend towards de-nationalization of the state, especially with reorganization of state capacities on a sub-national, national and supranational level. Typical examples are the regional blocs like the EU and NAFTA. Second, there is the de-statization of the political system – a shift from government to governance – in which the state loses its central role to a partnership of governmental, para-governmental and non-governmental organizations. Third, internationalization of policy regimes has meant that the key players in policy regimes now include foreign agents and institutions, and the state's increasing concern is with international competitiveness, rather than domestic development. As a consequence of these changes, many state theories seem to be agreed on 'dethroning the state from its super-ordinate position within society and analysing it simply as one institutional order among others' (Jessop, 2003). Therefore the state is seen as an emergent, partial and unstable system that is interdependent with other systems in a complex social order.

However, others have argued against this view. Poulantzos (1975, 1978) rejects this 'borderless world' on the grounds that 'every process of internationalization is effected under the dominance of the capital of a definite country' (1975, p. 73), because national states remain central to the reproduction of their bourgeoisies. Poulantzos also argues that nations retain their identity, because it is tied to factors which are not necessarily economic. These include territorial, linguistic, cultural, ideological and broadly traditional factors that unify a nation.

Even institutions previously at the heart of the Washington Consensus, like the World Bank, now reformulate their recommendation away from a reduction in state role towards an emphasis on the role of institutions in establishing regulatory frameworks. The 1997 *World Bank Report* has asked for a 'rethinking of the state's role', arguing that 'good government is not a luxury – it is a vital necessity for development' (World Bank, 1997, p. 15). Nevertheless, it still called for rolling back the state in a number of countries. It compliments the efforts of countries in Latin America and Africa during the structural adjustment programmes. Market failures (public goods, externalities, natural monopolies, incomplete markets, imperfect or asymmetric information and moral hazard), it claims, continue to provide powerful arguments for state intervention. The state can continue to provide pure public 'goods' (such as property rights, macro-economic stability, control of infectious diseases and safe water, roads and protection of the destitute), though some of these can also be provided by the private sector. Secondly, the state has some intermediate functions, including the management of externalities (pollution), the regulation of monopolies, and the provision of social insurance. Third, the Bank accepts the need for a limited activist role for the state. It can help to set up missing markets through co-ordination, as in the case of East Asia, where governments have tried to promote markets through financial and industrial policy. Finally, the Bank agrees that equity remains a central concern of the state. In Latin America, 69 per cent of citizens felt that the state should intervene to decrease income differences between the rich and the poor (World Bank, 1997, p. 111). The state's unique strengths are its powers to tax, to prohibit, to punish, and to require participation. Thus, the increasing acceptance that the East Asian miracle was a reflection of strong, strategic state intervention, and that the response to the 1997 East Asian crisis may well have been misguided (see box 10.1), has led to some softening of neo-liberal policy rhetoric the world over.

It seems clear that this debate will continue. The state has been a very significant player in many developing countries over the last half-century or more. 'Good' state intervention has helped many countries in East and South-East Asia to grow and develop at unprecedented rates. On the other hand, 'bad' state intervention has held back many more developing countries elsewhere in the world. The notion that the state is not effective (either in a good or a bad sense) in the face of globalization has still to be decided on.

Conclusion

This chapter has considered the role of the state in developing economies. We will revisit this issue time and again in the next few chapters. The state is expected to have a significant role when the goal is tangible and involves catching up with the West. While the 1960s and 1970s were the heyday of planning and state involvement in the economy, the 1980s saw a withdrawal in state intervention in many parts of the world, most notably of course, in Eastern Europe and Central Asia. Structural adjustment programmes have also ensured a reduction in state intervention in other developing countries.

In chapter 10, we will provide a historical review of three success stories in developmental terms. By subtitling the chapter 'The "Success" Stories', I do not mean to imply that these countries have 'achieved' development, with all its broad implications. Instead, I wish to show that two at least of these countries have advanced significantly from their position of a few decades ago, though in political and social terms their development may still be limited. I chose the three countries on the basis of their relative success and of the different paths followed by them. Thus, the UK was the first industrial nation, and as such had a unique experience of growth and development. South Korea followed a market-oriented but state-strategized model, while China followed a centrally planned model, to achieve similar developmental goals.

10

Development: The 'Success' Stories

As we have seen, development theories have tapped into a number of dichotomies – market orientation versus state planning, inward-versus outward-looking economies, industrialization versus agricultural development, top-down centralized approach versus bottom-up, decentralized, participatory approach (Brohman, 1996). In practice, however, most successful economies have found some locally appropriate combination of these strategies. Thus, they have combined market orientation with some state planning and inward orientation followed by export promotion, for instance. Before we move on to consider the impact of development on the domestic economy in Part IV, it is worth pausing to discuss the development experience of a few countries. How did these countries succeed? What characteristics did they possess? What policy trajectories, if any, did they follow? This chapter aims to take account of what we have read so far to show that there is no single blueprint for development. Most countries follow paths suited to their own particular conditions. But two factors stand out as significant, though in different ways in different countries. First, the state may be highly centralized or decentralized; it may adopt administrative planning or a market-friendly approach. Whatever the exact strategies adopted, a strong, focused state has been necessary for developmental success in almost all cases. Second, the contribution of foreign links has varied from country to country, and from one period to another, but the stance taken with respect to such links has defined development policy in different countries. Thus, development strategies have emphasized such links, whether in the context of attempting to minimize them (import-substituting industrialization) or in that of promoting them. In general, in most countries, export promotion has followed import substitution.

In this chapter, we will consider the development experience of three countries: Great Britain, South Korea and China. While we highlight the roles of the state and of foreign links, our discussion is neither systematic nor comprehensive. Each of the three models discussed in this chapter is similar with regard to its objective: that is, the Western conception of modernity, which accepts that 'the recent history of the West could be taken as evidence of the direction in which mankind as a whole *would* move, and flowing from this, *should* move' (Nisbet, 1969, quoted in Hettne, 1995, p. 29). Yet each of these models differs with respect to the means employed, partly because these had to be strategized in the light of already existing competition from the early developers.

What has motivated this choice of countries? I have chosen to consider the experience of two East Asian countries, in addition to that of Britain, for many reasons. Many writers within development argue that Britain is unrepresentative of developing countries today, because it had the advantage of being the first mover, while developing countries are burdened by their history as well as by the success of the early developers. Being the pioneer has meant that the British state did not have an objective goal to aspire to, as all later developers had. It also meant that Britain could take advantage of world trade and of its colonies, in a way that none of the less developed countries today can. The British development experience therefore has been unique in many ways. In spite of this, I have chosen to consider it on two grounds. First, there are a number of similarities (in kind, if not degree) that bear examining. Thus, Britain's experience with respect to urbanization, improvement in living standards and equity, and attitude towards industrial policy reflects important similarities with developing countries today. Additionally, though Britain is often held up as the original *laissez-faire* economy, we note that the state played a significant role in its development and that trade controls were also important (Chang, 2002). A historical consideration of its policies could provide important lessons for later developers, as we will see. Second, where there are differences, or where Britain was unique, it helps to recognize this, because it highlights the constraints facing developing countries today. Thus, while Britain was able to expand its exports almost without constraint, this cannot be true for any economy today, given the levels of international competition. While setting the goals for all countries that followed, Britain was able to progress relatively autonomously, at least initially. Of course, being an early starter also meant much slower rates of progress on many fronts. Thus, while it took many years for the death rate to decrease in Great Britain, this phase of the demographic transition (chapter 11) has been compressed in most contemporary developing countries through knowledge inherited from the early starters. Similarly, while democracy in the form of universal adult suffrage arrived in Britain only in 1918, most developing countries that do espouse democracy today have universal, rather than selective (based on income or status) adult suffrage (Chang, 2002).

I have chosen South Korea because it is one of a group of East Asian economies that has grown very fast over the last two or three decades. Today, South Korea stands thirty-second in the HDI rankings, above Portugal and just below other West European countries. In spite of the crisis in the late 1990s in East Asia, progress in this region has been unparalleled. Its success has generated an enormous literature, as well as a fruitful policy debate, which has held centre stage in Development Studies for the last two decades. It is therefore worth considering in more detail whether the East Asian growth experience can provide guidelines for other developing countries.

Both South Korea and China are relatively large countries. Their experience is therefore more generalizable than that of Hong Kong or Singapore, which are city-states. In addition, they have followed quite distinct paths to success. South Korea has followed a market- and export-oriented path, though with an efficient and strategically advanced state. China, on the other hand, followed a centrally planned and, even today (after many years of marketization), a relatively autarchic model. In spite of this, and contrary to all the literature regarding the miracle market economies, it has succeeded. China today stands 108th, which indicates a considerable improvement over its position a few decades ago. Has it been the accident of location that has contributed to its success and that of so many economies in this region? Or are there other factors?

We will look at each of these cases in more detail in what follows. We will begin with Britain, where the Industrial Revolution first created conditions for sustained growth over time.

The development experience

Britain: the first industrial nation

In Britain, the shift from an extensive growth[1] process to an intensive[2] one began between the 1740s and the 1780s, when agricultural productivity increased sufficiently to release resources from agriculture and enable changes in the structure of the economy. This process has been called the Industrial Revolution. While the term implies a sudden and very fast process, the pace of change in Britain, as we will see below, was slow, especially relative to later industrializers like Germany, the United States and Japan, or more lately South Korea.

The 1750s and 1760s saw many structural changes in the British economy. Enclosures of land and irrigation changed agriculture considerably.

The Enclosure Acts (1760–1830) forced peasants off the land, creating a relatively free and mobile labour force. Landless labourers now accounted for three-quarters of the agricultural workers in England and Wales. They were employed as wage labour both by capitalist farmers and by firms in the manufacturing sector, though by 1850, manufacturing had overtaken agriculture as a source of employment. The retail and distribution network was also becoming more sophisticated, with fewer people now shopping in markets or fairs and shops becoming more common. These changes in retailing were reinforced by changes that were taking place in commerce and transport (the building of canals).

Early industrial progress in Britain was distinguished by technical change. In the pre-industrial economy, technical change was intermittent, because workers learned their trade from their fathers and continued it in much the same way. In the industrial economy, however, change and improvement became the order of things, and pushed the economy towards faster growth. Technical innovations took place in a number of industries, beginning with textiles but including industries, like iron and steel and mechanical engineering by the nineteenth century. In no other country has industrial growth become synonymous with major industrial inventions as it did in Britain.

Real output increased from about 0.2 per cent per annum in the 1710–40 period to about 2 per cent per annum in the 1780–1800 period. The rate of growth of industrial output quadrupled, while that of agricultural output hardly increased at all. The growth rate of 2 per cent per annum, together with a rate of population increase of 1 per cent per annum between 1780 and 1800, meant an increase in real output per head of 1 per cent per annum (see table 10.1). Though higher than it had ever been before, this growth was generally slower than in the later industrializers.

Between 1750 and 1815, output per head in Britain increased by 2.5 times. While this increased the average standard of living, not everybody benefited. In fact there is considerable debate regarding the impact of growth on standards of living. Deane (1979) concludes that there is no firm evidence of an overall improvement in standards of living for

Table 10.1   Summary statistics for the British economy, 1710–1800

	Rate of growth (% per annum)		
	1710–40	1740–80	1780–1800
Real output	0.2	1.0	2.0
Real output per head	0.2	0.3	1.0
Population	0.0	0.7	1.0
Industrial output	0.7	0.9	2.8
Agricultural output	0.0	0.5	0.6

Source: Based on Deane and Cole, 1962

the working classes between 1780 and 1820. Living standards improved somewhat between 1820 and 1840, but it was not until after 1840 that a significant improvement was evident. This was largely the result of workers moving into higher-paid jobs and of decreases in unemployment.

It took almost a hundred years for the benefits of economic growth to trickle down to improvements in overall living standards. By 1851, the British economy had reached maturity, and had passed the point of no return in the process of industrialization. Soon after this, Britain began to be overtaken by other economies, especially the USA.

Proximate factors leading to development

From a developmental point of view, it would be interesting to consider what caused the Industrial Revolution, or the take-off, in Britain. The significance of this question for the performance of developing economies found its most explicit recognition in Rostow's use of the British growth experience as the foundation for his model of economic growth (see chapter 4). Of course, it is likely that a number of factors – Britain's favourable natural resources position, the role of Protestant ethics, increasing population, the advances in science, the will to economize, possession of sufficient economic resources to develop new sides of the economy, increased investment, the role of foreign trade, improvements in transport facilities and in financial institutions – came together in the late eighteenth century. None of these factors on its own would have been sufficient to result in sudden growth, but the conjunction of these factors seems to have been effective. We will consider some of these factors in more detail in this section.

The initial resource position in Britain was especially favourable (Mathias, 1983). The availability of coal and iron ore close to rivers or canals was important in an age when technology was making river transportation easier. Later, of course, the import of raw materials was also made possible through further improvements in transport. Improvements in road, canal and rail transportation, as well as changes in agriculture and industry, required considerable increases in investment. At the same time, the trend towards urbanization and industrialization necessitated investment in social capital, especially in urban housing, sanitation, water supplies, lighting and hospitals. Overall, the levels of investment doubled to about 11 per cent of GNP by 1790, a factor that was highlighted by Rostow (1960) and many later development economists as the catalyst for development. Later developers like South Korea and China have seen larger increases in investment (to about 25 per cent of GNP), and have benefited from an existing pool of technical and institutional knowledge, which they could tap into when planning investment expenditure.

After 1750, financial institutions developed to service the transactions and investments required by the new industries. There was very little imported capital to begin with in Britain. In fact, Dutch investment in

Britain during the early eighteenth century was drying up just when demand for capital was beginning to increase. In much of the period, investment was taking place elsewhere in the colonies, investment which would yield benefits later on in the process. Capital flows from England and France were especially important in supporting the movement of population to the USA, Canada, Australia, South Africa and New Zealand.

During this period, the social structure in Britain became more flexible, with the 'middling orders' becoming especially important. Commercial and professional interests began to gain political significance, which in turn increased their social standing. Protestant Nonconformism enabled and reinforced such social flexibility.

Thus, a number of factors came together to enable Britain's industrialization in the eighteenth century. We will consider two further factors – the role of the state and the role of foreign trade – in greater detail later in this chapter. Before we do so, however, we will consider South Korea's growth experience in the next subsection.

Korea: industrializing through learning

Britain did not retain her first mover advantage for long. By the mid-nineteenth century, a number of other countries in Europe and America had caught up with, and surpassed, it. The most recent examples of significant 'catch-up' have occurred in East Asia, beginning with Japan in the post-war period. Amsden classifies this latest phase of 'catch-up' as being based on learning (Amsden, 1989, p. 4).[3] Following on from Japan, South Korea began to emerge as a fast-growing industrial economy in the 1960s, and is today 'developed' at least in economic terms. As indicated earlier, it is now thirty-second in the HDI rankings (UNDP, 1997). The 1997 East Asian crisis (see box 10.1) has led a number of writers to

---

Box 10.1   The Asian financial crisis

Until 1997, the East Asian development experience was held up as a 'miracle', and attempts were being made to understand and imitate this miracle in other parts of the world (both developed and developing). The crisis in the late 1990s, however, caused a temporary reversal of opinion, with cries of 'cronyism' and predictions of doomsday. The achievements of these economies were being questioned, though some balance has since been achieved.

The crisis began with the Thai currency, the baht, which had been depreciating against the dollar. In an attempt to establish Bangkok as a rival financial centre to Hong Kong and Singapore, the Thai government had relaxed many of its regulatory restrictions and barriers to entry. This resulted in the rapid expansion of industry and a failure of prudential safeguards. By July 1997, the baht had to be floated, and by February 1998, the crisis had affected both Indonesia and South Korea.

The most surprising aspect of the crisis was that almost all economic indicators were quite healthy – domestic savings were relatively high, fiscal policy was prudent, inflation was low (being highest in Vietnam, which was relatively untouched by the crisis), the debt–GDP ratio was manageable, and international reserves were healthy. In addition, most of the South-East Asian economies grew relatively fast in 1996, and inflation was not a problem even in 1998 for any country except Indonesia. The only factor which with hindsight might have signalled a problem was the ratio of short-term to total debt. In South Korea, the share of short-term debt in total debt increased from an already high 43.7 per cent in 1993 to 58.3 per cent in 1996.

A number of reasons have been put forward for the crisis. Many blamed government policy (too much, too little, the wrong type, and so on). In many countries, attempts at financial deregulation had triggered the problem, because governments (whether in Thailand, Indonesia or South Korea) were not regulating the financial sector sufficiently. In South Korea, for instance, the Kim government was not even aware of the huge mismatch in the maturity structures between the borrowings of these banks (64 per cent, short-term) and lending (85 per cent, long term) on the eve of the crisis. Chang et al. (1998) maintain that the dismantling of traditional industrial policy in South Korea led to excessive competition, over-investment, low capacity utilization and falling profitability in the manufacturing sector. While cronyism had always existed in urban planning and in other government projects, it had now begun to spread to the manufacturing sector too. A number of writers (Krugman, 1998) maintain that the implicit guarantee provided by the South Korean (and other) states to business resulted in reckless investments and low efficiency (a kind of moral hazard). But Chang (2000) disputes this, arguing that while there is a state guarantee from the point of view of employees and consumers, it does not extend to the managers and owners who have caused the problems. In fact, the South Korean state made the disciplining of these managers and owners a condition of the 'bail-out' that it provided. While there is considerable disagreement regarding the causes of the crisis, there is some consensus regarding the role played by exchange-rate policy (fixed but adjustable exchange rates with fairly open capital markets) and weak and poorly regulated financial markets. These problems were reinforced by Japan's inability to play a major role in the recovery, due to its own recession, and by the IMF's pressure on governments with relatively conservative fiscal policies to tighten policy even further. Together with its mandated bank closures, this triggered widespread panic and collapse in financial institutions (H. Hill, 1998).

question South Korea's achievements in the last few decades. In retrospect, however, this seems over-hasty. Stiglitz (1998) argues that 'While Korea, Indonesia and Malaysia have only had one each [year of negative growth], India has suffered 4 contractions and the United States 5.' South Korea's long-term achievements remain considerable, even in the light of the 1997 crisis. We will consider these achievements and the factors underlying them in the rest of this section.

South Korean industrialization can be said to have begun in the 1870s, when the Japanese invasion shattered the Yi dynasty. But significant acceleration in economic growth did not occur until the 1960s, when South Korea emerged as one of the Asian newly industrializing countries. It is sometimes argued that the foundations for South Korea's development can be found in Japanese colonial policy between 1905 and 1945 (see chapter 9). Though there was considerable chaos and trauma in the fifteen years after the Japanese left, South Korea 'fell back into the grooves of an earlier origin (*the Japanese one*) and traversed along them, well into the 1980s' (Kohli, 1994).

In the 1960s and 1970s, the growth rate of GNP in South Korea was always above 5 per cent (see table 10.2), increasing to almost 10 per cent in 1967–71. While growth slowed down in the 1980s, it was higher than the 2–3 per cent per annum that Britain managed when it was industrializing. This is not surprising, of course, because as a late developer South Korea had the advantage of a pool of technical knowledge that it could tap. High growth rates could be maintained through the import of this technology, at least until the backlog was exhausted.

Structural change was also very rapid, with the contribution of agriculture to GDP decreasing from 38 per cent in 1965 to 7 per cent in 1994, while that of industry increased from 25 per cent to 43 per cent (see table 10.3). Life expectancy had increased to almost 71 years by 1992 and infant mortality had decreased to approximately 13 deaths per 1,000 births (see table 10.4). These changes took considerably longer in Britain, where the first two stages of the demographic transition were long drawn out.

Table 10.2   Growth of GDP in South Korea, 1962–1996

Years	Growth of GDP(%)[a]
1962–66	7.9
1967–71	9.6
1972–76	9.7
1977–81	6.0
1982–86	9.4
1987–91	9.6
1992–96	7.1

Source: Based on data from *International Statistics Yearbooks*, 1990 and 1997
[a] Five-year moving averages. Data up to 1977–81 are from the *International Statistics Yearbook*, 1990, and from 1982–86 onwards are from the *International Statistics Yearbook*, 1997.

Table 10.3   Structure of the economy in South Korea, 1965–1994

Year	% of GDP from agriculture	% of GDP from industry	% of GDP from services
1965	38	25	37
1977	27	34	39
1985	14	41	45
1994	7	43	50

Source: Based on data from *International Statistics Yearbooks*, 1990 and 1997

Table 10.4   Social development indicators for South Korea, 1972–1992

Year	Life expectancy (no. of years)	Infant mortality (no. of deaths per 1,000 live births)
1972	61.4	47
1982	67.7	30
1992	70.9	12.8

Source: Based on data from *International Statistics Yearbooks*, 1990 and 1997

Proximate factors leading to growth

In South Korea, and in most later developers, the development strategy adopted (with regard to trade, price setting, government intervention, industrial policies and so on) had a significant impact on the growth experience. We will consider this strategy in greater detail later on in this chapter. Here we will consider the proximate factors assisting South Korea's development.

The South Korean land reforms undertaken after the defeat of the Japanese in 1945 were amongst the most successful in the developing world. Whatever the reasons for the success of these reforms (see chapter 12), they did establish conditions likely to speed up growth and development. South Korea also benefited from the inflow of merchant capital, which was driven out of China by the Communist take-over there (Bagchi, 1989). In addition, US military activity, and the large expenditures it involved, helped traders and industrialists in the region. America's fears of a Communist revolution in the area also brought in large volumes of American aid into South Korea.

Many writers also argue that the early Japanese domination of South Korea had a significant impact on South Korean development. Japanese dominance meant that the local industrial bourgeoisie was not very strong and that when the Japanese were defeated, most industrial capital passed to the South Korean state. While this resulted in considerable corruption and the trading of favours,[4] it also enabled the foundation of the chaebols,[5] which went on to dominate South Korean industrialization.

Industrial interests in South Korea could therefore always be maintained subordinate to the state. Japanese foreign investment and technology supported early industrialization. The Japanese also carried out extensive agrarian reforms, creating relatively egalitarian rural structures. Jenkins (1992c) argues that the military threat faced by South Korea also pushed it to prioritize growth, industrialization and a strong fiscal profile (higher taxes and lower public expenditure).

In spite of these proximate factors, the most oft-cited reasons for South Korea's success relate to its development strategy – the quality of its state intervention and the model of export-led growth for which it opted – and the efficiency of its development institutions – the model of developmental state that it adhered to (see chapter 9). We will postpone discussion of these factors to a later section. We will consider the Chinese development experience in the next subsection.

China: planned industrialization

China still ranks as a developing country, the largest in terms of population. But it is one of the fastest-growing economies today, and this, together with its size, sets it on track to be a highly significant player in the world economy and polity in the twenty-first century. The Chinese experience of development is distinguished by its focus on a tangible (if moving) target – the standard of living of the developed world. Like most developing countries, it had an aim – that of catching up with the developed world in the shortest time possible, while minimizing social costs. Thus, Chinese economic policy aimed to 'steadily transform China from an agricultural into an industrial country and to build China into a great socialist state' (Mao Tse Tung, quoted in Singh, 1979, p. 588). To achieve this, the state took on a more consciously developmental role than it did in most early developers. The strategy adopted – administrative planning of resource allocation – was significantly more interventionist than in most other developing countries, too.

China has achieved very high growth rates since the beginning of planning. While the figures are not always reliable, growth was as high as 22 per cent in 1958, and 20–3 per cent in 1969–70. Though there were years of equally spectacular decreases (like 1960), the economy has grown consistently fast since 1969.

Table 10.5 indicates that GNP grew at more than 5 per cent in China between 1970 and 1980, and since then, it has grown even faster (at 9.77 per cent between 1980 and 1990 and 10.65 per cent since then). As in the case of Britain, industry has grown faster (10.5 per cent per annum between 1953 and 1974) than agriculture (2.4 per cent per annum during this period). Though GNP per capita grew at 3.4 per cent per annum during this period, in reality living standards improved faster through

Table 10.5   Summary statistics for China, 1950–1995

Years	Change in GDP at constant prices[a] (% per annum)	Life expectancy in years (figs for single years)	Infant mortality (no. of deaths per 1,000 live births) (figs for single years)
1950–60	12.02	—	—
1960–70	2.92	—	—
1970–80	7.53	64	70
1980–90	9.77	71	24
1990–95	10.65	72	17

[a]Averages
Source: Based on data from *International Statistics Yearbooks*, 1985 and 1997

direct redistribution undertaken by the state. Attempts at redistribution through investments in health, education and employment were highly successful. China managed to decrease chronic under-nourishment, and to improve the health of its people, so that by 1981, approximately 30 years after it began planning, life expectancy was 68 years and infant mortality was only 37 per 1,000 live births (Coale, 1993). While this trend is common to many developing countries today, and is partly a result of improvements in public health and hygiene (through new medicines, inoculations and vaccinations), it was also due to the priority given to health and education within the Chinese plans. Literacy rates in 1982 were 96 per cent for males and 85 per cent for females in the 15–19 age-group. Improvements in education, health and general living standards have therefore been faster in China than in Britain, where living standards took almost 100 years to improve significantly.

By the late 1970s, however, the problems with a planned economic system were becoming apparent (see also chapter 9). The informational burden of planned resource allocation is exceptionally heavy. Gathering the vast amounts of data required in the short time available, processing and analysing it and making decisions based on it, are very difficult. Secondly, there were problems with motivating individuals in the absence of monetary incentives. Finally, measuring output through physical targets reduces the sensitivity of the system to costs. Cost, quality and variety were therefore sacrificed in favour of meeting output targets. Growth was achieved in a wasteful manner with a large and increasing amount of capital. Thus, while 100 yuan[6] of accumulation resulted in a growth in national income of 57 yuan in 1963–5, this decreased to 26 yuan in 1966–70, only increasing to 41 yuan in 1981–5 (Nolan, 1990). In response to these problems, China undertook the marketization of its economy from the late 1970s (see box 10.2).

Box 10.2   China's marketization

China began to reform its economy in 1978 in a slow, experimental manner. Price liberalization was gradual, and a dual-track price system, in which both market and administered prices are used, still operates in China. China opened itself up to increased foreign trade and foreign direct investment in 1978. Though agriculture was de-collectivized, community ownership of land was retained. In the industrial sector, reforms were aimed at both the state-owned enterprises and the township and village enterprises (TVEs). In the latter, considerable competition was encouraged between regions and villages, and this has helped improve the performance of the TVEs. Unlike in much of Eastern Europe, the Chinese leadership went in for 'planned economic reform'. While this may seem like a contradiction in terms, it has been relatively successful in the last two decades. The Chinese leadership saw 'a strong state as a functional necessity for economic advance'. China's reforms also differed from those in many East European economies in adopting a slow, experimental, cumulative approach rather than a 'big bang' approach (see box 9.2). One of the most significant outcomes of the reforms is that the decision-making process in China is being decentralized relative to the one that existed in the pre-1978 period.

Proximate factors leading to development

It is often claimed that China's geographical proximity to Japan and the East Asian NICs has helped its development. To some extent, this is true, as it has gained from the regional division of labour and investments, which has followed a 'flying geese' pattern of development, with Japan at one end, then the Asian NICs, followed by the South-East Asian Tigers and then China. As wages have increased in Japan, Hong Kong and South Korea, so firms and investment have moved to China and other geographically proximate countries with lower wage rates. This can only be a small part of the explanation, however.

Another possible factor may be the death of Mao Tse Tung in 1976 and the characteristics of the leadership which took over in 1978. Perkins (1988) argued that though these leaders did not have a blueprint in mind regarding China's future, they had a 'strong distaste for many of the policies and values that played so large a role during that decade' (Perkins, 1988, p. 601). It was this change of leadership that has been seen as operative in China's subsequent economic development. We will consider these factors in the next section.

Development strategies considered

We have so far considered the development experience of Britain, South Korea and China, but have postponed discussion of the strategies they adopted (if any) for development. In this section, we will consider these in some detail. We will find that though the role of the state was significant in all three cases, the extent of state intervention varied considerably. Thus, while state intervention was all-encompassing in China (including price setting), it was more strategic, though still highly focused, in South Korea. In Britain, by contrast, it was less objective-oriented but nevertheless highly significant in attempting to maintain Britain's initial lead in manufacturing. Similarly, we find with respect to the role of trade that while Britain was careful in protecting her industries early on, she was also able to tap into captive export markets (in her colonies). South Korea also began by protecting her domestic firms, but her shift towards export promotion was highly successful. Finally, China began as a highly autarchic economy, but is also slowly opening up to export markets. Thus, it seems likely that initial import substitution is as necessary as later export orientation to foster growth.

Role of the state

While the proximate factors are important, and play a significant role in why and when some countries develop relative to others, development strategies (*vis-à-vis* the role of the state and of technological change and foreign links) determine the sustainability of such development, as well as the extent to which it is motivation rather than chance that leads to development. Though not all countries have had the same experience with respect to these factors, they have all had to make decisions regarding where they stand with respect to them.

Britain

While many early studies claimed that Britain, during the Industrial Revolution, was the original *laissez-faire* economy, it is now being increasingly accepted that the state played a significant and positive role even in the first industrial nation. On the eve of the Industrial Revolution, though there were many restrictions and regulations on the economy – usury laws, apprenticeship laws, Acts to control the quality of output and trade – the government was unable to enforce these laws effectively. Between 1760 and 1850, therefore, many of these laws were swept away. This has often been seen as a withdrawal of the state from the British economy. However, Deane argues that these reforms actually enabled the state to intervene 'more deeply and more effectively in the economy than it had ever done before' (Deane, 1979, p. 231).

'To the extent that the outcome of the first industrial revolution was something which no government could have expected consciously to contract it was indeed spontaneous. But it should not be supposed that government's role in the process was entirely passive' (Deane, 1979, p. 219). Mathias (1983) agrees, saying that 'Government, in terms of aggressive economic nationalism, actively underwrote the development of trade, bound up with imperial expansion and naval potential' (pp. 9–10). High tariffs were charged to pay for the war, but also helped to protect British industry.

Though this controversy is a precursor to the current debate surrounding the role of the state in developing countries today, there are some differences. To begin with, being the first industrial nation meant that the government had no target to achieve. Thus, the notion of 'catch-up' – a factor that has been significant in all later developers – was absent in Britain. In fact, it was this attempt to catch up that resulted in government involvement in a 'national project' of industrialization and development even in early industrializers like Germany and France.[7]

South Korea

British economic history reveals that the role of the state has always been a matter for debate in development. This debate, however, reached fever pitch in the 1980s when the causes of South Korean growth were being analysed. Both sides in the debate wished to 'claim' South Korea's success. Thus, there were those like the IMF and the World Bank who classified South Korea as a *laissez-faire* economy and used its success to prescribe *laissez-faire* and market economics to other developing countries (through structural adjustment programmes). On the other hand, a large, and growing, number of economists, institutional specialists and development practitioners argued that the South Korean economy was not a free market (Amsden, 1989; Chang, 1993, 1994). Thus, Singer concludes that 'The Republic of Korea is a country where a strong state overrides market forces without hesitation, with an effective, tightly-planned economy, with strict controls, an essentially nationalised banking system and a private sector organised in government sponsored trade associations for easier control. It is as far removed from free market policies as it is possible to be' (Singer, 1984, p. 86). The debate has culminated in a majority, including the World Bank (1993a), now accepting that South Korea was exceptional, not in having minimalist state intervention but in having strong, focused state intervention (see chapter 9).

Though not a planned economy, South Korea's industrial strategy, like that of many other developing countries, has been carefully determined by state policy. The state in South Korea has intervened, by protecting its industries and providing subsidies for investment. But, unlike in other developing countries, it was disciplinarian and kept its firms under control through the use of both carrots (subsidies) and sticks (threats to withdraw support) (see box 7.1). In every phase of industrialization the state played a significant role, through its use of fiscal and other financial incentives and through targeted industrial policies (see table 10.7). Companies were allowed to grow and merge and become very large,[8] and they diversified in an attempt to benefit from economies of scale and compete abroad. However, targets (usually export, production and operations management targets rather than financial ones) were set for these companies, and failure to meet them led to a withdrawal of support. All of this was done under close, strict state supervision. The government was able to exert control on the economy by

- nationalizing all banks (later privatized in the 1980s),
- using industrial licensing to determine 'what, when and how much to produce',
- imposing price controls on as many as 110 commodities by 1986,
- controlling capital flight and the remittance of liquid capital overseas,
- taxing the middle classes and providing very little in the way of social services for the poor.

Thus, the South Korean state was 'a highly pervasive and penetrating state that could be turned authoritarian, purged of corruption and made to refocus attention on matters economic, a state-dependent business strata that understood the benefits of co-operating with a purposive state; and a highly controlled working class' (Kohli, 1994, p. 1286). It has also been highly selective and strategic in its intervention, targeting specific areas and carrying out its policies effectively. The results of policies are closely monitored and revised, as necessary. Policies are also proactive rather than reactive. All this led, as we saw in chapter 9, to the South Korean state being classified as a 'developmental state' with a determined developmental elite, and a strong, independent bureaucracy with relative accountability. Some of this interpretation is being rewritten since the East Asian crisis in 1997, but the analysis still holds as a historical account of South Korea's development experience.

China

As we have seen above, the state played a significant strategic role in South Korea, though most resource allocation and pricing decisions were left to the market. In China, on the other hand, the state played a much more all-encompassing role. The Chinese economy is/was[9] a command economy (see chapter 9) in which resource allocation decisions are made in response to commands from planners rather than to price signals. The planners control a large volume of resources, and through this are able to command the whole economy (Naughton, 1995). The main characteristics of this kind of planning are state ownership of the means of production, political dictatorship, a mono-hierarchical system with the party leadership at the top, imperative and physical planning (Ellman, 1989).

In the USSR, often seen to exemplify such centrally planned economies, 25 per cent of GNP was reinvested in the economy, as opposed to approximately 11 per cent in Britain during the Industrial Revolution. China maintained gross investment at about 30 per cent of GNP throughout the late 1970s, and this figure increased to 35–7 per cent as the reforms progressed (Yusuf, 1994, p. 77).

Development strategy in China is operationalized through long- and short-term plans. Longer-term development plans set forth the leadership's political-economic strategy. Short-term plans, on the other hand, translate this broad strategy into a number of resource allocation decisions at firm, industry and regional levels. The plans specify output targets for each sector and for each enterprise within it (see box 9.1). They are operationalized through investment plans and by breaking down the targets for individual enterprises. Monetary flows within this system are subordinated to real flows,[10] and in this kind of command economy the plans are orders, which are binding on economic agents. They are often backed by some degree of state coercion. Thus, there is very little spontaneity in this process. Instead, it is carefully planned and controlled by the state.

In China, plans are five-yearly. The first plan, in 1952, gave greater priority to the industrial sector, and within this to modern, large-scale enterprises. In this, China followed the Soviet strategy, which greatly influenced Chinese leaders during this period. Thus, there was highly centralized planning, government control over the regions, priority given to heavy industry, and Soviet aid and technical assistance. From 1955, collectivization of agricultural land increased, and by 1956, approximately 90 per cent of peasant holdings were in co-operatives. Concern regarding the extent of inequality during this period, as well as the need to give more attention to agriculture, led to the launching in 1958 of the strategy of 'walking on two legs', or the balanced development of industry and agriculture. The Great Leap Forward, as it was called, was expected to help improve income distribution and welfare. During this period, People's Communes were created, with as many as 1,600 households on average in each one. However, it ended in disaster, with a slump in food grain production and consumption, as well as in industrial output. National income decreased by 50 per cent between 1960 and 1962 (Blecher, 1986, pp. 72–4; Selden, 1988, p. 14).

This was followed in 1978 (two years after Mao's death) by the marketization of the Chinese economy. Agriculture was de-collectivized, some private industry was established and the rural collective sector developed, prices were reformed, and the economy was increasingly opened up to

Table 10.6   Growth of Chinese output, 1953–1985

Period	Growth rate of net material product (1980 prices)
1953–57	6.61
1957–65	2.09
1965–76	5.11
1976–85	8.78

Source: Perkins, 1988, p. 628. By permission of American Economic Association.

foreign trade (see box 10.2). Since then, China's economic performance has strengthened.

Thus, as we can see from table 10.6, growth was fast between 1953 and 1957, but slowed down during the Great Leap Forward and the Cultural Revolution. Since the reforms in the late 1970s, however, growth has again picked up. China's reforms are part of a broad class of 'liberalization measures' undertaken across the world. The decrease in the role played by the state required by these policies has been achieved in many East European economies by a withdrawal of the state from the economy. In China, though, even the 'marketization' of the economy was carefully planned by the state so that there were no sudden changes and public opinion remained favourable to the reforms. It was therefore far from being the kind of 'big bang' approach favoured by some of the other transitional economies.

China's first step was to go in for price liberalization. However, it retained dual prices for a long time, only slowly increasing the list of prices that were determined by the market at the margin. Agricultural reforms have involved de-collectivization of agriculture, together with an increase in market incentives. This meant that excess output could be sold on the market, and that capital inputs/machines could be privately owned, though land was still owned by the community. Industrial reforms involved an increase in competition and market incentives. A larger proportion of profits could now be retained. Township and village enterprises (TVEs) from one village competed with those from other villages. Therefore, though they were still communally owned, they benefited from the hard budget constraints imposed by local authorities and by competition with TVEs from other regions. There has been very little privatization of large-scale enterprises. Trade reforms have also been undertaken, as we will see in the next section.

Role of foreign trade

Britain

Walpole's 1721 statement that 'it is evident that nothing so much contributes to promote the public well-being as the exportation of manufacturing goods and the importation of foreign raw materials' (Chang, 2002, p. 21) resonates in Britain's policy towards foreign trade during this period. Domestic manufacturers were protected until they were sufficiently competitive to survive without protection. The 1721 legislation decreased import duties on raw materials, increased duty drawbacks on imported raw materials for exported manufactures, abolished export duties on manufactures, increased duties on imported manufactures, increased export subsidies, and carefully regulated the quality of manufactures (Chang, 2002, p. 22). Many of these policies were similar to those used by South Korea in the late twentieth century, as we will see. Even in 1820, average tariffs were 45–55 per cent in Britain (Chang, 2002, p. 22).

Between 1750 and 1800, therefore, real GNP and exports from Britain doubled, while import volumes trebled. Between 1800 and 1850, GNP and imports increased by 3.5 times, while exports increased by 6.5 times in real terms (Deane, 1979). Thus, Britain's early start allowed her to expand her markets overseas in an almost unrestrained manner (Bagchi, 1989; E. A. G. Robinson, 1954) until the USA and other European economies began to grow behind protectionist barriers. Many writers claim that it was this link with the international economy that allowed the first industrial economy to develop spontaneously.

In fact, British industrialization promoted a new international division of labour whereby Britain imported raw materials and exported finished goods to a number of its colonies. The case of India is often cited. Britain used its power over India to manipulate import duties and appropriate colonial revenue so that the demand for domestic products decreased and India shifted (between 1813 and 1830) from being a textile exporter to being an importer. It was able to do this by deploying a number of policies, which encouraged primary production in the colonies, outlawed some manufacturing activities (like new rolling and slitting steel mills in America) in the colonies, banned the colonial export of products that competed with British products, and banned the use of tariffs by the colonial authorities (Chang, 2002, p. 52).

The big change came with the repeal of the Corn Laws in 1846, when tariffs on many manufactures were abolished. 'In 1846, Britain had 1,146 dutiable articles; by 1860 she had 48, all but twelve being revenue duties on luxuries and semi-luxuries' (Fielden, 1969, p. 82, quoted in Chang, 2002, p. 24). However, this free trade regime did not last for long. By the 1880s, many manufacturers were already asking for protection, and many tariffs were reintroduced in 1932.

Since very few countries have been able to tap into international markets with the same freedom as Britain did, many European countries developed behind trade barriers (Senghaas, 1985). This period of 'dissociation' from the world economy allowed them to restructure their economies, developing a capital goods industry and mass production of basic consumer goods before they reaffirmed their borders. Thus, European experience has indicated that, during the initial stages of industrialization, free trade was a luxury that few could afford. Other countries followed policies of economic nationalism, including state intervention, protection for infant industry, and temporary dissociation from international competition (Hoogvelt, 1990, pp. 354–5).

South Korea

Between 1900 and 1945, South Korea was an exporter of raw materials, food and other primary products, as well as handicrafts and light manufactures, much like other developing countries today. But in 1945, South Korean policy-makers were strongly influenced by the import-substituting industrialization doctrines then sweeping through the developing world. They began protecting their domestic industry through fiscal and financial schemes. This protection allowed manufacturing, especially in the consumer goods sector,[11] to grow. Table 10.7 summarizes the various stages in South Korea's trade policies. The first stage of import-substituting industrialization was followed by an export-led growth phase during which South Korea began to export labour-intensive products. To help increase the competitiveness of these products in export markets, the government devalued the won and provided financial and fiscal support to exporting industries. After 1970, South Korea combined its trade and industrial policies in an attempt to encourage exports. This led to a deepening of its industrial structure and an upgrading of its exports beyond simple labour-intensive products. South Korea's policy during

Table 10.7   South Korean economic policy, 1900–1990

Phase	Economic structure	Core policies
Primary product export phase (1900–45)	Raw materials or food exports, traditional agriculture, handicraft production and limited manufactures.	Colonial administration of economic activity.
Import substitution phase 1 (1945–64)	Growing manufacturing activity, especially consumer goods.	Protection, fiscal and financial supports to industry.
Export-led growth phase 1 (1964–70)	Manufacturing growth led by exports of labour-intensive goods.	Devaluation, selective liberalization, financial and fiscal supports to export industry.
Export-led growth, phase 2 (1970–90)	Industrial deepening coupled with upgrading of exports.	Targeted industrial policies.

Source: Haggard, 1990, p. 25, table 2.1. By permission of Cornell University Press.

this period was to encourage the huge chaebols or conglomerates to grow and export, setting them export-related targets.

South Korea's exports were only 3.4 per cent of GDP in 1960, but increased to 34 per cent of GDP by 1980. Between 1965 and 1980, her exports grew by 27.2 per cent, thereafter slowing down somewhat to a growth rate of 12.8 per cent between 1980 and 1990. In 1961, her top six export-earners were basic ores, iron ore, fish, raw silk, vegetables and swine. By 1976, this had changed to clothing, footwear, fabrics, electrical machinery, plywood and telecommunications equipment (Kiely, 1998, p. 101).

South Korea's timely shift from import substitution to export promotion has been seen as very significant in her economic success. In many other developing countries, strong domestic pressure groups built up in favour of protection, preventing such a shift. In the long run, however, the continuation of protection has prevented firms in these economies from maturing and becoming competitive. South Korean polity, however, was strong, and its developmental objectives were clear. It was therefore able to prevent domestic interest groups from unduly influencing its policy objectives.

China

China has been autarchic for long periods of its history. Its experience with colonialism reinforced its determination to be self-sufficient. Between 1977 and 1981, Chinese exports increased from US$7.6 bn to US$22 bn, or by 30 per cent per annum. By 1998, they had increased to approximately US$184 bn. In addition to this, China played a more active role in the World Bank and the IMF, even borrowing from them. A joint venture law was passed, encouraging foreign direct investment. The main benefits anticipated from FDI were not investment funds (as China already had a very high domestic savings ratio) but technological imports and market information. Special Economic Zones were created in Guangdong and Fujian provinces. Between 1975 and 1985, US$21.8 bn of foreign investment and credits were utilized by the Chinese economy. The rate of growth of FDI was particularly fast in the 1990s, when it increased from US$3.5 bn in 1990 to US$44 bn in 1998 (World Bank, 1999/2000).

The role of learning and the import of technology

The Industrial Revolution in Britain, as we have seen, was powered by a number of inventions, especially in transport, iron and steel and other manufacturing industries. The second industrial revolution in the United States and Germany involved innovations and the sale of new products and processes. The later industrializers, beginning with Japan and including South Korea and later China, have been learners. They have made use of the pool of technology already available in the developed countries to

power their growth. The advancement of science has commodified technology, and improvements in transport and communications have therefore made technology transfer easier. Many scientific operations have
become easier to learn as parts rather than as complete mechanical
operations. This transfer of technology has enabled the NICs to grow
fast, and has smoothed the path for later developers (Amsden, 1989).

The importance of technology, especially of imported technology, in
modern industrial processes has resulted in another significant aspect of
South Korean industrialization – the role of engineers. Engineers play a
very important role in current industrialization processes because they
now act as 'the gatekeepers of foreign technology transfer' (Amsden,
1989, p. 9). To enable such a transfer of technology, South Korea has
also invested heavily in education, so that its secondary and tertiary
enrolments (at 90 per cent and 40 per cent respectively) are at developed
country levels (Lall, 1996, p. 90).

South Korean industry used foreign technology to build up its R&D
capability. It was one of the largest importers of capital goods amongst
the developing countries, hiring foreign experts to resolve technical problems. The import of technology was promoted by tax and other incentives. The government even intervened in major technical contracts to
strengthen the position of domestic buyers. But it tried to minimize
foreign direct investment, and sought to keep control in local hands,
maximizing the participation of local consultants on many projects.

Social and political aspects

It has often been argued that many later developmental states, like South
Korea, have weak and subordinated civil societies in which media and
labour organizations have been strictly controlled (Leftwich, 1995; Jenkins, 1992c). In many of these states, civil rights have also been suppressed, sometimes quite brutally.

The weakness and disorganization of the working classes and domestic
capital in the Asian NICs strengthened state autonomy and permitted
rapid industrialization. This has meant that labour organizations are
strictly controlled and labour activism is repressed through restrictions
on freedom of association and other strict labour laws. At the same time,
legislation regarding working hours and conditions is relatively weak, so
that poor and hazardous working conditions are common. Many NICs
suppressed individual freedoms and promoted a type of 'puritanical
nationalism' enforced by authoritarian rule. In South Korea, the para-
military police force had approximately 150,000 men, and the Korean
Central Intelligence Agency (KCIA) was all-pervasive even in the social
and political sphere. This is quite different from Latin America, where
both the industrial bourgeoisie and organized labour were much stronger,
more vocal and more entrenched.

In spite of this, the position of the state has been legitimized by the wide distribution of the benefits of growth. Like China, South Korea has invested in education and health. In addition, though South Korea has had the longest working week in the world (Amsden, 1989, p. 10), its real wage growth rate may also exceed that of any previous industrial revolution. This implies that the standard of living of its workers is higher than at a comparable level of industrialization in Britain. This has provided an incentive to its workers to continue to work hard and accept their conditions.

Conclusion

Gerschenkron (1966), in his studies of European industrialization, stressed the role of banks and the state, and argued that the more backward the economy, the more centralized was the development effort. The primary agents of industrialization therefore have shifted from private entrepreneurs in Britain to investment banks in Germany and to the state in Tsarist Russia (Griffin, 1989).

In this chapter, we have considered the development experience of three countries – Britain, South Korea and China. Each of these countries followed a very different path to industrialization, and we have attempted to indicate the similarities and differences in their experiences, as well as the lessons they provide for future developers. The factors that stand out are that the first industrial nation did not have a target to achieve. It set the targets for all the countries that followed. Its state also did not have any real strategy to begin with. Countries that have followed it have had a target to follow, and consequently their states have been able to strategize to achieve this target. These countries have been able to tap into the experiences of the early industrializers as well as into their inventions and innovations through the import of capital and technology. Though backwardness implies that a backlog of technology exists that can be drawn upon, 'the more backward a country, the harsher the justice meted out by market forces' (Amsden, 1989, p. 13). The task is therefore both easier and much harder for the countries that are currently attempting to develop.

Part IV

The Domestic Sector

So far in this book, we have considered the definition and determinants of development and the roles played by the state and by international links in the process. We have only in passing considered the impact that development has on the domestic sector. This, after all, is the end-product of development – improvements in living standards and human welfare – and we concentrate on it in Part IV.

We saw in Part I that, among other changes, development results in a demographic transition, rural–urban migration and urbanization, an improvement in the education and health status of individuals, as well as a structural change in employment towards industry. Of course, these are 'stylized facts', and need to be qualified in a number of ways. In this part of the book, we consider these aspects of development in more detail.

We will consider some of the practical issues raised in the process of development. We will begin with the role of population, large-scale movements of people, and urbanization in chapter 11. We will then move on to consider agricultural change and rural development in chapter 12. Chapter 13 deals with issues relating to human capital formation (health and education), while chapter 14 considers labour market and employment-related issues.

11

Population, Migration and Urbanization

In this chapter, we will concentrate on issues relating to population growth in developing countries. World population crossed the 6 billion mark in 2000, and is growing at a rate of 1.2 per cent per annum. This growth is unevenly spread, with an average of 0.3 per cent per annum in the developed countries and 2.3 per cent per annum in sub-Saharan Africa. The uneven spread of population has, of course, given rise to large-scale movement of population, both within and across countries. The latter is constrained by international law and visa requirements, but the former is largely free, and has resulted in large numbers migrating from rural to urban areas. This is not surprising in the light of the structural change – from agriculture to industry – taking place in so many developing countries (see chapter 2). It has also resulted in the fast growth of cities across the developing world. This chapter will consider each of these three issues – population growth, migration and urbanization – in greater detail. We will begin with the impact of population growth on development in the next section.

Population

Population change is the net effect of births and deaths in a country. If the number of births is exactly equal to the number of deaths, then there will be no net growth of the population. Changes in birth and death rates as an economy progresses have been modelled within the demographic transition framework. This framework identifies the first stage in a country's population history as one of high birth and death rates. Populations during this stage tend to be relatively stagnant, as births are offset by deaths. However, as development occurs, improved hygiene and sanitation, as well as improvements in medical care, decrease the death rate. The birth rate continues to be relatively high, so that during this second stage, the population expands. Though population growth rates in many developing countries have decreased below the highs of the 1960s, they are still relatively high in a majority of these countries. As development progresses beyond this stage, however, birth rates also begin to fall. In stage 3, therefore, the rate of growth of the population begins to decrease, and in stage 4, it stagnates with low birth and death rates, as in many developed countries today.

Table 11.1 shows that industrial economies are in the fourth stage of the demographic transition, with very low crude birth and death rates. In fact, with birth rates being 13 per 1,000 people and death rates being 10 per 1,000 people in these countries, the net effect on population is only about 3 per 1,000. It is therefore not surprising that population growth (from 941 million in 1960 to 1,252 million in 1990) has been relatively slow in industrial countries. Populations in these countries are growing only at about 0.3 per cent per annum (last column, table 11.1). In developing countries, however, birth rates are significantly higher – at 27 per 1,000 people in all developing countries, close to 40 per 1,000 in the least developed countries, and 44 per 1,000 in sub-Saharan Africa. With death rates in even the least developed countries being 15 per 1,000 people, the difference between birth and death rates was approximately

Table 11.1   Birth, death and fertility rates, 1994

Region	Crude birth rate[a]	Crude death rate[b]	Total fertility rate[c]	Total population (millions)		Annual population growth rate (%)	
				1975	2015	1960–94	1994–2000
All LDCs	27.1	9.0	3.1	2,928	4,502.9	2.0	1.4
Least developed countries	39.8	15.0	5.3	372.2	568.4	2.5	2.2
Sub-Saharan Africa	44.2	15.8	6.1	303.1	555.4	2.8	2.3
Industrial economies	13.1	10.0	1.7	735.5	842.0	0.6	0.3
World	24.0	9.2	2.8	4,017.4	5,743.7	1.6	1.1

[a] Crude birth rate is births per 1,000 population per year.
[b] Crude death rate is deaths per 1,000 population per year.
[c] Fertility rate is the average number of children that would be born alive to a woman during her lifetime, if she were to bear children at each age according to prevailing age-specific fertility rates.
Source: Data from UNDP, 1999, p. 195 and p. 200, table 22
From *Human Development Report*, 1999, by United Nations Development Programme, © 1999 by the United Nations Development Programme. Used by permission of Oxford University Press.

28 per 1,000 in sub-Saharan Africa and 18 per 1,000 across all developing countries. Population numbers in the developing world have increased from 2,054 million in 1960 to 4,017 million in 1975 to 5,744 million in 2015 (estimated). The rate of growth is even faster in the least developed countries, where it has increased from 227 million to 620 million during this period.

This pattern of population growth has given rise to the view that the countries least able to afford it have the highest rates of population growth, leading to a controversy that is loaded in political and ethical terms. Is the right to have children a 'luxury'? Must the poor be excluded or rationed in some way? How would this affect the national and international distribution of birth rates? How can one protect the rights of children (to food, clothing and shelter) while protecting the rights of their parents to procreate? While this controversy has always existed, it is not much discussed in the academic literature. The irony, of course, is that many developed-country policies aim to increase rather than decrease population growth rates.[1] It is also true that, given the current distribution of incomes across countries (and across individuals within countries), a very high rate of growth of the population implies that already scarce resources are spread even more thinly across individuals, resulting in very low standards of living.

Since population is growing fastest in the least developed countries (and slowest in the most developed countries), it seems natural to ask whether the size and rate of growth of population is likely to affect the level of development of an economy. Alternatively, might the level of development of a country be affecting the rate of growth of its population? Does a large population provide better prospects for development? We will consider some of these questions in the next two sections, before we move on to look at large-scale population movements and urbanization.

The relationship between population and development

One of the first writers to focus on the relationship between population and development was Thomas Malthus. Writing in 1798, Malthus maintained that population would grow geometrically, doubling every 30–40 years. Food supplies, on the other hand, would grow only arithmetically, because land and capital would face decreasing returns over time. From time to time, the growth of population would cause per capita incomes to fall below subsistence level. The resulting famines and malnutrition would increase the death rate, bringing per capita incomes back above the subsistence level. As incomes began to increase significantly above subsistence level, population would begin to grow again, causing per capita incomes to fall. Living standards would therefore continue to hover around subsistence levels. The only way to emerge from this 'population trap', claimed Malthus, was to practise moral restraint and limit birth rates. Malthus's reasoning highlights the two-way causation between the rate of growth of the population and an increase in living standards. Since Malthus, a number of other writers have looked at this relationship between population growth and development, with varying degrees of pessimism.

In this section, we will consider both the effect that population growth may have on development and the impact that development has on population growth. The relationship between population and development preoccupied both demographers and developmentalists in the 1950s and 1960s. In recent years, however, the focus has shifted to the impact of population growth on income distribution, the position of women, and the environment (Furedi, 1997).

From population to development

Malthus's pessimistic conclusions regarding the effect of population growth on development were based on the assumption of diminishing returns to labour. In practice, technological change, first through the industrial and agricultural revolutions, and later through the continuous technical change that has accompanied economic growth, has resulted in increasing rather than decreasing returns to labour. Thus, Harrison (1993) argues that 'human ingenuity has so far been able to increase world food production in line with the increase in human numbers' (Harrison, 1993, p. 42), though he is pessimistic about its ability to do so in the future. In addition, the upsurge in population predicted by Malthus was contained in the UK, not by famines and disease, as Malthus predicted, but by voluntary choices made by individuals to have smaller families. Such choices have been made in conditions of prosperity rather than poverty. In fact, the Malthusian crisis has become a 'pollution crisis' rather than a 'resource crisis' (Harrison, 1993, pp. 53–4).

Turning now to look at the impact of population growth on development more generally, we note that it will depend upon the size of a country's population relative to its natural resources. A country that is underpopulated relative to its resources will experience an increase in growth when its population grows. But countries with large populations relative to their resources are unlikely to benefit from a further increase in population size.[2] As important as the size of the population and of the country's resources are the institutions and the social organization of a country, because these determine whether the population is deployed in the most efficient manner possible. Thus, in sub-Saharan Africa, with 18 per cent of the world's land and 10 per cent of its population, high population growth rates have resulted in the settling of nomadic populations and consequent over-cultivation. This has led to the erosion and desertification of land (as we saw in box 6.1). By contrast, higher population densities in large parts of Asia have been less problematic because of the relatively fertile land and the longer history of settled agriculture.

It is often argued that an increase in population will increase one of the inputs into the process of production – the labour supply – and may therefore be expected to increase growth. However, if the other inputs (specifically capital and possibly raw materials) remain constant, we would expect decreasing returns beyond a point as more and more labour is worked with fewer and fewer complementary inputs (see Solow's growth model in chapter 2). This has been called the 'capital shallowing effect', and is analogous to an increase in the population–resource ratio that we spoke of above. It has formed the basis of one of the most influential critiques of population growth, put forward by Coale and Hoover (1958). Another problem associated with an increase in population is that any output that is produced now has to be distributed across more individuals: living standards are therefore likely to fall. Additionally, as population increases, the number of dependants increases, and therefore the volume of consumption will increase. The consequent decrease in savings means that there will be insufficient funds for investment in the economy. However, this is mitigated by the fact that many children in developing countries work and therefore are not entirely dependent.[3]

In addition to diluting the level of investment in an economy, population growth may also change the nature of investment by diverting government expenditure into health and education instead of more 'productive', growth-oriented investments.[4] In the context of growing populations, increased expenditures on health and education may be ineffective in improving human capital, because *per capita* expenditure is constant or declining. This pessimistic view of the effect of population on development has influenced policy-makers and academics considerably. Enke (1966) concluded that the resources used to retard population growth are a 100 times more effective in increasing incomes per head than resources used to accelerate output growth. This result is based on the assumption that certain factors are fixed, technological change is insignificant, and individuals increase consumption but do not provide markets for output.

Though several models predict this negative relationship between population growth and development, empirical evidence is weak. Easterlin (1967), for instance, argued that a young population was more amenable to change, more receptive to new ideas, and more willing to shift resources from low to high productivity areas. Clark (1967) maintained that developing countries with the highest rates of population growth also had the highest rates of per capita output growth. Historically, periods of population growth precede and provoke economic growth. Proponents of this view claim that a growing population increases demand and stimulates investment, allows improvements in the labour force, and may encourage technical innovation, especially in agriculture. Thus, many modernization theorists saw increasing population pressure as necessary for social development, because it created problems which could only be resolved through a more productive use of land and increased division of labour. Marxists, in turn, saw increasing populations as necessary for the growth of capitalism, because they decreased the cost of labour and enabled large labour-intensive units of production (factories and plantations, for instance) to operate. In addition, a larger market size allows increased specialization and division between firms. It enables indivisible investment in roads, telecommunications and R&D, for example, which then give rise to economies of scale.

The view that a growing population may contribute to economic growth and power has been politically popular, though academic literature has tended to ignore it (Furedi, 1997). Thus, Mussolini is reported to have said in the 1920s that 'with a falling population, one does not create an empire but one becomes a colony' (quoted in Simpson, 1994, p. 31). More recently, a resolution adopted by the European Parliament in 1983 voted that 'population trends in Europe will have a decisive effect on the development of Europe and will determine the significance of the role which Europe will play in the world in future decades' (Gauthier, 1993, p. 149).

The relationship between population and development is still a matter of debate. It has been argued (Furedi, 1997) that this relationship has been used only to make population control more acceptable to developing countries. Furedi (1997) argues that it is in the interests of the West to decrease population growth in the Third World (for political and strategic reasons), and therefore the population–development relationship has not been 'talked up' by policy-makers. This relationship has been further complicated by the reverse relationship from development to population growth. While population influences development largely through its effect on economic growth, the reverse relationship (from the level of development to the rate of growth of the population) arises from more general improvements in basic needs, income distribution, education levels and the position of women in society. We turn to this next.

From development to population

The demographic transition model makes a clear link between the level of development and the rate of growth of the population. The effect of development on death rates is very clear. In England, the steady reduction in mortality rates at the end of the nineteenth century was caused by a reduction in food-, faeces- and water-borne diseases as standards of living improved. In developing countries today, however, the decrease in death rates has been caused by the application of scientific medicine, drugs and insecticides. Vaccinations and inoculations have proved to be low-cost, relatively reliable ways of preventing some diseases. Thus, diseases like diphtheria, measles, whooping cough, polio and tuberculosis have all been protected against. Smallpox has been eradicated. But diseases associated with insanitary living conditions, like cholera and typhoid, are still common, as is malaria. Today, however, AIDS is fast overtaking them in terms of the speed of its spread (see chapter 13). Death rates in the less developed countries have fallen to 9 per 1,000 people and in sub-Saharan Africa to 15.8 per 1,000. Life expectancy has increased to above sixty years in all regions of the world except sub-Saharan Africa (where AIDS-related deaths are worsening the life expectancy rates; see table 13.2), and infant mortality rates have decreased across the developing world (see table 11.2). These reductions have been helped by better diets and higher incomes associated with development, which have helped to decrease deaths from famine and malnutrition.

The effect of development on the birth or fertility rate of a country is less obvious and often lags behind. The decrease in birth rates occurs because development increases both the ability to control family size and the incentive to do so. Thus, contraceptive use increases an individual's ability to plan his or her family, while social, economic and environmental conditions make large families less necessary and small families more desirable. Many writers claim, for instance, that birth rates are high in developing countries because infant mortality is high.

Parents who have experienced child loss often over-compensate by having more children to insure against future child loss. However, the close spacing of births decreases the mother's physical resources as well as

Table 11.2   Life expectancy and infant mortality rates, 1970 and 1997

Region	Life expectancy at birth (years)		Infant mortality rate (per 1,000 live births)	
	1970	1997	1970	1997
All LDCs	54.5	64.4	111	64
Least developed countries	43.3	51.7	149	104
Sub-Saharan Africa	44.1	48.9	137	105
Arab states	50.6	65.1	125	53
East Asia	62.0	70.0	83	37
East Asia (excluding China)	61.0	72.8	46	15
South-East Asia and Pacific	51.0	65.9	97	45
South Asia	49.0	62.7	131	72
South Asia (excluding India)	48.8	63.0	132	75
Latin America and Caribbean	60.1	69.5	86	33
Eastern Europe and CIS	68.8	68.6	37	26
Industrialized countries	71.4	77.7	20	6
World	59.1	66.7	98	58

Source: Data from UNDP, 1999, p. 171. From *Human Development Report*, 1999, by United Nations Development Programme, © 1999 by the United Nations Development Programme. Used by permission of Oxford University Press.

the family's per capita resources, and in its turn increases the probability of infant mortality. Lappe and Collins (1977, p. 64) estimated that an Indian couple at that time would have to bear 6.3 children (on average) to be reasonably[5] confident that one son would survive. Economic development can break this cycle by decreasing infant mortality, increasing the chances of child survival, and therefore decreasing birth rates. However, this only occurs with a lag, and in the interim population may actually grow quite fast.

Economic development is also expected to influence birth rates by increasing female literacy. This relationship has spawned a large literature, wherein it is argued that female education helps to increase the age at marriage and improves a woman's knowledge of contraception and her ability and inclination to plan her life and that of her children. It therefore decreases women's inclination to have many children. Female education also often increases women's participation in the modern, formal labour force, and therefore increases the opportunity costs of maternity leave.[6] This, in turn, leads to a decrease in birth rates. Appleton (1996), for instance, finds that women who complete secondary schooling will start cohabiting four years later than those with no schooling and will breast-feed for eight months less.

Finally, by increasing living standards, economic development decreases the significance of children's contribution to household incomes. The existence of a social welfare infrastructure decreases the need for children to look after their parents in old age. The quality of children (their health and education) becomes more significant, and the costs associated with this lead to a restriction of family size. There are also those (Simpson, 1994) who maintain that there is a strong correlation between the proportion of population in agriculture and birth rates, because agricultural communities adhere to old customs and values. Development, which changes the structure of the economy towards industry, is therefore likely to decrease birth rates.

Conclusion

Thus, while population growth affects economic growth and development, the latter, in turn, influence the rate of growth of population. This, in fact, is one of the basic unresolved problems or conundrums of development. To achieve development, the rate of growth of population has to be controlled, but to control population growth, economic development is usually necessary. Emerging from this cycle takes considerable time, which most developing countries do not have. This relationship has been less significant in recent years. In fact, writers like Furedi (1997) argue that the population control lobby has found it more effective to highlight the impact of population growth on the position of women or on the environment, rather than on the economy. Thus, the population control lobby has become increasingly associated with the feminist and environmental lobbies across the world.

Large-scale population movements: migration

Migration involves the movement of people from one region to another. It can be distinguished on the basis of distance (rural–urban, national and international), duration (daily, seasonal, short-term and permanent) and causes (economic, social, cultural or natural disasters). Thus, black workers in South Africa entered the cities to work on a daily basis but always returned to their reservations at night. The millions who travel to Kolkata, Mumbai, Mexico City or Tokyo to work are also daily migrants, but are not influenced by political regulations. Seasonal migration occurs in response to shortages of farm-workers during harvests, and emigration occurs in response to insufficient employment in off-peak times. The many different types of migration can, of course, be interlinked. Rural–urban migration, for instance, can be daily (commuting), seasonal, short- or long-term. It can be caused by economic, social, cultural or natural factors. In the next subsection, we will consider rural–urban migration in more detail.

Rural–urban migration

Rural–urban migration has been very significant in terms of numbers in most developing countries. It is hard to obtain precise figures, because different types of migration occur (daily, seasonal, short- and long-term) and also because the precise cut-off point used to denote an urban settlement may vary from country to country.[7] It is also worth noting that larger urban settlements draw migrants from a larger hinterland. Thus, the cities of Mumbai and Delhi may draw migrants from all over India, while cities like Visakhapatnam and Baroda tend to draw migrants from a more limited region.

Rural–urban migration is affected by a number of push and pull factors. To begin with, the change in the structure of an economy from an agricultural to an industrial economy, a change that accompanies development (see chapter 2), drives the movement of people from rural (agricultural) areas to urban (supposedly industrial) areas. Thus, unemployment or underemployment in the rural sector, sometimes caused by increasing productivity in agriculture, is a key factor. In North Africa, however, urban drift has been caused by the increase in population density,[8] as well as the disruption of traditional agriculture. The abandonment of shifting agriculture and the inability of individuals to maintain rural living standards as costs of inputs into agriculture (credit, machinery, fertilizers, seeds and agrochemicals) increase more rapidly than output prices have contributed to urban drift. A rigid social structure, the need to conform, lack of amenities (schools, colleges and hospitals), lack of adventure as well as the low esteem in which rural life is held combine to push people out of villages. In fact, there are significant differences in child and adult mortality in rural and urban Africa. These differences bear out the perception that the town is the place where people feel most secure. Finally, events like droughts, floods and famines may trigger large-scale migration that is neither voluntary nor selective.

Cities, in their turn, exert a certain 'pull' effect. Urban employment provides higher returns to educated individuals. These include the greater potential for obtaining employment in cities, as well as the higher returns that such urban employment may provide to educated individuals. Cities also provide increased amenities in the form of better health, education and communication infrastructure than most rural areas. They are well-known centres for entertainment and leisure activities, which have been summed up in the literature as the 'bright lights'. Migration from rural to urban areas is thus seen to stem both from an economic motive (improved wages and working conditions) and from an extra-economic motive (the excitement engendered by the city, the broadening of horizons it entails, and the wider range of opportunities it offers for leisure activities).

Harris and Todaro (1970) have formulated a model of migration that takes some of these factors into account. They begin by assuming that the economic factors influencing migration far outweigh the effect of all other factors. Traditional migration models predict that migration will occur whenever the difference between *actual* earnings in rural and urban work is positive. However, in regions where there is considerable unemployment or underemployment, the probability that migrants will obtain employment when they move must also be taken into account. By including *expected*, rather than *actual*, earnings in their model, Harris and Todaro take both the probability of a migrant obtaining an urban job as well as the income earned in such a job into account. They therefore postulate that migration occurs when there are differences in the *expected* rather than *actual* earnings between rural and urban areas. It is clear that the probability of finding employment increases with time. Individual migrants therefore need to consider future incomes as well as present ones. The model therefore includes the present value of the future stream of expected urban income. The Harris–Todaro model is useful for seeing the kind of economic logic that might implicitly underlie migration decisions. But it is limited in that it deals primarily with economic factors. As already indicated, the motivations underlying migration are economic, social, political and natural.

Migration is often short-term to begin with. A young, male member of a family travels to the city in search of employment. He lives alone there until he finds work and has consolidated his financial position. During this period, he sends remittances home to his village. Once his position is stabilized, he sends for his wife and children (associational migration). This, of course, is a stylized picture. In reality, the vast majority of migrants in developing countries simply move from casual jobs in the rural sector to casual jobs in the urban informal sector. The economic outcome often does not meet the expectations held by the migrants when they move. It is worth noting in this context that many migrants return to their villages in the long run. It is, for instance, quite common to see 'urban dwellers loyal to a rural home' (Jones, 1990, p. 224), and many urban dwellers continue to maintain very strong contacts with their villages and will return to them.

A smaller, though in many ways equally problematic, type of population movement is international migration. The movement of workers between countries is highly restricted, and has implications for the countries' balance of payments. Unlike local migration, which entails an inter-regional transfer of these resources, it also involves a permanent loss of the resources embodied in a particular worker.

International migration and the brain drain

In an open world economy, one might expect the free flow of goods (trade) to be accompanied by the free flow of labour (migration) and of capital (foreign direct investment). In fact, if we accept neoclassical economic premisses, in a world of wage differences, labour should migrate in the direction of higher wages. High wages would reflect excess demand for labour. In reality, of course, labour flows are far from being easy or free. Most countries have very strict immigration controls, which help to maintain domestic wage levels. These rules are often relaxed for political immigrants or refugees, but are maintained quite stringently for economic migrants. It is sometimes argued that immigration is used as a 'regulatory valve in the advanced economies: the inflow of labour is increased and the rate of repatriation reduced when the economy expands and vice versa when the economy goes into recession' (Griffin, 1989, p. 86).

The major recipients of international migrants are North America, Western Europe, Oceania, the Middle East and some countries of Latin America. Migrants often tend to come from a small area, because information passes by word of mouth and experiences. Thus, Sylhet in Bangladesh, Ilocos in the Philippines and the North-West Frontier Province in Pakistan provide many migrants. Migrants also often tend to migrate to the same region and into similar economic activities. Many Sylhetis have gone into the restaurant business in the UK, for instance.

International migration has a number of consequences. In the labour-importing country, it helps meet excess demand for labour. Immigration of Turks into Germany or West Indians into the UK in the 1950s was of this kind. It also helps to cover temporary skill gaps that exist in many developed countries, as the immigration of doctors and engineers indicates. On the other hand, it contributes to racial, ethnic, economic and communal tensions in the host countries. The Black and Asian riots in the UK throughout the 1980s bear witness to such tensions.

In the labour-exporting countries (often the developing countries), such emigration is expected to help decrease unemployment and improve income distribution. While this is usually true, such migration also creates a 'brain drain' (or at least a skill drain) from these countries. International migrants are often middle-class, well-educated individuals, who can afford the costs involved in such movement. In addition, migrants (national or international) are also often highly motivated and dynamic individuals. Emigration can therefore be very costly for the exporting countries, which have already borne the expense of training these individuals (teachers, doctors and engineers) but are unable to reap the benefits of their investment.[9]

On the other hand, remittances from those who emigrate can help the labour-exporting countries by financing investment and providing scarce foreign exchange. Thus, in Bangladesh, remittances were almost 80 per cent of the value of exports, while in Pakistan they were 106 per cent of exports (see table 11.3). Remittances can therefore provide very large volumes of foreign exchange for these countries. Even though such remittances may increase consumption rather than investment in the first instance, they do at least re-enter the national flow of funds and increase incomes. They represent a relatively high proportion of GDP in many developing countries – 6.4 per cent of GDP in Bangladesh, 11.7 per cent in Pakistan, and 6.3 per cent in Sri Lanka.

Many writers maintain that one of the benefits of international migration is that it helps create skills which can be transferred to others when the workers return home. But, as Todaro (1985, p. 268) reminds us, this

Table 11.3   Migration and remittances in the early 1980s

Country	Year	Migrants as % of country's economically active population	Remittances as % of total exports	Remittances as % of GDP
Bangladesh	1981	0.58	79.7	6.4
India	1983	0.38	27	1.6
Pakistan	1981	3.60	106.5	11.7
Philippines	1983	2.44	19	3.8
South Korea	1984	1.31	5.1	1.9
Sri Lanka	1983	3.24–3.75	25.5	6.3
Thailand	1983	0.89	10.2	2.2

Source: K.B. Griffin, Alternative Strategies for Economic Development, 1989, Macmillan, p.88, reproduced with the permission of Palgrave Macmillan.

assumes that emigrants will obtain higher-skilled jobs abroad than at home, which is often not true. In fact, as already indicated, the individuals who emigrate are often the most skilled in their own countries, and it is quite common for them to work in less-skilled jobs in their host country. In addition, few of these workers return to their home countries. However, recent experiences of software engineers who migrate temporarily to work on particular projects fit this scenario (Kambhampati, 1999). The increased globalization of this industry has led to the notion of a 'brain circulation' rather than a 'brain drain' (Saxenian, 1999). Such migrants often gain skills and experience on their trips abroad, and many companies expect these skills to be transferred to others in the firm when they return home (Kambhampati, 1999).

Whatever the motivation and the precise pattern, internal and international migration in developing countries is very common. It increases the dynamism and flexibility of these societies, with all the problems that it causes. Internal migration, in fact, has resulted in the enormous growth of cities in most developing countries. We turn to consider this in the next section.

Urbanization

Early development literature saw rural–urban migration as beneficial, because people were expected to move from areas where the marginal social product[10] was low (or close to zero) to areas where the marginal social product was higher. Today, there are two views regarding cities. Gottman (1983) argues that large cities are an essential component of development. They help create wealth and are socially dynamic. McGee (1971), on the other hand, regarded cities as parasitic upon the surrounding areas, rather than as centres for the diffusion of development. The rampant growth of cities in many developing countries in recent years has increased support for the latter view. Urban populations in developing countries are growing at a rate of 3.7 per cent per annum, and the proportion of the population living in cities is forecasted to increase to 48.5 per cent by 2015. Thus, São Paulo grew from 12.5 million people in 1980 to 24 million people in 2000, while Mexico City grew from 3 million in 1950 to 16 million in the 1980s, and to 18 million by the year 2000. In sub-Saharan Africa the rate of growth of the urban population is higher, at more than 5 per cent per annum. This compares with a rate of growth of 0.8 per cent per annum in the industrial world, where 75 per cent of the population already lives in urban areas (see table 11.4).

Such rapid urbanization has placed tremendous pressure on the infrastructure in cities, resulting in the growth of slums and shanty towns with few utilities and extreme congestion. Thus, 'out of India's 3119 towns and

Table 11.4   Growth of urban populations

Region	Urban population (as % of total)			Urban population annual growth rate (%)	
	1960	2000	2015	1960–94	1994–2000
All developing countries	22	41	48.5	3.9	3.7
Least developed countries	9	26	34.5	5.7	5.4
Sub-Saharan Africa	15	35	42.7	5.6	5.1
Industrial countries	61	75	81.9	1.4	0.8
World	34	47.2	53.7	3.3	2.5

Source: Data from UNDP, 2000, p. 165. From *Human Development Report* 2000 by United Nations Development Programme, © 2000 by the United Nations Development Programme. Used by permission of Oxford University Press.

cities, only 209 had partial and only eight had full sewage and sewage treatment facilities' (UNCED, 1987). The mismatch between housing demand and supply has led to increases in property prices and rents. Sarre et al. (1991) report that in Mexico City, 40 per cent of families live at densities of more than two people per room, and 25 per cent live in a house with only one room. There are 2.75 million vehicles in the city, in addition to oil refineries, cement works and power stations. The low-paid and unemployed can neither rent nor buy homes, and therefore set up squatter settlements (without legal title to the land) around the cities, on sites unsuited to conventional housing or on vacant plots. Shanty towns are then built on these sites, with materials that can be easily and cheaply obtained – wood, board, metal and polythene sheets. Such settlements rarely have water or sewerage facilities. Electricity, when it is available, is pirated from illegal mains connections, and roads are simply dust tracks. These conditions increase social and political instability. In North Africa, the bidonvilles (shanty towns) were centres of political and social unrest, leading to riots in Morocco in June 1981, January 1984 and December 1990, in Tunisia in January 1978 and 1984, and in Algeria in October 1988 (Chapman and Baker, 1992).

From time to time, governments attempt to solve this problem by evacuating the slums and razing them to the ground. But this simply transfers the problem (and the slums) to other areas. Some countries help by giving squatters support in the form of titles to the land and by arranging refuse collection, water or electricity supplies. Squatting is thereby accepted and legalized. In other countries, land is demarcated for squatting, and in still others, streets are laid out, and plots with basic amenities are provided. In Zambia, for instance, the government has even built schools on the fringes of existing squatter settlements in anticipation of further inflows. They are then converted into self-built, unplanned

suburbs. Over time, there is evidence of self-improvement and consolidation, with improved housing, laid-out roads, electricity and water
supply, and sometimes sewerage.

However, such attempts to improve living conditions in the slums
through improved facilities, or in the job market through improved job
opportunities, have resulted in increasing the attraction of cities and
thereby further worsening conditions. Writers like Lipton (1977, 1980)
feel that government policies in the Third World show 'urban bias' and
reinforce the flow of migrants towards the towns.

Problems with urbanization

The concentration of population and economic activities in most cities has
given rise to many environmental problems. For examples, 75 per cent of
Thailand's factories dealing with hazardous chemicals are in Bangkok.
This, together with the volume of traffic in the city, has led to very high
levels of pollution. Additionally, the high levels of congestion have meant
increasing pressure on the existing water-supply, as well as pollution from
industrial and domestic waste, flooding and land subsidence. The city's
underground aquifers are being over-pumped to the extent that the land
surface is subsiding by approximately 100 mm per annum in some places.
The combination of sinking city, monsoon rains and removal of forest
cover has caused damaging and frequent flooding (Sarre et al., 1991). To
give another example, 'On the river Ganges, 114 cities, each with 50,000 or
more inhabitants, dump untreated sewage into the river each day. DDT
factories, tanneries, paper and pulp mills, petrochemical and fertiliser
complexes, rubber factories, and a host of others, use the river to get rid
of their wastes' (UNCED, 1987). The UNCED also reports that lung
cancer mortality in Chinese cities is four to seven times the national
average, because of greater air pollution in the cities. Table 11.5 shows
that air pollution levels (as reflected in peak levels of particulate matter in
the air) are about ten times higher in Beijing, Delhi and Calcutta than they
are in London or New York.

The only lasting solution to these problems of urban congestion and
pollution would be to develop rural areas and to improve job opportunities there. Bairoch (1973) argued that the disadvantages and problems
associated with rural underemployment are greater than those associated
with urban over-employment. In addition, the overhead cost of employment (in terms of the complementary resources required, including transport and social infrastructure) is higher in urban areas. Therefore, the cost
of creating an agricultural job is smaller than the cost of creating an
industrial job. Bairoch (1973) therefore argued in favour of stemming
rural–urban drift. But few countries have been successful in restraining
urbanization, as table 11.4 indicates. China is one of the few success
stories in this area (see box 11.1). Before independence, the growth of

Table 11.5   Air pollution levels in selected cities, 1982–1985

City	Peak levels of particulate matter	Peak levels of sulphur dioxide (mgm/m^3)
Brussels	97	205
Copenhagen	383	135
Frankfurt	117	230
London	77	171
New York	121	131
Warsaw	248	205
Bangkok	741	48
Beijing	1,307	625
Calcutta	967	188
Delhi	1,062	197
Manila	579	198
São Paulo	338	173

Source: World Resources Institute, 1988; reported in Sarre et al., 1991, p. 85. By permission of Kogan Page Publishers.

Box 11.1   China's urbanization policy

China is one of the few countries that has systematically tried to control the movement of people from rural to urban areas. China's urban population increased from 17.4 per cent of the total population in 1975 to 35.8 per cent in 2000. During this period, there have been times when urban populations have grown, and others when they have been 'rusticated' back to rural areas. In recent years, however, the Chinese leadership has indicated its willingness to allow cities to grow, possibly to 60 per cent of the total population by 2020 (*China People's Daily*, 17 May 2001).

   The Chinese government was able to control the levels of urbanization by restricting rural–urban migration. This was through two identity documents that all individuals were expected to hold:

- Permanent Registration Booklet: which identifies people as having urban or rural residence and thus prevents unauthorized movement from the countryside to the cities. Even marriage does not automatically entitle a person to move to their partner's place of residence. The system is quite strictly enforced.
- Work Identity Document: which is one way in which the system is enforced. This functions as an identity card, and is required for claiming a number of necessities, including foodstuffs, other consumables, access to schooling, child care, health care and other services.

   In addition to attempts to control in-migration, there have been periods when the authorities have forced out-migration of people from the cities.

This was common during the Great Leap Forward, for instance. Such mass deportations caused China's urban population to decrease in the 1960s. In addition, there have been attempts to enthuse young people to go to the countryside (up to the mountains and down to the villages), and between 1968 and 1978, around 17 million young people left the cities.

In recent years, efforts have been made to increase the levels of urbanization, since the latter is seen as the path to modernization. However, China plans to allow its small cities (less than 0.2 million people) and medium-sized cities (between 0.2 and 0.5 million people) to grow, rather than its large cities (more than 1 million people).

Source: Based on Ebanks and Cheng, 1990

urban areas in Central Africa was restricted by direct planning controls and by subtle social discrimination, which aimed to control the growth of the new indigenous middle classes who might challenge the European authorities.

In most developing countries, the problems associated with urbanization have been further exacerbated by the fact that there is a single primate city which has continued to grow. Historically, this has arisen because colonial trade patterns reinforced the importance of a single primate city close to a port.[11] All roads, rail and telegraphic links (usually established during the colonial period) lead to this city. Moving away from this pattern has been very difficult for most countries. Therefore, the primate city has continued to grow. Some developing countries have attempted to prevent such concentration by building 'new towns' in less developed regions, which they hoped would provide new growth poles. Ciudad Guayana in Venezuela is one such city, built using local mineral resources. It was hoped that it would provide an alternative to Caracas and Maracaibo. Similarly, in Brazil, Brasilia was built in the interior as the seat of government. Though it has grown somewhat, it has failed to counterbalance the growth of Rio de Janeiro and São Paulo.

The kind of urbanization now taking place in most developing countries is a far cry from that which occurred in Western Europe in association with its industrialization. In response to the history of urbanization in developed countries, early modernization theorists described towns as the catalysts for social development. Weber (1930) thought that cities inculcated a sense of individuality, because people in cities often did not know each other very well. While this meant that they could not depend on each other, it also meant that they could deal with each other as equals. Lerner (1964) thought that urban living encouraged specific features of modernity like literacy. This is required, for instance, if people are to be able to read street signs and timetables and move around easily. Thus, modernization theorists saw the urban centre as the locus of population growth, mobility and integration. People living in close proximity in towns were expected to create new life-styles because of the need to accommodate each other's ideas, desires and interests.

Third World urbanization has not resulted in such a modernization of life-styles, cultures or thought processes. It has therefore often been termed 'pseudo-urbanization'. People still live in conditions very similar to those in villages. Slums and shanty towns in most developing country cities reproduce the kinds of social networks and relationships that exist in villages. People are neither more distant nor more independent than they are in villages. While they have created new life-styles, this has occurred without an improvement in the life chances of a majority of the urban population.

Conclusion

In this chapter, we have considered issues relating to population growth and migration. We have considered the influence that population growth has on development, as well as the influence that the level of a country's development has on its population growth rate. We then moved on to a consideration of large-scale population movements, both rural–urban migration and international migration. In the next chapter, we will consider issues relating to agricultural changes and rural development. We will concentrate especially on institutional and technological changes in agriculture.

12

Agricultural Change and Rural Development

In chapter 11 we considered the movement of individuals from rural to urban regions within a country and the phenomenon of urbanization. As noted there, among the reasons for out-migration from villages are the poor employment opportunities and poor living conditions within the rural sector. In this chapter, we will consider the performance of this sector in more detail, and the changes that have taken place within it. The agricultural sector is often seen as synonymous with the rural sector. This association is not perfect, with many rural activities (mining, services) not being agricultural. In addition, rural non-farm employment is becoming increasingly important as a poverty-reducing strategy in developing countries. However, agriculture is still the major activity in rural areas; it employs a majority of the population, it influences the life-style and culture of rural areas, and is the backbone of most rural industry. We will therefore concentrate on it in this chapter.

The second qualification that we need from the outset is that neither rural nor agricultural sectors are the same the world over. The characteristics of the rural sector vary from country to country, often depending upon the type of production pattern being followed. Thus, nomadic agriculture (slash and burn, grazing or herding) results in relatively temporary, itinerant villages or societies. Plantation agriculture leads to societies that are concentrated within plantations but are otherwise dispersed, with the size of each settlement depending upon the size of the plantation. Intensively cultivated rice is associated with greater density of population than extensively cultivated wheat. Having said this, we need to note that there is no clear-cut causality. While the type of agriculture influences the types of settlements, the latter, together with population size, may influence the types of agricultural production chosen.

Differences in climate, soils and crops being produced have resulted in very different patterns of land ownership in different regions. In Asia, the pressure of population has resulted in small farms. Land tenure arrangements and inheritance rights have further reinforced this pattern. Thus, the right of all sons to inherit, rather than of the oldest alone, has led to the fragmentation of land and to small, economically unviable farms. At the other extreme, many large landholders rent their land out to sharecroppers or tenants.[1] In this context, absentee landlords are very common in Asia. Rural landlords often double up as money-lenders, since loans for consumption and investment are usually taken using land or labour as security.

By contrast, the relatively low population densities and infertile land in Africa have resulted in a pattern of shifting cultivation. In recent years, there has been a move towards settled villages and sedentary cultivation. Given the poor soil and climatic conditions, however, such settled agriculture has not been very successful. Land used to be held by the community rather than by individuals, and each family had access to land and water in the immediate vicinity. But this too is changing, as we will see.

Drawing general conclusions or discussing general patterns in the context of such variation is unlikely to be productive. Additionally, the literature in this area is very large, and we cannot do justice to it in a few pages. In this chapter, therefore, we will concentrate on three issues that have proved to be of major significance in this area. We will begin with a very brief look at rural development strategies, concentrating particularly on institutional reforms and technological changes in agriculture. We will also consider the poor performance of the agricultural sector in Africa. This, together with the recurrent problem of famines on that continent, has preoccupied analysts in this area in the last two decades. We conclude with a brief look at the role of the state in the agricultural sector.

Rural development

The World Bank (1975) has defined rural development as a strategy 'designed to improve the economic and social life of a group of people – the rural poor. It involves extending the benefits of development to the poorest among those seeking a livelihood in the rural areas. The group includes small-scale farmers, tenants and the landless.' Rural development can therefore be seen to encompass all efforts to increase farm and non-farm incomes through job creation, rural industrialization, and the provision of health, education and welfare services. It also involves decreasing inequalities in rural incomes and decreasing the disparity between rural and urban incomes.

Defined in its broadest terms, as the development of the rural sector, rural development involves improving the capacity of the rural sector to sustain and accelerate the pace of change. This can be achieved in a number of ways. In parallel with strategies for economic development generally, one can attempt to modernize the entire rural economy simultaneously (balanced development) or one can highlight certain sectors or regions (unbalanced development). If the latter, resources can be concentrated on a highly commercialized sector, for example. This would result in a dualistic structure of farm units.

The agricultural sector makes a number of contributions to a developing economy. First, it supplies food and raw materials to the rest of the economy. The pricing policy of this sector is therefore very significant in determining the profitability of the industrial sector. Secondly, agriculture provides labour to the non-agricultural sector. This has been incorporated into a number of dual-economy models of development (see chapter 2). Third, exports of agricultural products help a country's balance of payments. Fourth, it has long been recognized that the agricultural sector can help capital accumulation in the industrial sector. The ways in which this can be done – through taxes or changing the terms of trade of agricultural products – formed the basis for extensive debate in Soviet Russia after the revolution, and in many developing countries since then. Finally, agriculture plays an important role in increasing the size of the home market (Chakravarty, 1979).

The strategy chosen to develop the rural sector must be one that maximizes these contributions. It may involve land reforms and other institutional changes. In many countries, it has led to the commercialization of agriculture, a strategy that has often been blamed for Africa's poor agricultural performance. Given the seasonality of employment in the agricultural sector and the widespread poverty in rural areas, rural development strategies have often attempted to enhance employment opportunities both within farming and within other sectors of the rural economy. Thus, sustainable rural development requires a number of factors – non-farm economic growth, improvement in the well-being of the poor, sustainable management of natural resources – in addition to increased productivity in agriculture. The rural non-farm sector has become increasingly significant in recent years. While industry was initially expected to absorb the workers made redundant in the agricultural sector, it is now being recognized that this may not be sufficient. The rural non-farm sector helps employ some of this labour productively. Rural works programmes, which help create an infrastructure (schools, roads and housing), in providing such employment are often useful in this context. They also help by doing this *in situ*, thereby retaining the workers within the rural sector while helping to decrease migration into urban areas that have been unable to cope with this influx (Lanjouw and Lanjouw, 1995). Rural development strategies also aim to achieve changes in social attitudes that will lead to social modernization and help achieve certain social targets, like family planning ones, for example.

The literature on rural development and planning encompasses institutional changes, technical and technological changes, as well as a whole host of infrastructural, social and political changes in the rural sector. In what follows, we will concentrate on two aspects of such development: institutional reforms and technological change. The major institutional reforms undertaken in the agricultural sector over the years have been land reforms, which we will consider in the next section. Technological change in the 1960s and 1970s resulted in the introduction of high-yielding varieties of rice and wheat into agriculture. In the 1990s, however, technological change in agriculture has involved the genetic modification of a number of plant and animal species. We will consider both these types of technological change in this chapter.

Institutional change: land reforms

The rural development field places considerable importance on reforming institutions as a way of improving performance. Institutional change in the rural sector has ranged from the commercialization of agriculture, the institution of private property rights in Africa and in other parts of the developing world, as well as the move towards community ownership of land in many Socialist countries, including the former USSR and China.[2] In many developing countries, the aim has been to break up large farms, reduce the concentration of land ownership and let the tillers own their land. The rationale for this has been partly distributional and partly efficiency-related (smaller farms are seen to be more efficient, and ownership is seen to increase the incentive to invest). In this section, we will concentrate on land reforms that aim to redistribute landholdings.

Rationale for land reforms

Writing in 1980, Brandt reported that,

> in many countries, there are sharp disparities in land ownership: a minority of landowners and large farmers, often 5 to 10 per cent of rural households, may own 40 to 60 per cent of arable land. The rest of the rural populations are crowded on small, often fragmented pieces of land; many own no land at all. In many cases, a high proportion of rural land is held on a tenant or share-cropping basis with the landlords appropriating large shares of the total crop. Such agrarian structures are unjust and inefficient. In some countries, the large holdings are underutilized and output per acre is lower than on small holdings. To reduce poverty and increase food production, agrarian reform and the promotion of farmers' and workers' organizations are priority issues. (Brandt, 1980, p. 130)

This quote from the Brandt Commission Report brings out the two factors that most motivate land reform policies: the search for increased efficiency and the search for increased equity.

Search for increased efficiency

The debate on farm size, efficiency and equity pre dates the Brandt Report by many decades, but has yet to be resolved. Are small farms more efficient than large ones? The answer to this question depends upon a number of conditions, we will see below. Arguments in favour of large farms rely on increasing returns to scale in agriculture. It has been argued, for instance, that it takes a minimum amount of land to make full use of a tractor, combine harvester or other capital equipment. Small farms, as well as fragmented and spatially non-contiguous farms, do not offer scope for the use of machinery or technical innovations. Similarly, the processing and marketing of produce may also experience increasing returns to scale. Thus, tea requires careful marketing, but once the infrastructure for such marketing has been set up, the farm or firm can market any amount of tea through it, without an appreciable increase in costs. Finally, bigger farms have better access to credit (Banerjee, n.d.).

Even though most authors accept the above arguments, the arguments *against* large farms have carried greater weight. The main argument relates to what economists call 'agency problems': the difficulties relating to supervision and monitoring of work effort or output within agriculture. The difficulties arise because effort cannot be seen and the output from this effort in agriculture is the result of a combination of factors, including soil quality, weather, other labour inputs, and so on. The contribution made by a single worker cannot easily be distinguished. In addition, the output does not accrue immediately. Farmers have to wait until the harvest to know how efficient their workers have been. Supervising workers and incentivizing them are not easy in this context. Given these difficulties, smaller farms may be more productive than large farms for two reasons. First, they employ very little hired labour and rely almost entirely on family labour, which is better motivated than hired labour. Second, even when they employ wage labour, the smallness of the farm renders direct supervision easier.

Testing this relationship in India, Rosensweig and Binswanger (1993) found that the profit–wealth ratio for the smallest farmers was at least double that of the largest farmers. Lin (1992), studying the shift from a collective responsibility system to an individual responsibility system in China, found that productivity increased by only 14 per cent. Banerjee, Gertler and Ghatak (1998), analysing the impact of the reforms undertaken in West Bengal in the 1970s and 1980s, found that the productivity of the average sharecropper increased by almost 60 per cent.

Overall, it has been concluded that small farmers are more efficient in their use of land, while large farmers use labour more efficiently. Small farmers use more labour-intensive methods of production, often choosing labour-intensive crops like vegetables, rotating land use, leaving little land fallow, and using multiple cropping techniques. On large farms, owned by absentee landlords, the cultivators (often hired hands or tenants) have less incentive to work hard because they do not directly benefit from the gains. Many large farms therefore use more capital-intensive methods of cultivation. This increases the returns to labour, though it decreases the efficiency of land use. In many developing countries where land is the scarce resource, therefore, small farms are considered more appropriate for the factor endowments than large farms. Thus, output per *hectare* decreases with farm size, while output per *worker* increases with farm size. The optimum farm size, of course, would vary from country to country.

Search for equity

Apart from the potential increase in productivity when large farms are broken up, there is also likely to be an improvement in equity. Equity, as we saw in chapter 3, is desirable for itself. In addition, many writers argue that equity will increase efficiency in the long run. The redistribution of wealth may mean that the poor receive assets which they can use to improve their human capital or to obtain credit to improve their physical capital. In either case, the productivity of the poor is likely to increase. An equitable redistribution of land is also likely to create a more harmonious working and living environment in rural areas, which will in turn increase productivity. It helps to increase employment and improve the distribution of incomes. Some writers claim that it would be more direct to redistribute incomes rather than assets.[3] Finally, a more equitable distribution of land, and therefore of incomes, is likely to increase the size of the home market for manufactured products. Again, the argument that redistribution increases the number of consumers is reinforced by the fact that these consumers are also most likely to use domestically manufactured goods rather than imports.

The significance of land reforms lies in the fact that they may improve the productivity of agriculture and increase growth, while also decreasing inequality and directly contributing to poverty alleviation. Countries which have had successful land reforms have increased equality in rural areas and have built strong rural institutions like co-operatives, communes and farmers' associations. Land reforms have helped to retain people in rural areas, thereby spreading the benefits of development. They have also facilitated collective action, because equality decreases the ability of a small number of large farmers to usurp the benefits of collective action and also decreases social conflict. On the other hand, unsuccessful land reform can create more problems than it solves. It can destabilize the existing fragile equilibrium for peasants, and it can create a political vacuum by undermining the traditional power-holders (often rural landlords) before those with new economic power can gain political legitimacy. This political vacuum encourages social and political instability in which rebellions and revolutions are more likely.

The main alternative to land redistribution policies in developing countries is tenancy reform. In general, this attempts to increase tenancy rights by setting a limit on how much the landlord can demand as rent from the tenant, as well as restricting the eviction of tenants who have paid their dues. Such reforms increase the tenants' power as well as giving them a long-term stake in the land. This helps to increase investment in the land and is therefore likely to increase output. Another possible alternative is market-assisted land reform whereby the government makes a subsidized loan or grant available to individuals to buy land. This is purely market-driven. Only those interested are likely to come forward to buy land, and it may therefore be more efficient. But it is not so effective from the redistributive point of view.

Experience of land reforms in the developing world

The conviction that small farms are better from the point of view of both distribution and efficiency resulted in overwhelming pressure in favour of land redistribution in most developing countries in the 1950s and 1960s. Land reforms have varied across countries, from the transfer of ownership to tenants who already work the land (Japan, South Korea and Taiwan) to the transfer of land from large to small estates (Mexico); to rural co-operatives and state farms (Cuba) or to communes (China). In addition, land reforms involved the consolidation of small or fragmented holdings (India), abolition or reform of tenancy and the establishment of private property rights (sub-Saharan Africa).

While in most developing countries, land reforms have involved attempts to redistribute land and sometimes to consolidate it, in Africa they have involved changes in the form of ownership. Land reform measures in countries like Ethiopia have taken the form of co-operativization[4] and villagization. Co-operativization concentrates previously scattered units of production, and is expected to increase agricultural output. The requirement to sell all the output to the state at state-controlled prices and the consolidation of units have made them easier to control. But in spite of this, output decreased from an index of 100 in 1979–81 to 86 in 1996. Villagization is the social analogue of such collectivization. It brings together people living in dispersed homesteads and settles them in villages built according to government regulations. Unlike the earlier dispersed settlements, which were located close to water and fields, drainage and shelter, the new villages concentrate all the settlements in one area, and therefore are not able to take advantage of natural conditions. In

Tanzania, the original *ujamaa* concept anticipated a shift to living in nucleated villages and working on communal farms. It was hoped that farmers would be able to share machinery and equipment on such farms, but this proved financially unviable. In fact, the entire concept had to be abandoned because it was so unpopular (O'Connor, 1992). In southern Africa, the issue of land reforms has become inextricably linked with the racial question. Both in South Africa and in Zimbabwe, white farmers hold large farms, and redistribution, even after independence in the latter, has been made harder by political and racial factors.

In Asia, land reforms have involved both the redistribution of land and the consolidation of holdings. One of the most successful examples of land reform is the case of South Korea. In 1914, 1.8 per cent of households in South Korea owned 51 per cent of the land. In 1949, the government initiated a land reform programme which limited holdings to 3 hectares. Larger holdings had to be handed over to tenants, and 1.5 times the value of the land's annual production was paid to the owner in compensation. By 1953, this redistribution programme was mostly complete, and by 1974, only 1.4 per cent of farm households had more than 3 hectares. The success of the land reforms in South Korea, however, reflects the importance of many other factors. To begin with, especially after 1972, land reforms in South Korea were nested within a wider agricultural development programme. The increased ability of the urban-industrial sector to absorb the surplus rural population further decreased the costs of the reforms. The implementation of the reforms was eased by the disruption caused in the rural areas by the Korean War. Rapid inflation associated with the war also eroded the cost of compensation, and this, together with aid from the USA, helped to decrease the burden on the Treasury. The weakness of the agricultural lobby and the small contribution made by agriculture to exports also helped. All these factors were reinforced by government commitment to the reforms.

The significance of these factors can be seen from the unsuccessful land reform experiences of other countries in Asia. In the Philippines, for instance, dependence on agricultural exports gave large-scale farmers considerable power in preventing the enforcement of the reforms. In the face of their opposition, the government set the maximum size of holdings at 7 hectares, which is relatively large for a country as densely populated as the Philippines. In India and parts of Pakistan, the historical strength of the rural landlords (zamindars) helped them to fight the reforms. Many landlords were able to get around the ceilings by redistributing their holdings amongst family members, evicting tenants before the reforms, and winning local elections (sometimes through coercion). Since the reforms were unable to establish a new political power in the rural areas, the old landlords usurped political power within the new system.

In Latin America, Peru had widespread land reforms in which 10 million hectares changed hands. All large estates were expropriated, and many coastal plantations became co-operatives owned by permanent workers. Haciendas in the Andes merged into rural co-operative enterprises. Small farmers and landless labourers were excluded from the changes. Overall, neither productivity nor welfare has seen a marked improvement (Townsend, 1987). In Mexico in 1917, half of all farmland was reformed into communal tenure with individual rights. Since the land belonged to the community, people could not sell it, but it could be passed on to their heirs. Some state, collective and co-operative farms were also set up. Landlords lost power in these changes, but a new agricultural elite emerged. Today, foreign capital and national concerns are active in agriculture, and landlessness is increasing. In Chile too, many large estates were formed into co-operatives and administered by government officials and a farmers' committee. The reforms were intensified under the Allende regime, which took over 40 per cent of the agricultural land and set up 100 state farms. But when Allende was overthrown, many of these farms returned to their original owners (Simpson, 1994, p. 85). In Central America and Mexico, production contracting has helped farmers. Under this system, agribusinesses introduce new crops and techniques to peasants, who then grow the crop under specific conditions for sale only to the agribusiness. The agribusiness may also supply credit and inputs, thereby helping provide conditions for the commercialization of agriculture.

Land reforms: a package?

Land reform programmes are most successful when introduced as part of larger agricultural development programmes. In the past, many reforms have been unsuccessful because smaller farmers, having obtained the land, do not have access to information, credit and other inputs required to cultivate it (Dixon, 1990). This is true of many agricultural reforms. Inadequate access to, and use of, machinery on small farms can be overcome by hiring in machines from larger farms. But in cases where it is the *access* to credit, rather than the *cost* of credit, that is the problem, government support is often necessary (see last section of this chapter). Banerjee argues that 'publicly funded research on agricultural technology and agrobusiness, better extension services, public investments in infrastructure and marketing and improvements in credit access, should all be part of a broader programme that includes land reform' (Banerjee, n.d., p. 20). It is particularly important to have emergency income assistance programmes or work-relief programmes to help landowners who fall on hard times in the short run. In their absence, even minor cash-flow problems may lead landowners to resell land to the landlord, so that land distribution reverts back to its original levels in a few years. Of course, many countries legislate against such resale, in some cases banning resale of reformed land, and in others setting ceilings beyond which land cannot be purchased.

Technological change

Productivity increases in agriculture (as in other sectors of the economy) require technological improvements. These increases are an essential part of development, because a large proportion of the population depends upon this sector for its livelihood, and the rest of the population depends upon it for food and raw materials. There have been two major spates of technical change in agriculture: the Green Revolution in the 1960s and 1970s and the GM revolution in the 1990s. We will discuss them both in this section.

The Green Revolution

The most recent example of technological change in agriculture is the controversial introduction of genetically modified (GM) varieties of food and other agricultural products. The effects of this new technology are still under scrutiny, though many of the socio-economic factors being considered are very similar to those thrown up by the Green Revolution three to four decades ago. In this section, we will concentrate on the introduction of new seed varieties into the cultivation of rice and wheat in the 1960s and 1970s, since there is much to learn from that experience in the current introduction of new technology into agriculture. This, together with the accompanying change in fertilizer inputs and irrigation, has often been called the 'Green Revolution'. We will postpone discussion of the new issues thrown up by GM technology to the next section.

The Green Revolution began in the 1960s and involved the introduction and diffusion of high-yielding varieties (HYVs) of food grains, especially rice and wheat. Whereas the new varieties of wheat seeds were developed in Mexico, the new high-yielding rice varieties were developed in the Philippines. These new varieties increased yields considerably.[5] Aggregate statistics for India showed that the introduction of the new high-yielding varieties resulted in an increase in food-grain production from 95 million tonnes in 1967–8 to 130 million tonnes in 1980–1. Wheat production showed the greatest increases, tripling between 1963–4 and 1971–2 (Farmer, 1986). However, this increase in production required significant increases in the input of fertilizers, insecticides, implements and irrigation. Without fertilizers and controlled irrigation, the new seed varieties usually yielded 'no more and sometimes less than traditional strains' (Cleaver, 1972, p. 177). Simply applying the increased inputs to the old seed varieties was also unproductive, especially for rice. Thus, it was the entire package that worked, not its component parts alone.

It was generally expected that the Green Revolution would increase agricultural output and help developing countries to decrease the incidence of famines, hunger and malnutrition, much as genetically modified foods are expected to achieve in Africa today (Wambugu, 2000). It was seen to offer a number of advantages. First, since the central technology was the introduction of new varieties of seeds, it was seen to be scale-neutral: both large and small farms could introduce the HYVs with ease. Secondly, it was expected to create employment, especially in weeding and harvesting, and this in turn was expected to help spread the benefits of the innovation. Thirdly, the shorter growing season of the new varieties was expected to enable multiple cropping, and therefore increase output, which in turn would lead to lower prices.

There has been an enormous literature attempting to analyse each of these potential advantages (see Feder et al., 1985, for a survey; also Farmer, 1986). It has been found, for example, that though the technology itself was scale-neutral, the inputs required to complement it, especially fertilizers, irrigation, credit and education, were expensive and prone to economies of scale (Cleaver, 1972). They were therefore more likely to be used by larger farmers, at least in the beginning. By the time the smaller farmers adopted the new technology, the 'first movers' had appropriated most of the benefits, supply had increased, and prices were likely to have decreased. Production by smaller farmers then became relatively unprofitable (Rao, 1975). Ruttan (1977), however, concluded in his survey of the literature, that 'neither farm size nor tenure has been a serious constraint to the adoption of new high yielding grain varieties or has resulted in differential growth in productivity' (p. 17).

While the Green Revolution increased the demand for labour, this was met by household labour on smaller farms and by increased mechanization (especially tractors) on the larger farms. The employment of landless labourers therefore did not increase. Binswanger (1978) observed, for instance, that 'it is also clear to most observers that big farmers sometimes invest in tractors and other machines in order to avoid what – in their judgement – are problems of labour management, discipline and supervision, particularly in view of the fact that the high yielding varieties have led to increased labour demand and hence enhanced the bargaining power of labourers in the area where most tractor investment occurred' (p. 75). Ruttan (1977), in generalizing the findings of studies on the Green Revolution, disagrees, citing a number of studies to show that the demand for labour had increased. He does accept, however, that landowners have gained relative to tenants and labourers, and that the high-yielding varieties have contributed to a 'widening of wage and income differentials among regions' (p. 18).

The HYVs were found to be more sensitive to pests, disease and weather fluctuations than traditional varieties. Thus, the IR8 (the first high-yielding rice variety) proved to be very susceptible to pests and diseases under most South Asian conditions. It was also unadapted to dry conditions, conditions in which there was no irrigation, and to areas with prolonged monsoonal flooding (Farmer, 1986).[6] The new seeds also required significant inputs of fertilizer. A rise in fertilizer prices and the consequent decrease in quantities used affected output considerably, with the result that output became more variable after the new varieties were adopted. The increased use of fertilizers and pesticides was also criticized for its environmental impact.

Finally, the improvement in output was highly localized to certain crops, regions and sectors. In India, while the output of wheat and rice increased significantly (by 179 per cent between 1966 and 1977 for wheat, and by 62 per cent for rice), the effect on other crops was minimal. Additionally, the irrigation requirements of the new varieties resulted in their concentration in certain regions, so that the benefits were also highly localized. Thus, the adoption of new wheat varieties was primarily limited to the north and north-western states of Punjab, Haryana and western Uttar Pradesh in India. In Turkey, wheat adoption was limited to the coastal lowlands, and in Thailand rice adoption was largely in the central lowlands (Cleaver, 1972).

The Green Revolution has also been criticized because the decrease in food prices associated with the increased supply benefited urban populations disproportionately. Many commentators maintained that high profits in agriculture resulted in increases in land prices, thereby encouraging landlords to acquire more land and to convert their tenants into hired labour. This, together with mechanization, it was felt, also increased the number of unemployed in villages (Cleaver, 1972).

Many of these criticisms of the Green Revolution, however, relate to problems arising from its success rather than its failure. They are also a result of the poor administration of the changes, rather than of the changes themselves. As Ladejinsky (1977) put it, 'when all is said and done, it is not the fault of the new technology that the credit service does not serve those for whom it was originally intended; or that the extension service is not living up to expectations or wage scales are hardly sufficient to keep body and soul together' (quoted in Ruttan, 1977, p. 20).

In the Philippines, home of the Rice Revolution, for instance, there was an increase in total agricultural output, and the country attempted to achieve agriculture-led development by investing in roads, irrigation and marketing. While this helped to increase output and average rural incomes, a number of sectors suffered decreases in real wages and living standards, and there has been an increase in underemployment. The Green Revolution successfully enabled India to become self-sufficient in food and to build up stockpiles of grain to tide it over poor harvests.

Overall, one may conclude that while many of the criticisms have validity, at least some of them relate to the over-optimistic hopes pinned on the new technology. Others relate to the inability of the institutions within the adopting countries to cope with it. Before long, agricultural growth began to taper off, and countries began to look for other sources of growth.

Though the Green Revolution was very successful in increasing yields for a number of crops, population growth soon caught up with these gains. Whereas yields grew in the 1960s and 1970s, they began to decrease in the 1980s, for a number of reasons. First, price trends were unfavourable for growing staples. Second, staples production was extended into more marginal areas. Third, achievement of the most readily available yield gains required a shift from yield-enhancing to yield-protecting strategies (Lipton, 1999, p. 9). This led to a search for new ways of increasing productivity in the agricultural sector, especially in Africa, where the agricultural sector has collapsed (see next section). The new GM technology has been hailed as promising by a number of commentators and problematic by others. We will consider it in the next subsection.

The new revolution in agriculture: GM technology

It is estimated that by 2020, the world will require approximately 3,000 million tonnes of food grains annually (in addition to vast quantities of aquatic products and vegetables) to feed 8 billion human beings. But increasingly, developing countries are unable to add to the amount of land under cultivation (having already cultivated as much as they can). They are also faced with the loss of existing farmland and with decreasing resources of water and biological diversity. An increase in output under these circumstances requires an increase in yield per hectare. Increasing yields, in turn, require improved technology to be implemented.

One possible solution may be to adopt innovations in biotechnology in the agricultural sector in developing countries. 'Biotechnology' is short for a wide variety of biological manipulations – cell and tissue culture, embryo transplantation, transfer of DNA across sexual barriers – which provide opportunities for improving the products of tree, plant and animal species. The first transgenic plants were tobacco in 1983. Today, plants with new characters exist in maize, cotton, soybean, potato, tomato, tobacco, alfalfa and squash, amongst others. While the technology can be used to develop a number of traits in both plants and animals, it is currently being used to increase herbicide- and insect-resistance amongst plants. It also aims to increase the shelf-life of many products like tomatoes, as well as to create slow-ripening varieties. To date, its major uses have been in the commercial context of Western agriculture. While many of these modifications may also help farmers in the developing world, the research itself does not specifically aim to increase yields or to address the constraints facing farmers in the developing world. This is because the products targeted by the technology, as well as the traits being developed, are likely to be of greater use in developed country agriculture. The chief exception to this is the research aimed at the genetic modification of rice varieties in China.

GM technology has faced stringent criticism in the West, on many grounds. To begin with, there are fears of the development of 'super weeds', which will become resistant to insecticides and herbicides. Secondly, there are fears regarding whether crop varieties with multiple resistance to pests may contain toxins which will affect humans and animals. Tester (2001) also argues that 'allerginicity could cause problems that would be difficult to detect, as symptoms can take a long time to develop' (p. 11). Whereas extensive testing is required before the introduction of a new drug, new GM products can be introduced with much more modest testing regimes. This is especially problematic, because most GM products are likely to be consumed in larger quantities and more chronically than most medicines. This throws up a significant question in the context of developing country agriculture: are these problems sufficiently important for countries to forgo any benefits that GM technology may provide? Lipton puts it succinctly when he argues that 'it may make sense to take no extra risk for a longer-life tomato, but it makes no sense to take no extra risk to avoid blindness due to Vitamin A deficiency' (Lipton, 1999, p. 28). GM technology may help increase yields, as well as the incomes of farmers in developing countries, if it is appropriately developed and applied. This brings to the fore a number of other criticisms of this technology, which we will address below.

Much of the research into biotechnology is undertaken by large private corporations, and involves very large investments. This is a departure from the research undertaken for the Green Revolution by philanthropic organizations and governments. The nature of the financing of this research throws up a number of issues.

1   Will private companies allow their research to be made freely available to farmers in developing countries? There is already considerable unease about the way in which companies ensure that farmers cannot re-use or use seeds grown by them.
2   Developing countries are centres of biological diversity, and such diversity has been carefully nurtured over generations. But private companies have turned this biodiversity into biological productivity. While the companies must be properly compensated for the research undertaken, as well as incentivized to fund future research, is it equitable to grant a company a 100 per cent patent? 'What', asks Swaminathan (1990, p. 18), 'are the rights of the farm families who have conserved and selected genetic diversity in contrast to the rights of the breeders who have used them to produce novel genetic combinations?' There are also fears that such a patenting regime could result in a shift in research away from discovering the application of genes, towards the 'stockpiling' of intellectual property rights on genes.
3   There is concern regarding the areas in which such research is undertaken. Research in staples such as rice is most likely to help developing

countries. But most GM research to date has concentrated on maize, soybeans and cotton. The yellow-maize varieties and soybeans grown with GM tend to be designed as fodder rather than food crops, and are therefore mostly used in commercial, Western agriculture. Recently, Chinese researchers, together with the Rockefeller Foundation and others, have looked into GM rice varieties. But this research is still very small compared to research on maize, cotton and soybeans. Similarly, there is concern regarding the traits that GM sector research is spreading. Most research seems to concentrate on herbicide and insect resistance. These are less important for poorer farmers than varieties that increase yields.

4   Commercial firms, which produce this research, tend to target commercial farmers, as they are most able and willing to transport and pay for inputs, preferably with scale economies and avoiding dealer costs. While the scale advantage for large farmers was a criticism of the Green Revolution too, Lipton (1999) claims that it is a much more obvious failing of GM technology. In a debate reminiscent of the Green Revolution debate (see previous subsection), others argue that GM technology is a highly divisible technology, because it is reliant merely on farmers purchasing seeds, and because, unlike the Green Revolution technology, it does not require irrigation.

5   There are also questions regarding the practice of tying in contracts for seeds with complementary inputs like herbicides. This may have an exclusionary impact on some farmers.

Writers on GM technology argue that the way in which patents are awarded should be tightened, so that the contribution of the country in which the variety has been sustained over years is also acknowledged. Also, some research in this area by NGOs and other non-profit-making bodies would help to shift the balance towards areas where such research would increase public good in developing countries. Alternatively, private research companies can be incentivized (through taxes and subsidies) to shift some of their research in that direction. The debate on GM technology is on-going. There is still a long way to go before sufficient evidence can be gathered to judge whether this technology provides us with greater benefits or has larger costs. In the meantime, there seems to be some potential for helping with food availability in many developing countries, though the firms researching this area have to be carefully regulated and/ or incentivized if these benefits are to accrue.

Conclusion

Institutional and technological changes have been the main instruments used to improve agricultural performance and rural development in the last few decades. Each has had limited success, depending upon the country and the sector in which it was adopted. But neither institutional nor technological change has helped agricultural performance in Africa, as we will see in the next section.

Agricultural performance: the collapse of agriculture in Africa

When considering the performance of agriculture across the world, we encounter many diverse trends – from the extremely 'good' performance of the US and European food-producing sectors (reflected in their food mountains and lakes) to the 'collapse' of the agricultural sector in many countries in Africa. While Asia and Latin America have benefited (at least in terms of overall food production figures) from their attempts at agricultural development, whether through land reforms, the Green Revolution or both, Africa's agricultural sector has been relatively unsuccessful over the last few decades. As already indicated, in Africa, institutional change has resulted in the spread of private property rights and settled agriculture in place of community-held property and shifting agriculture. Technological change in the form of the Green Revolution has had less impact, though the commercialization of agriculture has become more widespread. These changes have resulted in significant decreases in food production per capita across countries in Africa, as table 12.1 indicates.

Of the thirty-two countries in table 12.1, only nine experienced increases in food production per capita between 1979–81 and 1996. In 1992, the FAO estimated that 10 million tonnes of food would have to be imported to meet Africa's needs. Even the daily per capita supply of calories had decreased in seventeen out of the twenty-eight countries for which there are data for both 1970 and 1996.

A number of factors have been put forward to explain the decrease in agricultural output in Africa. Inappropriate farming practices – especially the spread of commercial farming and the preference for settled agriculture on lands that have traditionally supported only nomadic cultivation or grazing – have resulted in desertification. This, together with the fact that the pastoralists are now driven into marginal land (e.g. the Afar pastoralists in Ethiopia), has increased the effect of drought on the local populations (see also box 6.1).

The huge, highly capitalized agricultural schemes favoured by most governments, together with attempts by donors to improve agricultural performance through model projects with up-to-date technology and farming and husbandry methods, has not helped the problem. Projects of this kind included those of the Kano River and the Sohoto Rima in northern Nigeria, and irrigation projects along the Senegal River in Senegal and Jahaly Pachar in the Gambia. During the 1960s and the 1970s, these projects were considered highly prestigious, and small projects were rarely ever given government support. Lofchie (1986) argues that in addition to being ineffective, these large projects contributed

Table 12.1   Food production in Africa, 1996

Country	Daily per capita supply of calories		Food production per capita, 1996 (1979–81=100)
	1970	1996	
Ghana	2,121	2,560	115
Cameroon	2,280	2,175	79
Kenya	2,180	1,971	83
Lesotho	——	2,209	70
Nigeria	2,254	2,609	129
Zaire	——	——	100
Zambia	2,140	1,939	99
Côte d'Ivoire	2,428	2,421	89
Benin	1,964	2,415	119
Togo	2,261	2,155	106
Yemen	1,763	2,041	75
Tanzania	1,749	2,028	76
Mauritania	1,868	2,653	81
Central African Republic	2,378	1,938	94
Madagascar	2,406	2,001	86
Angola	2,071	1,983	72
Sudan	2,167	2,391	76
Uganda	2,294	2,110	109
Senegal	2,546	2,394	111
Malawi	2,390	2,097	70
Guinea-Bissau	1,989	2,381	110
Chad	2,183	1,972	99
Gambia	2,108	2,332	76
Mozambique	1,886	1,799	77
Guinea	2,212	2,099	98
Burundi	2,094	1,708	92
Ethiopia	——	1,845	86
Mali	2,095	2,027	91
Burkina Faso	1,762	2,137	132
Niger	1,992	2,116	77
Rwanda	——	2,142	70
Sierra Leone	2,419	2,002	86
Sub-Saharan Africa	2,129	2,628	——
All LDCs	2,226	2,205	——

Source: Data from UNDP, 1999. From *Human Development Report*, 1999, by United Nations Development Programme, © 1999 by the United Nations Development Programme. Used by permission of Oxford University Press.

directly to the crisis by selling output produced on heavily subsidized farms in the open market at very low prices, thereby further decreasing the prices paid to local farmers. In the 1980s, therefore, the tide has turned in favour of smaller-scale projects.

The decreasing terms of trade[7] for primary agricultural exports have also decreased the prices obtained for Africa's agricultural exports and increased the price of its imports. This has been compounded by the fact that the demand for many agricultural commodities produced in Africa has been influenced by low income elasticities in general and by the production of substitutes in particular (see chapter 7 on export pessimism amongst developing countries in general). The former imply that as incomes increase beyond a certain point, people tend to consume more manufactures and fewer primary products. Thus, even in a growing world economy, the demand for agricultural production remains relatively stagnant, which reinforces the downward pressure on prices. Further, an increase in the prices of these commodities often decreases demand in the long run, by making the invention and use of synthetic substitutes more cost-effective. Thus, we find that synthetic rubber is substituted for natural rubber, and artificial fabrics for cotton and silk textiles.

This decrease in the terms of trade of primary products has been reinforced by the tendency of most African governments to restrict the prices of agricultural products. This has been part of the import-substituting industrialization strategy chosen by many African economies, and has led to the channelling of scarce investment resources into the industrial sector. This involves minimizing the prices of wage goods in the industrial-urban sectors and extracting surpluses from agriculture to invest in industry. Protection of the industrial sector at the expense of the agricultural sector has meant that farmers face high prices for their consumption and low prices for their output. This has had the effect of decreasing supply and eroding any agricultural surplus that existed to begin with. Thus, Robert Bates notes that 'the producers of cash crops for export . . . have been subject to a pricing policy that reduces the prices they receive to a level well below world market prices' (Bates, 1988, p. 28). This policy has been further reinforced by the over-valuation of many African currencies in an attempt to decrease import prices.

Thus, a number of factors have contributed to the continuing crisis of food production in Africa. This food crisis (together with a number of other factors) has manifested itself in the recurrence of famines in Africa (see box 12.1).

In response to this poor performance on the agricultural front, there are hopes that the 'new agricultural revolution' – the genetically modified (GM) foods technology – will help Africa. As Wambugu says, 'the Green Revolution which failed in Africa was alien. . . . Africa's farmers had to be educated in the use of fertilisers, for example.' However, she is very hopeful that GM crops may be more successful in Africa, because 'the technology – to control insects, for instance – is packaged in the seed' (Wambugu, 2000, p. 40). As discussed in the previous section, GM technology is relatively new, and there are considerable concerns regarding its safety. The

Box 12.1 Entitlements and famines in Africa

The traditional view of famines is that they are caused by a decrease in the availability of food. Therefore, they are expected to occur when droughts, floods or other natural disasters reduce agricultural output. Sen (1977, 1981) challenged this view by hypothesizing that famines are caused by a failure of entitlements rather than simply a reduction in food production. Entitlements, in turn, are determined by income-generating activities, the distribution of income and employment, as well as the legal and cultural frameworks in a country.

When considering famines in Africa, we may note that many African countries depend upon food output for employment and incomes, so that a decrease in food production may cause a decline in entitlements. In the East Asian economies, on the other hand, employment opportunities and incomes have been provided by other sectors, so a decrease in food production at home can be compensated for by purchasing food from abroad (Sen, 1997).[1] Countries like South Korea (which had a decrease of 1.7 per cent in food output between 1979–81 and 1993–5), Singapore (58 per cent decline) and Japan (12.4 per cent) have all faced decreases in food production between 1979–81 and 1993–5, but not famines.

Sen argues that many of Africa's major famines could have been avoided if food had been effectively distributed. The Ethiopian famine of 1972–4 was not accompanied by any significant decrease in food output, and in fact, even at its height in 1973, there was no major drop in food consumption per head. It affected some groups more severely than others. Thus, the pastoral people who had been pushed onto marginal lands by the spread of commercial agriculture and the agricultural community in the north-east were the worst affected. Similarly, it was largely the inequality in distribution rather than a decline in food production that caused the death of 100,000 people in the Sahelian famine (Mauritania, Senegal, Mali, Burkina Faso, Niger and Chad) in 1973. Problems with distribution and entitlements are often made worse by poor transport facilities. Thus, in Mozambique, rebel activities and damaged roads made the distribution of relief much harder, while in Namibia it was eased by efficient road and rail systems.

In many cases, poor government responses have made a bad situation worse. The government denied the 1984–5 famine in Sudan. This led to food hoarding and consequent price increases. Additionally, the drought in 1984 caused 80 per cent of the harvest to be destroyed at the same time that refugees were coming in from Tigray and Eritrea (Cammack et al., 1993). Sen (1997) argues that the prevalence of military dictatorships in Africa has decreased the importance of public opinion for the rulers and along with it the pressure to avoid famines at all costs. He makes a similar argument regarding the 1965–6 famine in China, as against the better record of India with regard to the avoidance of famines. In conjunction with the increased frequency of wars and revolutions, this has decreased health care provisions in Africa and has caused deaths through diseases.

Finally, political instability and wars in Africa have also contributed to the famines. The downfall of the dictatorial regime of Syed Barre in early 1991 in Somalia unleashed clan warfare. Faction fighters seized relief supplies and hampered their distribution. This, together with severe drought, caused one of the worst famines in Africa in Somalia. In the recent southern African food crisis (2002), it has been claimed that politics is influencing the distribution of food in Zimbabwe. Thus, Robert Mugabe's government is preventing the distribution of food via the public distribution system to areas and people supporting the opposition Movement for Democratic Change party.

Avoidance of famines therefore requires an increase in economic growth, in employment opportunities and in wages, the diversification of production, improvement in medical provisions, improved distribution of food, especially to the vulnerable (small children, deprived mothers), the spread of education, reduction of gender-based inequalities, and a general strengthening of democracy (Sen, 1997).

[1] See also Sen, 1981, and Dreze and Sen, 1989.

socio-economic literature on this technology is still relatively recent, as it has not yet been widely adopted. Though controversial, if it proves successful, it could provide considerable advantages for Africa, much as the Green Revolution (with all its limitations) did for Asia.

Role of the state in agriculture

The need for government intervention in agriculture (as in other sectors) relies partly at least on a number of 'market failures' in the rural economy. Farmers face significant risks (in terms of weather and demand conditions, and therefore of output and price too), but cannot insure themselves adequately against these risks because insurance and futures markets are not easily available. The poverty of individuals within this sector and their inability to provide collateral implies that they are unlikely to obtain credit from traditional sources like banks. At the same time, the nature of the agricultural sector, especially the seasonality of income, the uncertainty (relating to market conditions and the weather) in incomes, the need for regular investment (in machines, seeds and fertilizers), all imply that individuals within the sector often face cash-flow problems. They therefore require short-term loans to tide them over. But since the risk of default on such loans is relatively high, few traditional sources are likely to provide credit. Farmers therefore face usurious interest rates from landlords.[8] While these interest rates may reflect the higher risks of lending to farmers (who are often seen to default and cannot be forced to pay), they do imply that farmers will be less able to adopt new technology or capital equipment. This will have significant external costs on the rest of the economy (higher prices of farm output, smaller output, slower spread of the new technology to other farmers who may have learned from other farmers). This results in a less dynamic agricultural sector, which most countries wish to avoid. Therefore, governments often get involved in providing farmers with credit. This is especially important, because the provision of such credit has significant externalities in terms of furthering government policy objectives like equity in land ownership or adoption of new technology.

Governments also get involved in the provision of information to this sector. The adoption of new technology requires farmers to be 'aware' of it – that is, to have information regarding it. This is not always easily available, but while a farmer gains from such adoption, society (in terms of the entire farming community and its consumers) gain even more. Thus, the social benefits of such information gathering are greater than the private benefits, and governments therefore often enter the picture to provide agricultural extension services.

Another case where government intervention is necessary is when large-scale infrastructure or R&D projects are being considered. The provision of water through irrigation projects requires enormous investment, and provides the investor with monopoly power over a 'public' good – water. Governments, in their attempt to prevent the privatization of this natural monopoly, often provide this service themselves.

Similarly, many governments in the developing world (and in Europe and America) acknowledge the risks faced by farmers by attempting to stabilize the prices they obtain on output. This is done through buffer stocks and government purchases of excess production. However, such price stabilization does not help to stabilize incomes, which is what most farmers are concerned about.[9]

Finally, of course, as we have seen in this chapter, many governments intervene in the agricultural sector to redistribute assets (land) in the interests of equity and efficiency. This is generally not something that can be done privately, though there have been some suggestions for market-assisted reforms. Such redistribution has been accepted as part of government policy in the entire economy (see chapter 3), though the government's efficacy is questionable. Land reforms, for instance, have not been particularly successful in most countries that have undertaken them, and there are questions regarding government's efficacy in price stabilization and provision of agricultural extension services, for example. Overall, though, this relates to the efficacy of the government machinery rather than any real possibility that these activities could be undertaken in the private sector.

In spite of such attempts to help the rural sector, some commentators argue that government efforts continue to be skewed in favour of the urban sectors. In a series of writings on urban bias, Lipton (1968, 1977,

1980) highlights the potential sources of such bias. First, many government policies increase industrial prices relative to farm prices. This is done through ceilings on agricultural prices, as well as taxes on agriculture to extract surplus that can be invested in industry. The higher industrial prices increase the costs of inputs into agriculture as well as the costs of consumption in this sector. Second, governments concentrate investment in industry and provide tax incentives and subsidies to industry. Third, many governments undervalue their currencies, and this decreases the domestic currency receipts from agricultural exports. Finally, there is greater government expenditure on education, training, housing, plumbing, nutrition, medical care and transport in urban, than in rural, areas.

In addition to such direct measures, the government's macro-economic policy also affects the agricultural sector through its impact on demand in other sectors of an economy, on exchange rates, which in turn determine the prices that agricultural products obtain in export markets, and on taxes and subsidies for this sector. The agricultural sector has a significant impact on the rest of the economy, as we have seen in this chapter, because it provides food for the rest of the economy and because it provides inputs into manufacturing, as well as demand for the output of the manufacturing sector. The performance of this sector is therefore a key to the performance of most developing economies, and few governments are willing to leave this to the vagaries of the market.

Conclusion

In this chapter, we have considered some of the experiences of change in rural areas in developing countries. A large majority of people in developing countries live in rural areas and work in agriculture. However, problems facing the rural areas and the attraction posed by urban living have meant that urban areas are growing faster than they can cope. Many attempts are being made, on paper at least, to stem this by improving conditions in rural areas through rural development initiatives: institutional and technological reforms. However, these have not been successful in improving living standards in rural areas generally, or in decreasing hunger and poverty.

In the next two chapters, we will consider issues relating to human capital formation (chapter 13) and employment (chapter 14). Education and health improve both human capital (and therefore contribute to growth) and human welfare (they contribute to development and are part of it). We will consider them in some detail before we turn to look at rural and urban labour markets and employment opportunities in chapter 14.

13

Human Capital and Human Welfare: Health and Education

While a large population may increase the size of a country's labour force, the skills and quality of this labour force become pertinent when considering its effect on growth. It is often maintained that developing countries are quite generously endowed with labour in quantitative terms but that the quality of this labour falls short of what is required for industrialization and development. Many countries (especially in East Asia) have attempted to overcome this shortcoming by investing in human capital as a first step towards development. This includes investment in health facilities and services like the provision of minimum nutrition and preventive medicine which increase the ability of individuals to work. It also includes investment in education: formal education at school and university, on-the-job training, adult education programmes, and agricultural and rural extension services. All of these activities might be expected to improve the knowledge of individuals and therefore their productivity. This has been captured in the more recent growth theories, in which a human capital term is included in the production function, which is separate from the physical capital term (see chapter 4).

The above seems to imply that education and health are important because they are instrumental in improving growth prospects. While this is true, it is clearly not the whole story. Education and health are also desired because they determine human welfare, and it is recognized that they are essential if individuals are to realize their full potential. Most definitions of development in fact see education and health as *part* of development, rather than simply the *cause* of development. This has been made explicit in indices like the Human Development Index (see chapter 1), which include some measure of health (life expectancy, infant mortality) and of education (number of years of schooling, enrolment rates or literacy rates). Thus, education and health are 'both the seed and the flower of economic development' (Harbison and Myers, 1965, p. xi). They improve the prospects for future development, but are also part of the development that is taking place.

It is therefore not surprising that of the seven international development goals put forward by the World Bank (2000/1), two relate to education – enrol all children in primary schools and decrease gender disparities in education – and three relate to health – decrease infant and child mortality, decrease maternal mortality, and improve access to reproductive health services. The Bank also includes lack of access to good health care and education, together with vulnerability, in its multi-dimensional definition of poverty.

In this chapter, we will look at these two aspects of human welfare in greater detail. We cannot do justice, of course, to the wealth of literature in these fields, but we wish to consider a few key issues. On the health front, the main issues discussed are the changes in health patterns over time and across developing countries, as well as the ability of developing countries to cope with such change. We will also consider the concerns raised by the spread of HIV/AIDS in the Third World. On the education front, we will consider the significance of education (both its public and private benefits), returns to education, and ways in which the educational needs of developing countries can be met. We will conclude with a look at the role of state policy in these two fields.

Health

While the day-to-day definition of health – absence from disease and infirmity – is relatively well accepted, the notion of health as a state of 'complete physical, mental and social well-being' is rather more elusive. Status indicators reveal the health of a country through its outcomes – infant mortality, life expectancy, deaths from communicable diseases like AIDS, and so on. While status indicators may measure both morbidity (sickness) and mortality (death), morbidity statistics are rarely reliable. This is partly because individuals are often unable or unwilling to visit a doctor when they are unwell. Since they are not formally diagnosed, they are therefore never counted in the morbidity statistics. Sometimes individuals are not even aware that they or their children are unwell. This is especially true in cases of chronic ill health and low-level malnutrition that people accept as facts of life. Service indicators, on the other hand, consider health status from the point of view of inputs. These include sanitation facilities, doctors per 1,000 of the population or per square mile, and so on.

Causes of sickness and death: the epidemiological transition

The demographic transition (chapter 11) models the *effects* of changes in health, while the epidemiological transition models the changes in the *causes* of ill health and death (Armstrong and Fellman, 1998, p. 79). In the *age of pestilence and famine* (stage 1 of the epidemiological transition), the main causes of death are infections, respiratory and parasitic diseases and malnutrition. This was true of many developed economies in pre-modern times and is still true of many developing countries today. It also corresponds to stage 1 of the demographic transition (see chapter 11). In stage 2 – the *age of receding pandemics* – there is an improvement in average life expectancy and a decrease in mortality rates through medical and nutritional improvements. These lead to an increase in population (as in stages 2 and 3 of the demographic transition). Finally, in the *age of degenerative and man-made diseases*, mortality decreases, and fertility becomes important in sustaining growth. During this stage, diseases of the circulatory system and cancer are the chief causes of death (see table 13.1).

This transition is clearly seen in the case of the East Asian NICs, with gastro-intestinal and respiratory diseases being the major causes of death in the early stages of their growth, and cancer, cardiac and other chronic diseases gaining predominance by 1993. Most developing countries, however, are still at stage 2 of this transition, where mortality rates are decreasing but are not at developed country levels. The chief causes of death in these countries can be categorized into three types (Gonzalez and Norwine, 1998):

1   *Diseases carried in human faecal matter*, like diarrhoea, typhoid, cholera, hepatitis A and poliomyelitis. They are the result of poor sanitation and unsafe drinking water.

Table 13.1   Leading causes of death in East Africa

Taiwan		Korea, Rep. of		Singapore		Japan	
1952	1993	1965	1993	1968	1993	1950	1993
Gastro-intestinal	Cancer	Respiratory	Cancer	Infectious	Cancer	Tuber-culosis	Cancer
Pneu-monia	Cerebro-vascular	Gastro-intestinal	Cardiac	Parasitic	Cardiac	Pneumonia	Heart attack
Tuber-culosis	Accidents	Accidents	Organ disease	Tuber-culosis	Diabetes	Heart attack	Stroke
Cardiac	Cardiac	Cardiac	Hepatitis/liver	—	—	—	—

Source: Gertler, 1995, as quoted in Mundle, 1998, p. 668. Reprinted in *World Development*, 26 (4), S. Mundle, Financing Human Development: Some Lessons from Advanced Asian Countries, pp. 659–72, © 1998, with permission from Elsevier.

2   *Diseases transmitted from person to person*, and associated with over-crowding and poverty. These include tuberculosis, measles, pertussis, pneumonia, hepatitis B and sexually transmitted diseases.
3   *Vector-borne diseases*, like malaria, yellow fever, sleeping sickness and river blindness. Malaria is still one of the major causes of sickness and death in developing countries, especially in Africa (where 90 per cent of the cases are concentrated). There are about 300–500 million cases of malaria each year.

Given the conditions prevalent in most developing countries with respect to overcrowding, slums, pollution and congestion, as well as inadequate sanitation, nutrition and water supplies, it is not surprising that death rates remain higher than developed country levels. The relationship between poverty and health is significant, and has resulted in the term 'diseases of poverty' (Parker and Wilson, 2000). But the relationship is not straightforward. While poverty causes ill health because it decreases access to sanitation, nutritional and medical facilities, ill health in its turn causes poverty, because it decreases an individual's ability to work and increases expenditure on medicines and doctor's visits. In most countries, however, once a child survives the first five years, life expectancy rates begin to converge to those of adults in developed nations. Thus, an average new-born boy in Bangladesh would not expect to survive to 46 years, while a five-year-old could be expected to survive to 59 years (Gillis et al., 2001, p. 349). This pattern is changing with the increasing incidence of AIDS amongst the young in many developing countries, especially in Africa (see table 13.2).

The problem in most developing countries is that an improvement in health requires improved living standards, while the latter, in turn, require an improvement in the health status of individuals. Governments have attempted to break into this cycle through the provision of public health care facilities, but have been faced with rising costs and a fiscal crunch. These rising costs have been reinforced by the epidemiological transition, as we will see. Thus, two-thirds of the medical care in countries like Ghana, Côte d'Ivoire, Kenya and the Republic of Tanzania is from public health facilities, and the other one-third is from private non-profit organizations.

Given their limited resources, governments have to consider expenditure strategies in this sector very carefully. Until recently, selective biomedical intervention was favoured, though in recent years, primary health care has been emphasized.

1   *Selective biomedical interventions* tend to target a small number of diseases for prevention. In the 1980s and 1990s, such interventions included vaccination programmes against measles, neonatal tetanus and whooping cough; the distribution of oral rehydration salts,

vitamin A supplements (to prevent blindness), and bed nets to prevent malaria. They have been very effective in the past in preventing deaths from communicable diseases like smallpox, typhoid and cholera, and have been central in pushing most developing countries into stage 2 of the demographic transition. The problem with this approach, though, is that while it gives quick results when a single disease causes a large number of deaths and also when the diseases are easily transmitted, it is less effective in other circumstances. This is because while vaccinations are relatively low-cost measures, the provision of oral rehydration salts or bed nets is harder both to undertake and to sustain for most cash-strapped health systems.

2 *Comprehensive primary health care*: the WHO defined primary health care as education concerning health problems, prevention and control, promotion of food supply and nutrition, safe water and sanitation, family planning and maternal and child health care, immunization and so on. Thus, it emphasizes preventive over curative care. China provides one of the best examples of this strategy.

While selective biomedical interventions were very popular in the 1980s and 1990s, the pendulum is tilting in favour of comprehensive primary health care today. This is not surprising. The diseases which could be easily controlled by hospital-style treatment have already been controlled. Others, like diarrhoea or respiratory disorders, are better prevented than cured, and this requires an improvement in socio-economic conditions. There are, of course, still a few (vector-borne) diseases that can be controlled by more specific interventions. Thus, China, for instance, has made progress against schistosomiasis through mass campaigns aimed at ridding rivers and lakes of snails that transmit this disease. However, the eradication of diseases like diarrhoea and hepatitis A requires an improvement in sanitation, while the eradication of diseases caused by overcrowding, like TB and hepatitis B, requires an improvement in general living conditions. In both these cases, the general socio-economic environment must be dealt with if health is to be improved. In the case of attempts to improve infant mortality figures, female literacy has been found to be very effective, *whatever the family income*. This is because a mother's awareness of (and willingness to try) recommended health, hygiene and nutritional practices is often the most important determinant of a child's health.

Each of these strategies – biomedical interventions, primary health care and socio-economic development – is likely to be effective under different circumstances and given different types of disease patterns, as seen above. The epidemiological transition also throws up new issues in this context. While infections and parasitic diseases can be dealt with quite effectively through preventive health care programmes at relatively low cost per capita (Mundle, 1998, p. 668), chronic diseases are more expensive to treat and must be approached on an individual basis.

Human immuno-deficiency virus (HIV) and AIDS

The single most significant threat to world health today is the spread of HIV/AIDS. AIDS is caused by the human immuno-deficiency virus (HIV). It has two distinct phases: the first, when individuals contract HIV, which can lie dormant and undiagnosed for many years. The second stage – the fatal one – when these individuals contract AIDS. By the time AIDS is diagnosed, the disease is usually too far advanced to treat. At the level of the population, therefore, AIDS epidemics usually signal the peak rather than the start of the crisis.

AIDS was first diagnosed in the early 1980s, and has since reached epidemic proportions in many parts of the world (particularly in Africa and now parts of Asia). In the UK, the spread has been less exponential, with fifty-one cases in 1983 and 14,431 cases by 1997 (Barnett and White-side, 1999). The largest group with AIDS in the UK is still the gay community, followed by people with links abroad and injecting drug-users (Barnett and Whiteside, 1999). In Africa, where 14 million people were infected with HIV in 1996, the heterosexual community (amongst them women) has been hardest hit. Here the disease has spread through heterosexual sex and also from mothers to their infants during pregnancy and lactation. The World Bank (1997a) estimated that 15–20 per cent of all HIV infections in Africa are amongst infants infected by their mothers. This has given rise to considerable concern regarding the recommenda-tion that mothers should continue to breast-feed their babies. It is clear that breast-feeding has many advantageous side-effects, especially in communities where drinking water supplies are unsafe and unreliable, and where the resistance to disease provided by breast milk is highly desirable. However, with the risk of HIV infection, the recommendation is now under scrutiny.

The impact of the disease on Africa is enormous. In a large number of countries, it has actually resulted in a decrease in life expectancy rates, a clear reversal of the demographic transition in these countries. Thus, in Botswana, life expectancy decreased from 65.2 years in 1996 to 52.3 years in 1997 (see table 13.2). This has, in turn, had a huge impact on human development, causing Botswana to fall from 71 in the HDI rankings to 97, a fall that has also occurred (though to a smaller extent) in Zambia, Zimbabwe, Togo and a number of other countries in Africa.

While table 13.2 clearly reveals the humanitarian costs of such a crisis, the socio-economic costs are less obvious. Since HIV/AIDS strikes the sexually active age-groups, it is the young who are most affected by it. This has meant that in many families, it is the chief earner who has died, leaving the family emotionally and economically distraught. In agriculture, prod-

Table 13.2   Changes in the Human Development Index for four African countries

Country	HDI rank		Life expectancy	
	1996	1997	1996	1997
Botswana	71	97	65.2	52.3
Togo	140	147	55.2	50.6
Zambia	136	143	48.6	42.6
Zimbabwe	124	129	53.4	49

Source: Whiteside, 1998, pp. 4–5, using data from UNDP *Human Development Reports*. Reprinted by permission of the International Health Exchange.

uctivity has decreased because many young farmers have lost their lives and are being replaced by older, less energetic farmers. In addition, Gillis et al. (2001, p. 351) argue that with lower life expectancy, both individuals and firms have less incentive to invest in education and training. Further, it is increasingly being found that firms that used to provide very generous health, retirement and death benefits can no longer afford to do so, in the face of the increasing claims brought on by this epidemic.

The only hopeful sign at the moment is that the epidemic shows signs of having passed its peak in Africa. The prevalence of HIV has decreased in Uganda (Parker and Wilson, 2000), though the reasons are not entirely clear.[1] On the other hand, the incidence is increasing in Asia, where, however, it seems to be localized amongst certain groups and in certain regions.

Conclusion

The demographic and epidemiological transitions have been criticized as being ethnocentric, based as they are on the experience of the developed countries. However, it is clear that some degree of transition has taken place in most developing countries, though the details of the transitions may vary. Thus, with medical knowledge borrowed from the West, the second stage of these transitions has been compressed in the developing world today, leading, as we saw in chapter 11, to a population explosion. The new crisis – in the image of Malthus's age of pestilence – today is AIDS. This has significantly decreased population growth rates in many countries in Africa, inverting the population pyramid by killing the young and able and leaving large numbers of dependants – children and the old – without support. We have touched on the role played by governments in controlling diseases in this section. We will consider the role of policy in health (and education) in greater detail at the end of the chapter. In the next section, we will consider the second aspect of human capital development – education.

Education

Just as improved health is expected to increase the productivity of individuals, so too education is seen as an input into human capital formation which will influence both growth and development. In fact, Machlup (1970) observed that the literature on the subject of education and economic growth is almost two hundred years old. The functionalist view of education, which was reinforced by the new growth theories (chapter 4), sees it as the provider of basic skills – literacy and numeracy – as well as the more technical and specialized knowledge required for modern activities (whether in farming, industry or commerce). As technology advances, modern industry is becoming skill- rather than labour- or capital-intensive. In addition, of course, the process of education is seen to encourage self-discipline, hard work and an achievement orientation, characteristics pin-pointed by modernization theorists as being necessary for the transition from tradition to modernity. Education also helps provide administrative and leadership skills, which are especially important in many developing countries, where the withdrawal of colonial rule left an administrative and managerial vacuum. Education may contribute to aggregate growth rates by creating a more productive and skilled labour force.

In addition to these effects on growth itself, education also influences development in a number of other ways. It creates a more 'modern' attitude to life (according to modernization theories), and increases the ability of individuals to participate in the social, cultural and political activities surrounding them. Education, in an indefinable way, is also expected to broaden people's minds and horizons, and can help to reduce communal, racial, tribal and other tensions. Educated individuals improve their living environment and benefit all others living within it.

Women's education has been particularly emphasized by development practitioners, as we saw in chapter 11. The secondary schooling of women, it is argued, has a powerful impact on decreasing fertility (Appleton, 1996) as well as on decreasing infant mortality, even when mothers do not work in the market-place. Handa (1996), studying maternal education and child achievement in Jamaica, for instance, finds that in male-headed households, maternal education gives mothers greater bargaining power within the household and is seen to significantly assist children's educational attainment.

We have so far spoken of education as a determinant of growth and development. It is equally true that, just as in the case of health, it is hard to separate the effect of education on incomes from the effect of increased incomes on the demand for education. This endogeneity of education has, in fact, been highlighted as one of the chief weaknesses of growth literature (Mankiw, 1997). Education yields benefits both to the individual (private benefits) and to society (social benefits). The effects of education on growth and, more especially, development can be seen as among the social benefits of education. They arise from knowledge gained and from having a more literate population, irrespective of formal school attainment levels. For social benefits to accrue, therefore, the knowledge or skills gained – the ability to read and write, converse or take part in discussions – are more important, and therefore literacy and informal education are equally useful. On the other hand, education also yields benefits to individuals who undertake it, in the form of improved career prospects, increased incomes, improved ability to think and appreciate issues, and so on. Maximizing the private benefits of education requires a formal education system within which the grades or levels attained signal the ability of the individual to future employers.

The social returns from education can be higher than the private returns if education leads to technological progress not captured in the private returns to education, or if education produces positive externalities like a reduction in crime rates and social security pay-outs, or more informed political decisions. While technological progress would require an increase in tertiary education, the other benefits are more likely to accrue with an increase in education at lower levels (Krueger and Lindahl, 2000). It is unclear whether social returns from education really do exceed private returns, though the positive externalities mentioned above are more likely to accrue from investments in disadvantaged than advantaged groups (Heckman and Klenow, 1997).

Many writers have attempted to study the benefits of education at the level both of individuals and of the country. Psacharopoulos (1985) finds that returns from education are higher in developing countries than in developed countries. Psacharopoulos and Woodhall (1985) also indicate that, in developing countries, average returns from investment in education are higher than those from investment in physical capital. Among human investments, primary education is the most effective for overcoming absolute poverty and decreasing income inequality. Psacharopolous (1994) shows that there is a higher return from primary schooling than from secondary or tertiary schooling. In spite of such findings, many planners in developing countries have prioritized secondary and tertiary education so as to meet the immediate need for skilled labour.

Evidence regarding the impact of education on growth at the macro level is mixed. National-level studies seem to show that it is the initial stock of human capital, rather than changes in this stock, that matters for economic growth. Thus, educational investment may take quite a long time to have an effect. Additionally, secondary and tertiary education are more important for growth than primary education. In spite of considerable anecdotal evidence regarding the importance of education, cross-country studies have not found much evidence of a relationship between educational attainment and economic growth. Thus, Barro and Sala-i-Martin (1995) and Benhabib and Spiegel (1994) conclude that changes in schooling have an insignificant impact on GDP growth. In fact, Benhabib and Spiegel (1994) conclude that their 'findings shed some doubt on the traditional role given to human capital in the development process as a separate factor of production' (p. 144). This could be because of measurement errors in cross-country education data. More specifically, it is well known that school enrolment, or mean years of schooling (Barro and Lee, 1993; Kyriacou, 1991; Benhabib and Spiegel, 1994), provide a very poor indication of educational achievement. Formal educational achievement, in turn, provides a poor indication of the usefulness of this attainment. Krueger and Lindahl (2000) find that once measurement errors in education are accounted for, change in education is positively associated with economic growth. Thus, there is some conflict between the micro and macro evidence on the education–income/growth relationship.

There is also considerable disagreement regarding the effect of female education on economic growth. As we saw in chapter 11, female education helps to decrease fertility rates and therefore the rate of growth of the population. This has been associated with an increase in economic growth. Barro (1997), however, found female education to have an insignificant and sometimes negative effect on economic growth, while Caselli et al. (1996) found the opposite.

While the results of empirical analysis are still being debated, most countries, at a policy level, have prioritized investment in education in their expenditure plans. This has resulted in a significant improvement in school enrolment rates (table 13.3) and in adult literacy levels (table 13.4). Primary school enrolment rates have increased in many developing countries in the last few decades. In Africa, countries like Kenya have shown substantial increases in enrolment rates, from 50 per cent in 1965 to 95 per cent in 1987. In Tanzania too, enrolment rates increased from 30 per cent to 65 per cent during this period, though the record in Somalia was very poor, increasing only from 15 per cent to 20 per cent (UNICEF, 1990). Similarly, while enrolment rates were between 98 per cent and 100 per cent for East and South-East Asia, they were as low as 56 per cent in sub-Saharan Africa and 78 per cent in South Asia. These figures are also reflected in the levels of adult literacy achieved in these countries.

Literacy rates have increased across all groups of countries in the last two decades, with the average across developing countries increasing from 43 to 64 per cent. The high HDI developing countries (which include most of East and many countries in South-East Asia), in fact, do well (with adult literacy at 93 per cent in 1994) even in comparison to the developed countries of the North (100% in 1994). The level decreases progressively, to 80 per cent in the medium HDI countries and 50 per cent in the low HDI countries. There seems to be a clear correlation between

Table 13.3   Net enrolment rates and expenditure on education, 1993–1996

Region	Net enrolment ratio			
	Primary (as % of relevant age-group)	Secondary (as % of relevant age-group)	Children not reaching grade 5	Public education expenditure/ GNP
All LDCs	85.7	60.4	22	3.6
Least developed countries	60.4	31.2	—	—
Sub-Saharan Africa	56.2	41.4	34	5.4
Arab states	86.4	61.7	10	—
East Asia	99.8	71.0	6	2.7
East Asia (excluding China)	97.9	93.7	—	3.5
South-East Asia and Pacific	97.8	58.3	14	3.0
South Asia	78.0	56.5	38	3.3
South Asia (excluding India)	80.9	45.2	—	3.0
Latin America and Caribbean	93.3	65.3	23	4.5
Eastern Europe and CIS	—	—	—	4.6
Industrialized countries	99.9	96.2	—	5.1
World	87.6	65.4	—	4.8

Source: Data from UNDP, 1997, p. 179. From *Human Development Report*, 1997, by United Nations Development Programme, © 1997 by the United Nations Development Programme. Used by permission of Oxford University Press.

Table 13.4   Literacy rates

Country category	Adult literacy (%)		Adult literacy (%) (North = 100)	
	1970	1994	1970	1994
High HDI	80	92	81	93
Medium HDI (excluding China)	55	79	56	80
Low HDI (excluding India)	28	49	28	50
All LDCs	43	64	43	64

Source: Data from UNDP, 1997, pp. 166–7. From *Human Development Report*, 1997, by United Nations Development Programme, © 1997 by the United Nations Development Programme. Used by permission of Oxford University Press.

the level of development and the rates of literacy. As usual, however, the direction of causation – literacy to development, or development to literacy – is not clear.

In spite of government commitment to education (see table 13.3, last column, and next section), many countries still do not have an adequate number of schools or teachers, especially in rural areas. In addition, schools that exist in many developing countries lack resources. They also tend to emphasize formal education which inculcates a value system and a knowledge base that are often irrelevant to the problems of development. For example, heart surgery is usually ranked above tropical diseases as a significant specialism in developing countries. Similarly, the emphasis on English as a medium of education is often inappropriate for the needs of these countries.

From time to time, attempts have been made to reform these tendencies, but the political and social power bases in these countries have usually defeated these attempts. In Bangladesh, for instance, the attempt to make Bengali the sole language in primary schools was seen as a way of giving peasant children and their teachers (who were generally poor English-speakers) a better chance to do well. However, it faced considerable opposition from the English-speaking elite who feared that their children would lose their monopoly benefits, and in 1978 the scheme had to be abandoned (Dove, 1981). Thus, the elitist system of education pursued in many former colonial countries continues to have repercussions today. While the system was pursued in the past because it provided the colonial masters with an able, willing, co-opted bureaucracy, today these elites are unwilling to give up their advantages.

Many developing countries have also been criticized for concentrating resources on tertiary education, in spite of findings that the returns to primary education are higher than to secondary or tertiary education (Psacharopoulos, 1981, 1985). Thus, in 1993–6, Venezuela spent 35 per cent of its educational budget on higher-level education, as did Turkey (UNDP, 1997). Countries like Zambia, Togo, Senegal and Congo all spent more than 20 per cent of their educational budgets on higher education. Since private returns to education are highest at university level, emphasizing tertiary education is likely to increase inequalities between individuals and to benefit the elites in developing countries disproportionately. It also tends to encourage migration in search of higher private benefits abroad (see chapter 11). This emphasis on tertiary education has also been criticized for causing qualification escalation, intense pressures on education budgets, and further neglect of primary in favour of tertiary education (Dore, 1980). This is because as education levels increase, higher qualifications are required for the same job, so more and more education is sought. Dore (1980) has termed this the 'diploma disease'. It must be said, however, that tertiary education is also seen to have a greater impact on growth than primary education, so that it may not simply be pressure from elites but also the pressure for growth that has caused tertiary education to be emphasized over primary education in developing countries.

In addition to these supply-side problems, the levels of development of an economy also influence the uptake of these benefits. Thus, even where schools exist, the opportunity cost of school attendance (in terms of what the children could be doing at home or at work) is sometimes sufficiently high for parents to keep children at home. In this context, it is possible that children may be enrolled but may not attend school regularly.

Alternatively, when the quality of schools, or of the education, provided is poor, parents may see attendance as a waste of time. Analysing education patterns in four South Bengal villages, Kambhampati and Pal (2000) found that on average the children who did not attend school were from poorer families (with total incomes of Rs. 7,179 as opposed to average total incomes of Rs. 12,908 for the families of children who regularly attended school).

In addition to the effect of incomes, many studies have found that girls have to give way to the education of their male siblings (Parrish and Willis, 1993). Kingdon (1996), for instance, finds that boys had a 38 per cent higher probability of being enrolled in a fee-paying school than girls in urban India. In East and North Africa, education programmes have gone some way towards redressing this imbalance between female and male education, though not at the tertiary level. In Tanzania and Kenya, primary enrolment rates for boys and girls are at parity today, though in Somalia, little equalization has occurred.

In response to such problems, many authors argue that a less formal mode of education would have greater benefits in developing countries. This approach encourages the development of 'informal apprenticeships' and the passing on of skills from one individual in a village to another. Sometimes, this would involve a weaver teaching his craft to other villagers, while at other times it might involve a numerate or literate person passing on their numeracy and literacy to other people. It also includes attempts to pass on scientific and technical farming skills to farmers through adult education or women's education classes (Webster, 1990, p. 127). Thus, 'any organised, systematic, educational activity carried on outside the framework of the formal system to provide selective types of learning to particular subgroups of the population, adults as well as children' (Coombs and Ahmed, 1974) would be more beneficial than the formal education currently in favour in developing countries.

Though this appears to be a practical solution, it has faced considerable opposition, because formal education is seen as the best way to improve the employment prospects of individuals. Most governments, as seen above, have in fact emphasized formal tertiary education because of its impact on growth. In the next section, we will consider the role played by policy in human capital formation.

Role of policy

The experience of countries like Sri Lanka and China has shown that appropriate government policies can help to increase both literacy and life expectancy, even when incomes do not increase commensurately. In Sri Lanka, this has been achieved through free medical care, training more doctors, and a tripling of the number of nurses and paramedics. This has enabled the extension of primary health care into rural areas. Sri Lanka also has near universal literacy, and this in turn has helped its health performance. Life expectancy is 72 years, almost at developed country levels.

In many developing countries, health care is dominated by the public sector. Education, on the other hand, is provided through a combination of the state and the private sector, though state regulation and subsidization are significant. The commitment of developing country governments to education can be seen from the size of government expenditure on education. Table 13.3 indicates that expenditure on public education was 3.6 per cent of GNP in all developing countries taken together in 1993–6. In sub-Saharan Africa, governments spent 5.4 per cent of GNP on education, while the figure was 4.5 per cent of GNP in Latin America and the Caribbean.

What is the rationale behind government provision of health and/or education? Both health and education are merit goods. They provide private benefits to individuals receiving them in the form of increased productivity, earnings or quality of life. They also result in large externalities, so that the communities around these individuals also benefit. This is clearest in the case of communicable diseases, where attempts to control the disease help society overall. Under the circumstances, the external benefits of health care (especially in the first and second stages of the epidemiological transition) are very high. As indicated earlier, education too has large external benefits. Improved education helps decrease crime rates and welfare pay-outs and increase the general quality of life of the community. In addition, the equity argument suggests that an individual's ability to access educational and medical facilities must not depend upon his income level.

Finally, there is the argument first put forward in chapter 4, that improvements in health and education help increase growth rates and are therefore good for the economy. This, in fact, is an externality/spillover benefit of these expenditures. Leaving health and education to the market in the face of such externalities would result in 'too little' being spent on them (individual expenditure depends upon the perceived private benefits rather than the benefits that may accrue to society at large). Most governments therefore have attempted to intervene in these markets to directly provide health care as well as to regulate private sector providers. The problem is that such intervention is becoming increasingly hard to finance. Thus, while infections and parasitic diseases could be controlled at a low cost per head, the epidemiological transition to chronic diseases has increased the cost of health care per head, because cancer and heart disease require individual treatment that is expensive. Such treatment has few externalities in terms of preventing other cases of the same diseases, for instance. Increasingly, therefore, governments are having to resort to a combination of state-led and private provision of facilities. While this in itself is no bad thing, provided it is carefully regulated, there is also the need for such provision to be carefully monitored, so that the state continues to provide services for the poor, while the rich can opt out of this system and into private care.

The public goods case for education to be provided by the public sector is less clear. It is clear that primary education has the largest external benefits, and therefore has greatest claim to being publicly funded. Then comes secondary education, and last is tertiary education. In fact, as seen above, many empirical studies indicate that tertiary education has higher private than social benefit, and there is therefore a case for it to be privately funded. But most developing country governments spend more on it than its social benefits warrant. Increasingly, funding for education is also coming under strain. It is becoming necessary to include a significant private component in the provision of education facilities.

Mundle (1998), studying the case of four advanced Asian economies (AAEs) – South Korea, Taiwan, Singapore and Japan – found that these countries prioritized health and education in their public expenditures. About 30–40 per cent of spending was allocated to social services in the AAEs, as compared to 20 per cent in the OECD and developing countries (this excludes expenditure on welfare benefits). Thus, the AAEs concentrated expenditure in areas with the highest social returns. Equally important has been targeting the right areas. The AAEs, for instance, laid great emphasis on primary and lower secondary schooling, so that by 1960 (just prior to their high growth phase) enrolment was around 100 per cent. Only after a minimum threshold level had been reached in primary education, did the AAEs shift emphasis to secondary and higher education. Since primary education has been seen to have the highest social benefits, it was publicly funded in the AAEs. Tertiary education, on the other hand, had relatively high private benefits, so an increasing proportion of costs was left to be borne by the individuals benefiting from such education. Mundle (1998) also reveals that though these countries had very high pupil–teacher ratios, performance was exceptional, because teachers were highly paid and therefore highly motivated.

Conclusion

Education and health are significant in developmental terms both because they influence human capital (and through this, the prospects for growth) and because they influence human welfare (an aspect of development).

While there is considerable rationale for government provision of both education and health, budgetary constraints restrict pure government provision. Some optimal combination of public and private provision must be arrived at. In the next and final chapter, we will consider employment and labour markets in developing countries.

14

Labour Markets and Employment

Employment provides one way in which the benefits of growth can trickle down. In general, the closer an economy is to full employment, the more equitable its income distribution. This was why employment was so strongly emphasized by the ex-Socialist economies. However, full employment is rare, even in developed countries. In these countries, being out of work but able and willing to work is a tangible phenomenon, made more so by a relatively effective social security network. Such unemployment can be both voluntary (where people do not wish, for whatever reason, to take up the available jobs) and involuntary (where the number of jobs available is in any case less than the number of people looking for employment). In the absence of a social security network in developing countries, however, unemployment generally means destitution. It is therefore more common for people to be underemployed, using a number of strategies for survival. They are often 'self-employed', rarely utilizing their potential and scarcely extracting a living from their work, often simply performing odd jobs. It is therefore not surprising that the trickle-down mechanism has failed in most developing countries (chapter 3).

The 1970s ILO country missions were the first explicit recognition that unemployment had become chronic in most developing countries. More significantly, these missions provided an early acknowledgement that unemployment in developing countries had three dimensions: lack of employment opportunities, lack of adequate sources of income (i.e. employment not providing sufficient incomes) and a volume of unutilized or under-utilized labour (ILO, 1970). Thus, unemployment, underemployment, unproductive employment and employment with inadequate incomes were all problems.

In this chapter, we will analyse issues relating to employment in both the rural and the urban sectors. We will consider the strategies employed by workers unable to obtain formal sector employment (see section on the urban informal sector). Before we do this, it is worth briefly considering the structure of employment in developing countries.

The labour force in developing countries is approximately 47 per cent of the total population. Table 14.1. also indicates that 61 per cent of workers in developing countries and 74 per cent in the least developed countries were employed in agriculture in 1990. As against this, only 10 per cent of the labour force in developed countries is employed in agriculture. Whether this structure is the cause or the result of under-development is not clear, as we saw in chapter 2. We will not consider this any further. Instead, we will move on to look at labour markets in the next two sections. While agriculture and rural labour markets are often seen as synonymous, the same is not true of industrial and urban labour markets, as we will see.

Rural labour markets

A majority of the rural population derives its income from land, as landlords, tenants or labourers (both permanent and casual). Much of the employment within this sector is seasonal and casual, with labour being employed for short durations, sometimes on a daily basis (Dreze and Mukherjee, 1987). In rural Brazil, there are 15 million migrant workers, or 'cold lunch people', who move jobs every few days (D. Preston, 1987). In this context, it has been argued that permanent contracts are simply a means of providing an incentive for harder work when effort cannot be easily monitored[1] (see also chapter 12). Since these contracts provide a higher wage and greater security of employment, they

Table 14.1   Structure of employment, 1960–1990

Region	Labour force as % of total population	% of labour in agriculture		% of labour in industry		% of labour in services	
	1990	1960	1990	1960	1990	1960	1990
All LDCs	47	77	61	9	16	14	23
Least developed countries	47	86	74	5	10	9	17
Sub-Saharan Africa	45	81	66	7	9	12	25
Industrial economies	49	27	10	35	33	38	57
World	48	61	49	17	20	22	31

Source: Data from *UNDP*, 1997, p. 183, table 16. From *Human Development Report*, 1997, by United Nations Development Programme, © 1997 by the United Nations Development Programme. Used by permission of Oxford University Press.

are both attractive and scarce. This makes the threat of dismissal costly and credible, and helps to extract effort, especially in conditions of an excess supply of labour (Bardhan, 1984a; Eswaran and Kotwal, 1985). As opposed to this, some writers (Rudra, 1982) argue that workers *choose* casual contracts because they do not want to be tied down permanently.

The seasonality of output and employment in agriculture is reflected in seasonal increases in poverty in the rural sector. To cope with this seasonal reduction in incomes, rural labourers, small farmers and tenants borrow from the landlord. Loans are taken both for consumption and, with the commercialization of agriculture and the Green Revolution (see chapter 12), increasingly for investment purposes – seeds, fertilizers, machinery and irrigation. Rural credit organizations set up by govern- ments as part of their extension services have not been very effective in reaching the poorest people. This is because the risk of default on loans to tenants and small farmers is high. In the context of their poverty, legal safeguards are rarely sufficient to induce repayment (Basu, 1983). Even today, therefore, in the absence of more formal sources of finance, many farmers borrow from landlords. The landlord doubles his gain from this transaction because in addition to earning interest on the loan, the increased investment undertaken by the tenants yields larger returns on his land and therefore higher rents.[2] Providing loans to some workers also helps to 'tie' them to the landlord so that they are compelled to 'work off' their loans during the peak season when labour is hard to find (Bardhan, 1984a). Finally, the lender is able to decrease the risk of default by exercising some control over the borrower.

In addition to agricultural work of this kind, cottage industries and homeworkers produce traditional handicrafts and implements of simple design, like basic furnishings and agricultural tools aimed at low-income consumers. This provides employment at off-peak times and increases the diversity of rural livelihoods.

The preponderance of casual contracts, seasonal unemployment and poverty help 'push' workers towards cities and industrial employment. In recent years, this has been reinforced by a reduction in subsidies and credit available to farmers. The structural adjustment programmes have imposed stringent budget constraints on many developing country gov- ernments, which in turn have decreased expenditure on the agricultural sector. It is feared that these cut-backs could affect the small farmers most (ILO, 1995). In many countries in southern Africa, migration of key household members has created a shortage of certain types of labour, and has therefore undermined the productivity of small farms. In such communities, the permanent population – dominated mostly by women, the young and the old   is highly dependent on migrant remittances.

Does the migration to cities signal better living conditions there? We have already seen in chapter 11 that cities are congested, polluted and expensive to live in. Do they, however, provide better employment opportunities and labour market conditions than rural areas? We will turn to consider the characteristics of urban labour markets in the next section.

Urban labour markets

While a majority of the rural population continues to be employed in agriculture, employment in urban areas is much more diverse. Only a small proportion of the urban population is employed in factories and other manufacturing establishments. With increasing out-migration from villages, the supply of urban workers in many developing countries far exceeds the demand, resulting in very high rates of unemployment and underemployment in cities. In the absence of a social security system, survival requires that they take part in some activities, however casual or short-term. This has given rise to a very large 'grey' economy which Hart (1973) termed 'the informal sector'. While the informal sector exists in the rural labour market too, its manifestation in the urban sector is quite distinct.

The formal sector is generally taken to mean wage labour in permanent employment and usually implies work situations which are officially registered in economic statistics. It therefore includes a set of interrelated jobs which are part of a composite, internally well organized labour structure, with working conditions which are protected by law (Breman, 1976). Thus, the formal sector not only has jobs that are permanent and generally well established, but it also benefits from government regulations and trade union activism. We will consider this particular characteristic of the formal sector – the organization of workers into unions – in more detail later in this chapter. But before we do so, we will consider the urban informal sector in the next section.

Urban informal sector

The informal sector is not easy to define. It is often described just by listing the activities included within it: porters, hawkers, shoe-shine boys, rickshaw-pullers and vendors. While this gives us a rough idea of what is meant by the informal sector, it is very *ad hoc*. The alternative has been to treat this sector as a residual, so that any activities not included in the formal sector are automatically classified as informal. This has been criticized as being purely tautological. In general, informal sector activities are characterized by ease of entry, reliance on indigenous resources, family ownership of enterprises, small scale of operations, labour intensity and adapted technology, skills acquired outside the formal schooling system, and unregulated and competitive markets. They are 'largely ignored, rarely supported, often regulated[3] and sometimes actively discouraged by the government' (ILO, 1976, p. 6). By contrast, the formal sector is characterized by obstacles to entry, reliance on imported resources, capital intensity and formally acquired skills, corporate ownership and large scale of operations, as well as protected markets.

Concentrating on one aspect of this definition, Mazumdar (1976) claims that 'the basic distinction between the two sectors turns on the idea that employment in the formal sector is in some senses protected so that the wage-level and working conditions in the sector are not available, in general, to the job seekers in the market, unless they manage to cross the barrier of entry somehow' (p. 656). This kind of 'protection' may arise from the actions of trade unions, of governments, or of both acting together. The informal sector has therefore variously been termed the 'bazaar economy', the underground economy, the shadow economy, the black economy, the subterranean economy, and so on. It is often so classified on the basis of labour status (undeclared labour, no social benefits, and avoidance of minimum wage rules), unreported income or tax evasion, and unregistered enterprises whose output does not enter into the national statistics. It relies on strong social networks characterized by the 'friend of a friend' relationship, and has been seen as synonymous with the small self-employed sector.

This crude classification ignores the diversity within each sector, as well as the spectrum of activities between these two extremes (Breman, 1976). Breman, for instance, attempts to get beyond this binary classification by dividing urban workers into four categories: the labour elite, the *petit bourgeoisie*, the sub-proletariat and the paupers. Those employed on a regular basis with standardized working conditions and leading a relatively comfortable existence are classed as the labour elite. This includes workers in factories and in government offices. Then there is the *petit bourgeoisie*, which includes the owners of small-scale enterprises, self employed craftsmen, retail traders and other one-person firms, as well as those engaged in economic brokerage – money-lenders and rent collectors. They are a relatively entrepreneurial class and inject some dynamism into this sector. The third category includes casual and unskilled workers, as well as those employed by small-scale workshops, and the labour reserve of large enterprises, also termed the 'sub-proletariat'. Thus, Breman stresses the spectrum of possibilities, and moves away from a consideration of the two extreme sectors. Extending this classification, one could speak of the urban labour market as 'fragmented' rather than dichotomous (Breman, 1976).

Much of the early literature saw the urban informal sector as a residual sector encompassing the 'reserve army of labour'. It was seen as a sector where the marginal productivity of labour was very low, but which provided some income and employment, however small and irregular, to the people working within it. New migrants were therefore seen as entering this sector and progressing into jobs in the formal sector. In the early days, the informal sector was seen as encompassing a large army of marginally employed individuals who hampered collective action and exercised downward pressure on wages and working conditions.[4] This view was criticized on the grounds that the formal and informal sectors are non-competitive. Workers in the formal sector are recruited on the basis of standard and impersonal procedures, and it is very difficult for informal sector workers to break into the formal sector. These critics, implicitly or explicitly, accept the view of the informal sector as a residual category.

Attempts have been made to move away from this notion of the informal sector being a residual or buffer zone with low productivity towards one where the informal sector is seen as dynamic and as providing jobs using appropriate technology (Breman, 1976; ILO, 1995). In 1973, the ILO launched a major initiative to study this sector in a number of cities across the world. The main aim of this initiative was to consider whether the informal sector could provide a productive, viable option for employment generation in developing countries, rather than simply being a residual sector which includes the unemployed and the unemployable. The ILO's Kenya Report concluded in 1972 that 'the informal sector is capable of creating more jobs and growing faster than the formal sector', and that 'the bulk of employment in the informal sector far from being only marginally productive is economically efficient and profit making' (p. 5).

More recently, in its 1995 *World Employment Report*, the ILO reiterates that the 'informal sector typically consists of both dead-end survival activities and small-scale activities with the potential for growth and technical upgrading' (ILO, 1995, p. 92). Making administrative procedures simpler and more flexible would encourage the dynamism of the sector and increase its ability to provide productive employment. The picture varies, of course, from region to region. In Africa, informal sectors are still dominated by low-productivity, survival activities, whereas in East Asia, a thriving base of small-scale enterprises has been created (ILO, 1995, p. 93). The informal sector in Latin America lies between these extremes, exhibiting both 'sponge' and dynamic characteristics.

The concept of the informal sector has been very useful in allowing us to analyse employment and earnings patterns, as well as the life-styles of people in urban areas in developing countries. It feeds into the notion that rural–urban migration in many developing countries is leading to pseudo-urbanization, in which very little real formalization of economic and other relations is occurring. Before we end the chapter, we will consider formal sector employment, especially the role of trade unions in developing countries.

Urban labour market: trade unions and formal sector employment

As already indicated, the two main factors distinguishing the formal sector from the informal one are government regulations and the role played by labour activism. In this section, we will consider the latter – labour activism and industrial democracy – in greater detail. What role might trade unions be expected to play in a developing country? Will they help or hinder development? Will their effect be purely economic or political and social too? Many models of trade unions have been built on two functions fulfilled by unions – the defence or protection of workers' interests and their contribution to the national effort to attain development.

The effect of trade union activity on growth and development has been a matter for considerable soul-searching in developing countries. On the one hand, unions fight to increase their members' wages. While this is a useful activity in a situation where the excess supply of labour may push market wages to levels below subsistence, an increase in the share of national income going to wages reduces profits and may decrease investment which is financed from such profits. Strikes and industrial stoppages which accompany such bargaining can also repel potential investments from multinational enterprises. On the other hand, wage pressures can lead to growth by reducing profit margins and stimulating the rationalization of production. An increase in wages also helps increase demand, and can therefore be expansionary. In addition to these effects on growth, trade unions can assist the wider process of development by helping to redistribute the benefits of economic activity. They provide the institutional context within which their members can be integrated into industrial work and into the fight for democracy (as in Latin America and Africa).

In Latin America, tripartite bargaining between the state, companies and unions has become the norm. Such bargaining has helped the transition to democracy in countries like Chile. Though their participation in populist alliances brought with it the recognition of workers' interests as legitimate, it also decreased the autonomy of these unions. Workers' interests were co-opted by the state. In the 1960s, however, authoritarian regimes in Brazil, Argentina, Chile and Uruguay attempted to exclude labour unions rather than co-opt them. With liberalization and their new autonomy under such regimes, labour militancy took the form of political strikes directed at the overall socio-economic situation.

In East Asia, high wages and a social security system have helped authoritarian governments prevent industrial unrest in spite of very long working hours. South Korea's working week has always been very long, peaking at 50.5 hours in 1989, and Taiwan's at 47.2 hours per week. In recent years, however, with labour markets becoming tighter, there have been calls for wage restraints. There is considerable debate regarding the nature of labour markets in East Asia. On the one hand, there are those who claim that the NICs are characterized by very efficient labour markets that adjust easily to changing demands (Galenson, 1992; World Bank, 1993; Chowdhury and Islam, 1993). On the other hand, it is argued that workers here are repressed and docile (Deyo, 1987). Collective bargaining in East Asia is decentralized, and though pay has been the traditional variable of concern, such bargaining is being extended to other issues like working hours and worker participation in management.

In Africa, as in Latin America, trade unions had a more significant political role. Their legitimacy and status arise from their participation in freedom struggles in many countries. In addition, the existence of transnational corporations and old colonial interests in industry have meant that the role of trade unions in extracting benefits for their members is much more straightforward. But the transition from independence to their role today has not been easy for them (Gordimer, 1971). Structural adjustment has had a major impact on industrial and public sector employment in Africa, and therefore threatens trade unions more on this continent than elsewhere in the world.

Overall, unions have played a significant role in many countries. By organizing workers, they have provided a 'voice' for a significant mass of individuals in developing countries. However, given that a very small proportion of people work in factories and in formal public sector employment, unions continue to unionize the 'elites' among the workers. Most people work in occupations that are not unionized, like agriculture, or in enterprises that are not, like those in the small and cottage industrial sector. Their significance is constrained by this. In India, for instance, only 8–10 per cent of workers are unionized, even though unions themselves play a relatively significant role in the economy (especially the public sector unions).

Women in the labour market

Approximately 40 per cent of the adult labour force in most countries is composed of women, and approximately 33 per cent of income is earned by them (see table 14.2). Though women are employed in both the rural and the urban labour markets, we have chosen to look at their experiences separately in this section, because irrespective of the sector they work in, they have certain common problems and issues to deal with.

The role of women in the agricultural sector was first studied by Esther Boserup in her book on women and development (Boserup, 1970), which became the forerunner of a large literature on the role of women in development (see chapter 6). Working women generally have two roles – that of paid worker outside the home and that of unpaid worker (as wife and mother) within the home. The latter role involves reproductive activities – housework, food preparation and child care – which can be

Table 14.2 Share of women in employment and incomes

Region	Women's share of adult labour force (%)		Earned income share (%), 1994	
	1970	1990	Female	Male
All LDCs	37	39	31.7	68.4
Least developed countries	43	43	33.1	67.2
Sub-Saharan Africa	43	42	35.5	64.6
Industrial economies	40	44	37.7	62.4
World	38	40	33.3	66.9

Source: Data from UNDP, 1997, p. 183. From *Human Development Report*, 1997, by United Nations Development Programme, © 1997 by the United Nations Development Programme. Used by permission of Oxford University Press.

very time-consuming. In developing countries this is compounded by the fact that water-carrying and fuel-gathering activities often take many hours every day (Agarwal, 1983). Outside the home, women have traditionally been involved in many agricultural activities. Amongst shifting cultivators men clear the land and cut down trees, women sow the crop, weed and harvest, and prepare the crop for storage or consumption. Within settled agriculture, women use their income from subsistence farms to supplement other sources of income. They also form a reserve of labour for seasonal work.

Many aid projects have begun to recognize women's contribution. The Jahaly–Pacharr project in the Gambia, for instance, saw female family labour as the pre-condition for meeting project objectives – 'women are better than men as far as transplanting is concerned and they are also better than men as far as working in the water ... so quite frankly we expect a lot of labour from women, more so than from men' (Carney and Watts, 1990, p. 226). While this explicit recognition of women's role has helped, it has also increased women's work considerably. Women continue to perform most of the reproductive tasks, in addition to working on these projects. This, of course, is not new. Women have always been involved in a number of activities to help men and earn a subsistence income. Thus, the wives of the Ewe seine fishermen in south-east Ghana bought the fish from the net owners' company, preserved it (by smoking), and resold it, often at a profit (P. Hill, 1970). Similarly, markets in Ghana were mostly operated by women (Arhin, 1979). Garlick (1971), in his study of Ghana, found that some women dealing in imported textiles in the mid-1950s 'had incomes of several hundred pounds a year and some had incomes running into 4 figures' (p. 49).

While women in Africa are still generally involved in subsistence agriculture, women in Asia are increasingly being employed in cash crop cultivation on plantations (Sri Lanka) and in factories (East and

South-East Asia). Thus, women constituted 40 per cent of the work-force in East Asia in 1990, and 35 per cent in South-East Asia. This compares with 39 per cent in the developed countries and 29 per cent in Latin America (Cammack et al., 1993, p. 220). Many women in East Asia are employed in textile or garment factories and on assembly lines making bulbs and microchips, for instance. They are often young and leave school early to help pay household expenses and fund their brothers' education (Parrish and Willis, 1993). Though women in East Asia have been working for more than a generation, they are not autonomous agents within the labour market. They are controlled by their families, before entering into relatively late marriages. In spite of their increasing activity and involvement, these women continue to have little control over their output or earnings (Carney and Watts, 1990). Of course, the precise situation varies from country to country, and even across tribes and families in the same country.

In South-East Asia, there is greater female autonomy. Families tend to be matrilocal and matrifocal, with daughters inheriting family land in equal shares.[5] Young women in countries like Thailand and Indonesia work in factories producing textiles and electronics. But, unlike women in East Asia, they tend to retain much of their earnings. They make the decision to go to work in factories themselves, and it has been noted that women workers in Bangkok (like those in Latin America) are often more militant and more likely to engage in trade union activities than men.

Within the urban informal sector, women tend to be employed in domestic services. This is especially common in Latin America, where domestic service is seen as an entry point into the labour market for women who have migrated from the villages. While they generally hope to move upwards, this rarely happens because domestic service does not enable them to make contacts or learn other skills. In fact, exit from such employment usually occurs only when they get married. In India too, such domestic service is very common. In addition, women are also employed in cooking and providing lunch boxes to office workers in cities like Mumbai and by the city authorities for cleaning services. Employment in the informal sector tends to be precarious, poorly paid, and lacking in legislative protection.

The 1989 UN report on the world social situation showed that female wages were between one-half and three-quarters of male wages in a cross-section of developed and developing countries. Table 14.3 indicates that in the UK, for instance, they were only 68 per cent. In South Korea they were less than half, while in Sri Lanka they were 76 per cent in 1986. This difference in male and female wages, is both because women are employed in lower-paid work as well as because they are paid less than men even in these jobs. In addition to earning much less than men, in some countries women are unable to retain the benefits of their labour, having to pass it on to their families. Even married women generally use

Table 14.3   Wages of females as a percentage of the wages of males

Country	1977	1986
Developing countries		
Cyprus	49.6	56.1
El Salvador	80.8	81.5
Hong Kong	—	77.9
Kenya	55.6	75.6
Singapore	—	63.4
South Korea	44.7	48.5
Sri Lanka	—	75.5
Developed countries		
France	75.8	79.5
Greece	68.8	76.9
Japan	46.0	42.5
New Zealand	73.3	71.8
Sweden	87.4	90.4
UK	70.8	67.9

Source: United Nations, 1989, p. 13. Reprinted with permission of the United Nations from *Report on the World Social Situation*, United Nations, Geneva, 1989, p. 13

most of their income for family expenditure, while men retain part of their income for their own use.

Another point of concern is the small proportion of women in professional and managerial jobs. Table 14.4 shows that very few women enter politics or hold seats in parliament even in developed countries, and the proportion in management is even fewer, at 10 per cent in the developing countries. The proportion in professional and technical work seems to be higher, at approximately 37 per cent in the developing countries.

Table 14.4   Sectoral spread of women's employment

Region	Seats in parliament (% women)	Administrative and managerial (% women)	Professional and technical (% women)
All LDCs	12.7	10	36.7
Industrial economies	13.6	27.4	47.8
World	12.9	14.1	39.3

Source: Data from UNDP, 1997, p. 152. From *Human Development Report*, 1997, by United Nations Development Programme. © 1997 by the United Nations Development Programme. Used by permission of Oxford University Press.

While the employment of women in paid work might be expected to improve their social and political situation, the rate of change is very slow, as we have seen above. In fact, the situation often worsens to begin with, because women now have to work harder to keep their jobs and homes functional. Momsen (1991), in her study, showed that while men in Sri Lanka worked for 426 hours per month in peak seasons, and 350 hours per month in the slack season, women were working for 560 and 530 hours per month in each of these seasons respectively. Additionally, while men spent 294 hours and 370 hours per month in sleep/leisure activities, women spent only 160 and 190 hours per month in such activities in each season. While the situation may be expected to improve, the change is very slow.

Conclusion

Employment reflects people's involvement in the economy as well as their opportunity to benefit from its performance. In general, fast-growing economies provide more employment, *ceteris paribus*, than slow-growing ones. However, even increasing employment levels cannot keep pace with fast-growing populations in most developing countries (chapter 11). The result is underemployment and a vast army of workers employed in the informal sector. This sector is both a highly dynamic one as well as one which is simply a residual sector with sponge-like characteristics, providing survival opportunities but no real employment. If good 'quality' employment exists when the economy is growing fast, then equity is taken care of. In its absence, growth is not accompanied by equity, and we return to the issues discussed in chapter 3. This is why governments in the West have always been so preoccupied with the employment objective.

Conclusion

This book is about development in broad terms. While the notion of progress across a number of fronts seems clear enough, closer scrutiny reveals that there is little consensus regarding what constitutes 'progress'. There is also little agreement regarding the various 'fronts' along which such progress must take place – economic, social, political, cultural and human rights. In this book, we have abstracted from the second question, but have considered the former.

Until recently, 'progress' in Development Studies was defined in Eurocentric terms. Movement towards the European model – in economic, political or social terms – was considered to be progress. Thus, maximizing growth was important for progress, but so too were structural change towards industry, social change towards urban living, and political change towards democratization. In recent years, however, this notion of progress has attracted considerable criticism. The environmentalists have argued that maximizing growth is not desirable. In fact, from the point of view of sustainability and the future of the planet, they argue that it may actually be regressive. We discussed their arguments in chapter 6. They have also argued, along similar lines, against industrialization. While the environmentalists argue against industrialization and excessive growth the world over, the neoclassical theorists argue against industrialization particularly in developing countries. Thus, while the former argue that industrialization has adverse consequences in terms of pollution, over-consumption of natural resources, and so on, the latter argue that it is inappropriate given the resource endowments of developing countries. We discussed these issues in chapters 6 and 7.

Defining 'progress' in social and political terms has, if anything, been even more contentious. Early modernization theorists argued that development required a shift from 'tradition' to 'modernity'. This, in turn, required a change in attitudes away from emotional/sentimental thinking to rationality, away from community towards the individual, away from rural living towards urbanization. This notion of 'progress', based as it was on Western experience, was strongly criticized from the late 1970s onwards. We considered a number of these critiques in chapter 5. In response to these criticisms, there have been attempts to consider development 'from below', to see what progress means for individuals living in developing countries, rather than imposing a notion of progress on them. Such attempts have been advocated by the participatory rural development school, as well as by gender theorists.

These attempts to shift the concept of development away from one based purely on the experience of the Western nations have been successful in highlighting the problems associated with such progress. In spite of this, however, this book leads us to conclude that many of these changes are required for development. Development requires an increase in average incomes, but, more importantly, it requires a decrease in poverty. This implies that equity must accompany growth. Development also requires structural change, which in most cases requires industrialization if it is to be successful. But if this industrialization is to be sustainable, then it must be environmentally 'friendly'. These changes on the economic front will imply changes on the social front – increasing rural–urban migration and urbanization. Since these are, to a large extent, inevitable, development requires that they be regulated in such a way that the worst consequences of such change (see chapter 11) are avoided. In addition to providing people with economic freedom, development must increase their political rights too. In spite of some controversy regarding the imposition of Western-style democracies on countries that have never been democratic, some increase in people's rights to be represented and heard, as well as to make decisions, must accompany development. Of course, this also requires change at the grass-roots level (participation in rural development, industrial democracy, and so on).

The second aspect that we have considered throughout the book is whether anything can be done by countries that wish to develop. We have considered the possible factors that contribute to development in some detail. We have, for instance, looked at whether industrialization leads to growth, whether population growth encourages or hinders development, and whether improvements in education and health enhance prospects for development, and so on. What emerges from our analysis is that all of these factors (and many more) certainly contribute to growth and development. Yet there are other known (and unknown) factors that also play a part in development. Equally, each of these factors, in its turn, is influenced by many other factors. Thus, industrialization depends upon the natural resource base of a country, investment levels, managerial and labour skills, government policy and international economic and commercial conditions, and so on. The interlinkages between each of these factors are complicated and impossible to separate. They lead us to conclude that the causes of development are hard to separate from its consequences. Thus, as we noted in the Introduction, industrialization leads to growth, and growth leads to industrialization; education leads to development (or is part of it), but development also helps improve educational levels and so on.

In such a situation, what can be done to achieve development? It is clear that some government input is necessary. While the debate regarding state intervention in an economy has been put forward in binary terms – *dirigisme* versus *laissez-faire* – with neither extreme being plausible, experience has shown that the most successful countries in developmental terms have been the ones in which state intervention has been clear, strong and strategic. Thus, improvements in human welfare (health and education) in Sri Lanka and Costa Rica relate to government intervention in these countries. Equally, the strong economic performance of both South Korea and China relates to a strategic and determined role played by state policy. Of course, state intervention is not always successful. One has only to look at countries in Africa and some parts of Euro-Asia for this to become clear. It is the quality of state intervention, rather than state intervention *per se*, that is significant. Equally significant in the twenty-first century is the possibility that globalization has reduced the power of the state, so that governments can no longer help (or hinder) their countries' development. In this context, developing countries will increasingly reap the consequences of international economic conditions.

Thus, while the role of the state constitutes one axis of the development strategy, international links constitute the other. Once again, the traditional literature has dichotomized the options available into inward- and outward-looking policies. But our analysis in this book indicates that the most successful economies have used both, usually sequentially. In most cases, some early protection has been followed by greater openness and a search for export markets (see chapter 10).

This book does not have an explicit regional focus. However, from time to time, we have highlighted successes and failures on different fronts. Thus, for instance, the South Korean (and East Asian) success on the economic front is referred to throughout the book. What also emerges from our analysis is the different development experience of different parts of the world. In fact, with the relative position of Africa worsening over the last two decades (Toye, 1993) and many countries in Asia having improved their position to the extent that they can now graduate into the ranks of the developed countries, it is becoming increasingly hard to talk of the Third World as a single entity and of it having common problems. Of the thirty-one least developed countries (LLDCs), two-thirds are in Africa. The increasing polarization within the Third World is reducing the possibility of these countries speaking with one voice.

Thus, as we saw in chapter 12, Africa was bypassed by the Green Revolution. Food availability has fallen in a number of African countries, and so has calorie intake. This is unprecedented in most other parts of the world. Figures are superfluous in this context. A passing knowledge of the number of famines hitting the continent is sufficient evidence. Of course, famines are not caused merely by food availability. They are also influenced by entitlements (chapter 12), which in many developing countries are socially and politically determined. This brings us back to the failure of the political system to ensure these entitlements in Africa.

We also noted the worsening health situation in Africa. The spread of AIDS has reduced life expectancy in many countries, which is unprecedented given the improvements in death rate, both historically and across the rest of the developing world. We saw that this has pushed a number of African countries down in the HDI rankings (see chapter 13). A look at the 2001 Human Development Index indicates that of the thirty-six low HDI countries, twenty-nine are in Africa.

The challenges facing Africa are immense and clearly worrying. While we have not dealt with them in detail in this book, they have nevertheless emerged as significant from our analysis. Both poor state policies and poor international links must take their share of the blame for this. Undoubtedly, domestic conditions have been difficult, and a number of proximate factors have caused both the famines and AIDS. But they have not been helped by the international community, as we saw in our analysis of the debt crisis and of agricultural performance in Africa. More important, however, is the failure of the state in Africa. If East Asia was helped by a strong state, Africa has been let down by its states. Political instability and repression have been rife on the African continent. *Coups d'état* have been common in a number of countries, including Ghana, Nigeria, Mauritania, Burkina Faso, Uganda and Sudan. Even where governments were democratically elected initially, they have succeeded in stifling opposition parties and setting up one-party systems – Tanzania under Nyerere, Uganda under Obote, Zimbabwe under Mugabe, and so on. In addition to this, many countries have experienced civil war and inter-ethnic strife – Somalia, Rwanda-Burundi, Eritrea-Ethiopia. Thus, Africa has been unfortunate in that, in facing problems that are much more extreme or challenging than those elsewhere in the world, it has had governments that have been distracted by political and military exigencies. Attempts to indicate solutions to such complex problems are naïve, but it is clearly imperative that both states and the international community prioritize the problems facing the African continent.

Notes

Chapter 1   Growth and Development

1 The exact form of this quotation is from Ray, 1998, p. 47.
2 For a more detailed and comprehensive analysis of the evolution of development thinking, see Oman and Wignaraja, 1994.
3 GNP = GDP + net national income from abroad. Net national income (NNI) from abroad is the income earned by nationals of the country from abroad (through labour and investment abroad) – income from work and investments undertaken by foreigners in the domestic economy (as this is repatriated abroad).

Chapter 2   Structural Change, Industrialization and Economic Growth

1 After a certain stage, however, the demand for manufactured products becomes saturated, and the tertiary/services sector begins to grow. This is true of many developed countries today.
2 Manufacturing can be said to experience increasing returns to scale (or economics of scale) when a proportionate increase in all inputs leads to a more than proportionate increase in output. For instance, output more than doubles when all inputs are doubled.
3 For a range of other such dependencies, see Weiss, 1990, p. 96.
4 The output produced by each extra unit of labour is the marginal product of labour (MPL). In theory, it is often assumed that each unit of labour is paid its marginal product. In reality, however, this need not be true. When the MPL is low, it is possible that the wage it would yield is below that required for subsistence.

5 Between 1960 and 1980, the proportion of output produced by the manufacturing sector in the UK decreased from 32.1 per cent to 20.7 per cent. This was
accompanied by a decrease in jobs in manufacturing to 23.6 per cent.
6 Manufacturing excludes activities like mining, gas and electricity generation,
and transport, which are included within the industrial sector.
7 The arguments in favour of, and against, a reliance purely on agriculture or
mining are delayed to chapter 7, on trade and development.
8 India's industrial performance shows both the successes and the failures of
such a strategy. On the one hand, it is a highly diversified industrial structure,
producing a vast range of products. On the other hand, it is a relatively high-
cost industrial structure in which capital under-utilization is rife.
9 It is important to note that distortions do not necessarily mean government
interventions. Agarwala (1983) notes that while some governments like South
Korea actively intervened to bring prices into line with assumed economic
values, others do not intervene even when prices move away from equilibrium.
The latter countries will show higher distortions than the former, even though
they have lower government distortions.

Chapter 3   Growth, Distribution and Equity

1 However, it has been shown that even in the UK, the poor suffer from poorer
health than the rich.
2 Though it is possible that wages will increase in agriculture too, as people
transfer out, and will decrease in industry, as more people enter.
3 Redistributive policies have been important, and the trickle-down is not
automatic as many early growth/development studies have assumed.
4 More recent studies claim that once energy requirements are taken into
account, the gender bias in consumption is eroded (Institute of Nutrition
and Food Science, Bangladesh, quoted in Sen, 1984).

Chapter 4   Theories of Growth

1 In general, the current period will have a greater weight in such a measurement
than the far distant future.
2 The capital–output ratio is the ratio between the value of capital and the value
of output, and is meant to indicate how much capital is required to produce a
unit of output, or the capital intensity of production. Of course, it is complicated by the fact that valuing and adding up different types of capital is not
easy.
3 'Exogenous' in this context implies that it is not explained within the model.
Thus, the KO ratio is taken as given and unchangeable.
4 Changes in labour quality can be included in investment in human capital, but
changes in labour quantity cannot.

5   Readers wishing to do so can skip this section without losing the thread of the argument so long as they acquaint themselves with the basic conclusion of the model.

6   If technical change is neutral, it does not change the proportions in which capital and labour are currently being used. More commonly, however, it tends to be labour-saving, like computers or automated textile looms, for example. Capital-saving technical progress is also possible (and much intermediate technology falls into this class). It is very important for most developing countries, which have insufficient capital to begin with. Such technical progress, however, is less common than labour-saving change, because most R&D takes place in countries which are capital-rich and labour-scarce.

7   Nadiri (1972) gave capital a weight related to its contribution to GNP in the country concerned.

8   The growth of output per unit of input measures productivity growth. Total Factor Productivity (TFP) is the growth of output with respect to all inputs.

Chapter 5   Development and the World

1   The major contribution of this school of thought to later development thinking is the idea of comparative advantage and trade specialization (views that influenced the import-substituting versus export-oriented industrialization debates of the 1950s and 1960s (see ch. 7). Even today these views form the foundation of neo-liberal arguments in favour of liberalization across the world.

2   Horizontal linkages are the commercial connections between firms at similar stages in the process of production. Vertical linkages connect firms at different stages in the process of production. Thus, the links between a farmer producing wheat, the miller who grinds it into flour, the baker who bakes it into bread, and the retailer who sells the bread are vertical linkages. On the other hand, the links between different farmers or between different bakers (or other food producers) would be classed as horizontal linkages.

3   This was the infant industry argument that led to the protection of firms in developing countries, through taxes and subsidies, against international competition. It led to the import-substituting industrialization (ISI) argument (see ch. 7). One of the reasons advanced for the late industrialization of Russia, for instance, was that the capitalist sector within Russia had to compete not only with the pre-capitalist sector, but also with the more efficient industries in advanced countries.

4   Except for oil and similar cartels.

Chapter 6   Beyond the Impasse: Development Theory in the 1990s

1   This section has relied quite considerably on Visvanathan et al., 1997, an excellent selection of readings on the subject.

Chapter 7   Globalization, Trade and Development

1   Robertson (1992) saw three sources of cleavage in the cultural arena: religious, legal and industrial. The religious cleavage is between fundamentalist Islam and Christianity (a cleavage that many would say is highlighted by events in the twenty-first century). The legal-diplomatic cleavage is between democracies and absolutist states (the East–West divide). The industrial cleavage is between cultures that emphasize rationality, individuality and impersonal authority and those that do not (the North–South divide).
2   Though these figures seem very high, given the nature of the exports of these countries, they may also reflect the low value of their primary product exports.
3   There are those who claim that these measures are a response to perceived protectionism in East Asia.
4   This is especially true when general tariffs or exchange-rate manipulation are used.

Chapter 8   International Financial Flows

1   While modernization theorists accepted that the net flow of funds was from developed to developing countries, dependency theorists maintained that in the long run the flow was in the opposite direction – from less developed countries to the developed ones.
2   This was in spite of the fact that countries like Mexico had already defaulted on loans.
3   The cost of debt is debt servicing and includes both the liquidation of capital and payment of interest. However, when the debt is foreign, the payments have to be in foreign exchange, and therefore require developing countries to be exporting more than they import – i.e. be making balance of payments (BOP) surpluses if they wish to pay loans back.
4   The increase in utility/happiness of the poor will offset the decrease in happiness of the rich when they forgo their excess wealth.
5   This was given theoretical focus by the work of modernization theorists, who claimed that aid would help countries to reach the level of investment required for 'take-off' (Rostow, 1960).
6   Note that this is the opposite of aid flows, which predominantly went to Africa.
7   Transfer pricing arises when two subsidiaries of a firm trade with each other. Since this involves inter-company trading, the books are adjusted to allow for this. The problem is that because the transaction does not take place on the open market, market prices are not used to value the transaction. This is especially true when pricing technology whose price is hard to determine in any case. It creates a problem, because a TNC subsidiary in a high-tax country can price technology so that it shows lower profits than a low-tax country subsidiary. In addition to country's losing tax revenue in this way, equity-holders earn smaller dividends in high-tax countries.

Chapter 9   The State, Growth and Development

1   On the other hand, in Latin America, it is often claimed that the interests of private capital dominate (Evans, 1987, p. 212).
2   In fact, defining democracy in such broad terms leads us on to the issue of 'human rights'. Attempts to measure the extent to which human rights and freedoms are exercised by people in different countries have given rise to indices like the Human Freedom Index (UNDP) and the Gastil Index (Freedom House). These indices attempt to bring together a number of different measures of such freedoms. Thus, the HFI lists forty rights and freedoms, including social and economic equality for ethnic minorities, freedom for an independent press, and freedom from capital punishment. Very few countries really observe all of the freedoms. Sweden and Denmark, which top the list, observe thirty-eight out of the forty on the list. But there are some democracies – India (14), Colombia (14), Israel (19), Spain (26) – which have very low scores. At the bottom of the list are countries like Iraq (0), Libya (1) and China (2). Overall, however, according to Sorensen, although there is considerable variation across countries, it does look as though democracies are better at respecting human rights than authoritarian systems. But a transition towards democracy may lead to a breakdown of authority, which can lead to violation of human rights.
3   Details of this categorization can be obtained from Sorensen, 1993.

Chapter 10   Development: The 'Success' Stories

1   Extensive growth occurs when population and production grow at about the same rate, hence there is little improvement in standards of living.
2   Intensive growth, on the other hand, occurs when per capita output begins to rise (Reynolds, 1983).
3   Thus, while industrialization 'first occurred in England on the basis of invention', this was followed by industrialization 'in Germany and the United States on the basis of innovation' (Amsden, 1989, p. 4).
4   The 1950s are often seen as the period of illicit wealth accumulation in South Korea (C. Edwards, 1992).
5   Chaebols are large industrial houses in South Korea, much like the zaibatsu in Japan. They are highly diversified and own enterprises in a number of industries.
6   Chinese currency.
7   In Germany, for instance, after the 1870s, most major products were regulated by price cartels and import controls, and marketing was through a single agency or marketing syndicate. In addition to tariffs, monopoly grants and cheap supplies from royal factories, the main instrument used by Germany was direct involvement by the state in key industries (Chang, 2002, p. 33). In France, the government promoted the growth of large industrial complexes shielded from competition (Kiely, 1998, p. 31). This has meant that the level of

government involvement required has increased as the gap between the early and late developers has widened.

8   This is in contrast to the anti-trust policies practised in most developed countries and in many developing countries like India.

9   In what follows, I will describe the Chinese command economy in the present tense, even though attempts have been made since 1978 to reform this system. It is therefore currently in the process of transition.

10   Where real flows imply the flow of goods and services, while monetary flows imply the flow of money to pay for these goods and services. In some instances, when prices are 'correct' and inflation is low, the flows may be expected to be the same or at least similar. However, in the centrally planned economies, prices are not representative of scarcities, and therefore the two flows are often very different.

11   This sector is usually the first to take off because it has easier technology to emulate and there is latent domestic demand for its output.

Chapter 11   Population, Migration and Urbanization

1   Furedi (1997) argues that much of the pressure to decrease population growth in less developed countries arises from 'competitive fertility', whereby each society eyes the growth of other societies with suspicion. He argues that though such competition exists, it is rarely talked about, especially in academic literature, and has become one of the 'significant silences in the literature on demography' (Furedi, 1997, p. 163).

2   In economic terms, the argument can be illustrated by this simple example. If an economy has 5 hectares of land, each requiring one person to cultivate it optimally, then an increase in labour from four to five people will increase the output of the land. However, increasing labour beyond five to six, seven or even eight workers will decrease output per unit of land because the workers now begin to get in each other's way and do not have sufficient land to work on.

3   Note that both the very old and the very young are dependants. While an increasing birth rate might decrease savings because it increases the number of young dependants, a lower birth rate may also do the same, because the ageing of the population increases the number of older dependants (as is true in many Western economies today). The former, in fact, is the more optimistic scenario, because it holds out the prospect, in the medium to long term, of an increase in incomes when these babies enter the labour force.

4   Note, of course, that according to the new growth theories (ch. 4), such investments are expected to increase the *quality* of human capital and to increase growth as well (see ch. 13).

5   At 95 per cent level of probability.

6   It has been found that female labour force participation decreases birth rates only when women work in modern, high-prestige jobs and not in traditional employment (Kabeer, 1994).

7   In Iceland, a 200-person settlement has many urban functions, whereas in southern Spain or Italy, a settlement with even 8,000–10,000 people may be

called a village. In China, a large urban settlement is one with more than 1 mn people, while a medium urban settlement is seen to have between 0.5 mn and 1 mn people.

8   Population density has increased as administrative and political conditions have become more settled. Public health measures have also helped to eradicate malaria from the Moroccan plains.

9   Some developing countries are trying to get round this by requiring their students and workers to sign bonds.

10 The extra product produced by an additional unit of labour, which does not accrue to the labour producing it. It is therefore a benefit to society.

11 The colonial city grew to serve the needs of the colonial investors who used the city for administrative and commercial purposes, exporting raw materials to Europe from here and importing manufactures. The city was also seen by them as a place where they could cut themselves off from the local culture and where they could re-create certain aspects of 'home'.

Chapter 12   Agricultural Change and Rural Development

1   Sharecroppers pay a share of their output as rent, while tenants pay a fixed rent.

2   This has again been reversed in recent years, with moves towards breaking up and/or privatizing communes in these countries.

3   However, the redistribution of assets is likely to have a longer-run impact because incomes can more easily be misused. A number of studies, for instance, have found that the male head of the household misuses redistributed income in the short run, leaving his family vulnerable in the longer run. Many land reforms therefore make the resale of redistributed land illegal.

4   The property rights school (Coase, 1960) maintains that the inability to exclude others from access to the land or even to sell it has meant that farmers are often unwilling to invest in the land. Evolutionary theorists, on the other hand, take a more dynamic perspective, and see rights as evolving spontaneously towards economically efficient forms. The main idea of these theorists is that new institutions evolve whenever changes of factor endowments and/or technical change create disequilibrium between marginal returns and marginal costs of factor inputs (Platteau, 1991).

5   Thus, the dwarf wheat varieties exported to India in 1965 produced 4,450 kg/ha under experimental conditions, while the indigenous Indian varieties produced only 3,200 kg/ha. Significantly, however, under non-experimental conditions, the yields were only 1,200 kg/ha (Dixon, 1990).

6   Later varieties (often bred in the countries themselves) attempted to overcome these problems.

7   The terms of trade for primary agricultural products refer to the price of primary agricultural products relative to the prices of industrial products or to some other prices. This implies that primary agricultural product prices are decreasing relative to other prices.

8   Landlords are able and willing to lend them money, since they interact with these tenants in other markets (land and labour) and can therefore enforce repayment of these loans (see ch. 14).

9   There is a large literature on whether governments should stabilize prices or incomes or whether they should leave this to the private sector (Newbery and Stiglitz, 1981).

Chapter 13   Human Capital and Human Welfare: Health and Education

1   Some claim that it is because deaths have decreased the number of people that currently have the disease, while there is no change in the number of new infections. Others claim that it has been brought about by greater use of condoms and better treatment of other sexually transmitted diseases.

Chapter 14   Labour Markets and Employment

1   Monitoring may be difficult because labour is dispersed spatially or because the output accruing from effort is not apparent until the crop is harvested at the end of the season.
2   However, tenants will also gain from such innovations, and as their incomes increase, they will borrow less for consumption, and therefore interest incomes will decrease. Depending on the magnitudes of each of his sources of income, the landlord's total income may actually decrease, and he may therefore refuse to adopt the new technology (Bhaduri, 1973).
3   In Peru, for instance, the acquisition of a licence to operate a street kiosk takes 43 days and costs five times the minimum monthly wage (ILO, 1995, p. 93).
4   Thus, although the decrease in employment in the formal sector in the cotton textile industry in India has eroded the membership of the monopoly trade union in the sector, this union does not consider recruiting the growing number of informal sector workers into the ranks of its members, as feasible. Organizing these workers has therefore been left to a non-governmental organization called SEWA (Howell and Kambhampati, 1999).
5   The youngest daughter, rather than eldest son, is responsible for looking after her parents in their old age. She therefore also inherits their house.

Bibliography

Agarwal, B. 1983: Diffusion of Rural Innovations: Some Analytical Issues and the Case of Woodburning Stoves. *World Development*, 11 (4), 359–76.

Agarwal, B. 1989: Rural Women, Poverty and Natural Resources: Sustenance, Sustainability and Struggle for Change. *Economic and Political Weekly*, 24 (3), WS 46–65.

Agarwal, B. 1991: *Cold Hearths and Barren Slopes – The Woodfuel Crisis in the Third World*. London: Zed Books.

Agarwal, B. 1997: The Gender and Environment Debate: Lessons from India. In Visvanathan et al., 1997b, pp. 68–75.

Agarwala, R. 1983: *Price Distortions and Growth in Developing Countries*. World Bank Staff Working Paper, no. 575. Washington, DC: World Bank.

Agnihotri, S., Palmer-Jones, R. and Parikh, A. 1998: Missing Women in Indian Districts. Mimeo.

Ahluwalia, M. S. 1974: Income Inequality: Some Dimensions of the Problem. In H. B. Chenery et al. (eds), *Redistribution with Growth*, Oxford: Oxford University Press, pp. 3–37.

Ahluwalia, M. S. 1976: Inequality, Poverty and Development. *Journal of Development Economics*, 3 (4), 307–42.

Ahluwalia, M. S. and Chenery, H. B. 1974: The Economic Framework. In H. B. Chenery et al. (eds), *Redistribution with Growth*, Oxford: Oxford University Press, pp. 38–51.

Ahluwalia, M. S., Carter, N. G. and Chenery, H. B. 1979: Growth and Poverty in Developing Countries. *Journal of Development Economics*, 6 (3), 299–341.

Ahluwalia, M. S., Carter, N. G. and Chenery, H. B. 1979: *Growth and Poverty in Developing Countries*. Washington, DC: World Bank.

Alesina, A. and Perotti, R. 1996: Income Distribution, Political Instability, and Investment. *European Economic Review*, 40, 1203–19.

Alesina, A. and Rodrik, D. 1994: Distributive Politics and Economic Growth. *Quarterly Journal of Economics*, 108, 465–90.

Allen, T. and Thomas, A. (eds) 1992: *Poverty and Development in the 1990s*. Oxford: Oxford University Press and Milton Keynes: Open University Press.

Allen, T. and Thomas, A. (eds) 2001: *Poverty and Development into the 21st Century*. Oxford: Oxford University Press and Milton Keynes: Open University Press.

Amin, S. 1976: *Unequal Development*. New York: Monthly Review Press.

Amsden, A. 1989: *Asia's New Giant: South Korea and Late Industrialisation*. New York: Oxford University Press.

Anderson, J. H. 1998: *The Size, Origins and Character of Mongolia's Informal Sector*. World Bank Working Paper, no. 1916. Washington, DC: World Bank.

Appleton, S. 1996: How does Female Education Affect Fertility? *Oxford Bulletin of Economics and Statistics*, 58 (1), 139–66.

Apter, D. E. 1965: *The Politics of Modernization*. Chicago: University of Chicago Press.

Apter, D. E. 1987: *Re-thinking Development: Modernization, Dependency and Post-modern Politics*. Beverly Hills, CA: Sage Publications.

Arhin, K. 1979: *West African Traders in Ghana in the Nineteenth and Twentieth Centuries*. London: Longman.

Armstrong, R. W. and Fellmann, J. D. 1998: Health: One World or Two? In Gonzalez and Norwine, 1998, pp. 75–92.

Armstrong, W. 1987: Imperial Incubus: The Diminished Industrial Ambitions of Canada, Australia and Argentina (1870–1930). Conference paper quoted in Griffin, 1989.

Aslund, A. 1995: *How Russia Became a Market Economy*. Washington, DC: The Brookings Institution.

Bagchi, A. K. 1987: Industrialization. In J. Eatwell, M. Milgate and P. Newman (eds), *The New Palgrave*, Basingstoke: Macmillan Press Ltd, pp. 797–803.

Bagchi, A. K. (ed.) 1995: *Democracy and Development*. London: Macmillan.

Bairoch, P. 1973: *Urban Unemployment in Developing Countries: The Nature of the Problem and Proposals for its Solution*. Geneva: ILO.

Balassa, B. 1978: Exports and Economic Growth. *Journal of Development Economics*, 5 (2), 181–9.

Balasubramaniam, V. N. 1998: Globalisation. Mimeo, University of Lancaster.

Banerjee, A. V., Gertler, P. and Ghatak, M. 1998: Empowerment and Efficiency: The Economics of Agrarian Reform. Mimeo, Department of Economics, MIT.

Banerjee, A. V. n.d.: Land Reforms: Prospects and Strategies. MIT mimeo, World Bank website (*www.worldbank.org/research/abcde/washington_11/pdfs/banerjee. pdf*).

Baran, P. 1957: *The Political Economy of Growth*. New York: Monthly Review Press.

Barbera, S. 1995: Comment on 'On the Relationship between Economic Development and Political Democracy'. In Bagchi, 1995, pp. 56–7.

Barbier, E. B. 1987: The Concept of Sustainable Economic Development. *Environmental Conservation*, 14, 101–10.

Bardhan, P. K. 1980: Interlocking Factor Markets and Agrarian Development: A Review of the Issues. *Oxford Economic Papers*, 32 (1), 82–98.

Bardhan, P. K. 1984a: *Land, Labour and Rural Poverty*. Delhi: Columbia University Press and Oxford University Press.

Bardhan, P. K. 1984b: *The Political Economy of Development in India*. Oxford: Blackwell.

Bardhan, P. K. 1988: Alternative Approaches to Development Economics. In H. Chenery and T. N. Srinivasan (eds), *Handbook of Development Economics*, vol. 1, Amsterdam: North Holland, pp. 40–71.

Barnett, A. and Whiteside A. 1999: HIV/AIDS: Case Studies and a Conceptual Framework. *European Journal of Development Research*, 11 (2), 220–34.

Barro, R. J. 1991: Economic Growth in a Cross-section of Countries. *Quarterly Journal of Economics*, 106 (2), 407–43.

Barro, R. J. 1996: Democracy and Growth. *Journal of Economic Growth*, 1 (1), 1–27.

Barro, R. J. 1997: *Determinants of Economic Growth: A Cross-Country Empirical Study*, Lionel Robbins Lectures. Cambridge, MA: MIT Press.

Barro, R. J. 1999: Determinants of Democracy. *Journal of Political Economy*, 107 (6), S158–S183.

Barro, R. J. and Lee, J.-W. 1993: International Comparisons of Educational Attainment. *Journal of Monetary Economics*, 32 (3), 363–94.

Barro, R. J. and Sala-i-Martin, X. 1995: *Economic Growth*. New York: McGraw-Hill.

Basu, K. 1983: The Emergence of Isolation and Interlinkage in Rural Markets. *Oxford Economic Papers*, 35 (2), 262–80.

Bates, R. 1988: Markets and States in Tropical Africa. In R. Bates (ed.), *Toward a Political Economy of Development*, Berkeley: University of California Press, ch. 10.

Bauer, P. 1991: *The Development Frontier: Essays in Applied Economics*, Hemel Hempstead: Harvester Wheatsheaf, pp. 38–49.

Bauer, P. T. and Yamey, B. S. 1957: *The Economics of Underdeveloped Countries*. Cambridge: Cambridge University Press.

Baumol, W. J. 1986a: *Microtheory: Applications and Origins*. Brighton: Wheatsheaf.

Baumol, W. J. 1986b: Productivity Growth, Convergence and Welfare: What the Long Run Data Show. *American Economic Review*, 76, 1072–85.

Becker, G. S. 1964: *Human Capital*. New York: Columbia University Press.

Beckerman, W. 1974: *In Defence of Economic Growth*. London: Jonathan Cape.

Beckerman, W. 1992: Economic Growth and the Environment: Whose Growth? Whose Environment? *World Development*, 20 (4), 481–96.

Bello, W. 1992: Export-Led Development in East Asia: A Flawed Model. *Trocaire Development Review*, 11–27; reprinted in R. Ayres (ed.), *Development Studies*, Dartford, Kent: Greenwich University Press, 1995, pp. 342–54.

Beneria, L. and Sen, G. 1997: Accumulation, Reproduction and Women's Role in Economic Development: Boscrup Revisited. In Visvanathan et al., 1997b, pp. 42–50.

Benhabib, J. and Spiegel, M. 1994: The Role of Human Capital in Economic Development: Evidence from Aggregate Cross-Country Data. *Journal of Monetary Economics*, 34 (2), 143–74.

BEQB 1991: The LDC Debt Crisis. *Bank of England Quarterly Bulletin*, 31 (4), 498.

Berg, A. 1994: The Logistics of Privatization in Poland. In Froot Blanchard and J. D. Sachs (eds), *The Transition in Eastern Europe*, vol. 2, Chicago: University of Chicago Press, pp. 165–86.

Berg-Schlosser, D. 1984: African Political Systems: Typology and Performance. *Comparative Political Studies*, 17 (1), 121–51.

Bernstein, H. 1971: Modernisation Theory and the Sociological Study of Development. *Journal of Development Studies*, 7 (2), 141–60.

Bernstein, H., Crow, B. and Johnson, H. 1992: *Rural Livelihoods: Crises and Responses*. Oxford: Oxford University Press and Milton Keynes: Open University Press.

Bhaduri, A. 1973: Agricultural Backwardness under Semi-feudalism. *Economic Journal*, 83 (329), 120–37.

Bhagwati, J. 1988a: Export-Promoting Trade Strategy: Issues and Evidence. *World Bank Research Observer*, 3 (1), 27–57.

Bhagwati, J. 1988b: *Protectionism*. Cambridge, MA: MIT Press.

Bhagwati, J. 1995: Democracy and Development: New Thinking on an Old Question. *Indian Economic Review*, 30 (1), 1–18.

Binswanger, H. P. 1978: *The Economics of Tractors in South Asia: An Analytical Review*. New York and Hyderabad: Agricultural Development Council and ICRISAT.

Birdsall, N. 1977: Analytical Approaches to the Relationship of Population Growth and Development. *Population and Development Review*, 3 (1 and 2).

Black, J. 1991: *Development Theory and Practice: Bridging the Gap*. Boulder, CO: Westview.

Blaney, B. L. and Pasha, M. K. 1993: Civil Society and Democracy in the Third World: Ambiguities and Historical Possibilities. *Studies in Comparative International Development*, 28 (1), 3–24.

Blecher, M. 1986: China: Politics, Economics and Society, Boulder, CO: Lynne Rienner Publishers.

Bock, G. and James, S. (eds) 1992: *Beyond Equality and Difference – Citizenship, Feminist Politics and Female Subjectivity*. London: Routledge.

Boone, P. 1996: Politics and the Effectiveness of Foreign Aid. *European Economic Review*, 40, 289–329.

Booth, D. 1985: Marxism and Development Sociology: Interpreting the Impasse. *World Development*, 13 (7), 761–87.

Booth, D. 1991: Timing and Sequencing in Agricultural Reform – Tanzania. *Development Policy Review*, 9 (4), 353–80.

Booth, D. (ed.) 1994: *Rethinking Social Development*. London: Longman.

Bornstein, M. 1997: Non-Standard Methods in the Privatisation Strategies of the Czech Republic, Hungary and Poland. *Economics of Transition*, 5 (2), 323–8.

Boserup, E. 1965: *The Conditions of Economic Growth*. London: Allen and Unwin.

Boserup, E. 1970: *Women's Role in Economic Development*. New York: St Martin's Press.

Boserup, E. 1981: *Population and Technological Change: A Study of Long-Run Trends*. Chicago: University of Chicago Press.

Brada, J. C. 1996: Privatization is Transition – Or is It? *Journal of Economic Perspectives*, 10 (2), 67–86.

Braidotti, R., Charkiewicz, E., Hausler, S. and Weiringa, S. 1997: Women, Environment and Sustainable Development. In Visvanathan et al., 1997b, pp. 54–61.

Brandt, W. 1980: *North–South: A Programme for Survival*. London: Pan.

Brandt, W. 1983: *Common Crisis: North–South Co-operation for World Recovery*. London: Pan.

Breman, J. C. 1976: A Dualistic Labour System?: A Critique of the Informal Sector Concept. *Economic and Political Weekly*, 11 (48), 1870–5, (49), 1905–8, (50), 1939–44.

Breman, J. C. 1980: *The Informal Sector in Research: Theory and Practice*, Rotterdam: Comparative Asian Studies Programme: Erasmus University.

Brohman, J. 1996: *Popular Development: Rethinking the Theory and Practice of Development*. Oxford: Blackwell.

Burnell, P. 1997: *Foreign Aid in a Changing World*. Buckingham: Open University Press.

Burnside, C. and Dollar, D. 1997: *Aid, Policies and Growth*. Policy Research Working Paper, 1777. Washington, DC: World Bank Development Research Group.

Byres, T. J. 1981: The New Technology, Class Formation and Class Action in the Indian Countryside. *Journal of Peasant Studies*, 8 (4), 405–54.

Cammack, P. 1997: *Capitalism and Democracy in the Third World*. London: Leicester University Press.

Cammack, P., Pool, D. and Tordoff, W. 1993: *Third World Politics*. Baltimore: Johns Hopkins University Press.

Cardoso, F. H. and Faletto, E. 1979: *Dependency and Development in Latin America*. Berkeley: University of California Press.

Carney, J. and Watts, M. 1990: Manufacturing Dissent: Work, Gender and the Politics of Meaning in a Peasant Society. *Africa*, 60 (2), 207–47. Repr. in S. Corbridge (ed.), *Development Studies: A Reader*, London: Edward Arnold.

Caselli, F., Esquivel, G. and Lefort, F. 1996: Reopening the Convergence Debate: A New Look at Cross-Country Growth Empirics. *Journal of Economic Growth*, 1 (3), 363–89.

Cassen, R. and associates 1994: *Does Aid Work?* Oxford: Clarendon Press.

Chakravarty, S. 1979: On the Question of the Home Market and Prospects for Indian Growth. *Economic and Political Weekly*, special number.

Chakravarty, S. 1987: *Development Planning: The Indian Experience*. Oxford: Clarendon Press.

Chambers, R. 1983: *Rural Development: Putting the Last First*. Harlow: Longman.

Chambers, R. 1985: *The Crisis of Africa's Poor: Perceptions and Priorities*. Brighton: Institute of Development Studies, University of Sussex.

Chang, H.-J. 1993: The Political Economy of Industrial Policy in Korea. *Cambridge Journal of Economics*, 17 (2), 131–57.

Chang, H.-J. 1994: *The Political Economy of Industrial Policy*. London and Basingstoke: Macmillan.

Chang, H.-J. 2000: The Hazard of Moral Hazard. *World Development*, 28 (4), 775–88.

Chang, H.-J. 2002: *Kicking Away the Ladder: Development Strategies in Historical Perspective*. London: Anthem Press.

Chang, H.-J. and Nolan, P. (eds) 1995: *The Transformation of the Communist Economies: Against the Mainstream*. London: Macmillan.

Chang, H.-J., Park, H. J. and Yoo, C. G. 1998: Interpreting the Korean Crisis: Financial Liberalisation, Industrial Policy and Corporate Governance. *Cambridge Journal of Economics*, 22 (6), 735–46.

Chapman, G. P. and Baker, K. M. (eds) 1992: *The Changing Geography of Africa and the Middle East*. London: Routledge.

Chatterjee, S. and Ravikumar, B. 1997: *Minimum Consumption Requirements: Theoretical and Quantitative Implications for Growth and Distribution*. Working Paper, Economic Research Division, Federal Reserve Bank Philadelphia 97–15, Philadelphia.

Cheema, G. Shabbin 1998: Equity within Diversity: State Reform and Renewed Citizenship in Asia. Paper presented at International Seminar on Social and State Reform, 26–9 March 1998, São Paulo, Brazil.

Chenery, H. B. (and Elkington, H.) 1979: *Structural Change and Development Policy*, Oxford: Oxford University Press.

Chenery, H. B. and Syrquin, M. 1975: *Patterns of Development, 1950–1970*. New York: Oxford University Press.

Chenery, H. B. and Taylor, L. J. 1968: Development Patterns: Among Countries and Over Time. *Review of Economics and Statistics*, 50, 391–416.

China People's Daily, 17 May 2001.

Chowdhury, A. and Islam, I. 1993: *The Newly Industrialising Economies of East Asia*. London: Routledge.

Clague, C. and Rausser, G. 1992: *The Emergence of a Market Economy in Eastern Europe*, pt 4. Cambridge, MA: Blackwell.

Clapham, C. 1992: *Third World Politics: An Introduction*. London: Routledge.

Clark, C. 1967: *Population Growth and Land Use*. London: Macmillan.

Claude, A. 1996: *Democracy and Development in Africa*. Washington, DC: Brookings Institution.

Cleaver, H. J. 1972: The Contradictions of the Green Revolution. *American Economic Review*, 62 (1–2), 177–86.

Cline, W. R. 1982: Can the East-Asian Model of Development be Generalised? *World Development*, 10 (2), 81–90.

Cline, W. R. 1994: *International Debt Re-examined*. London: Longman.

Coale, A. J. 1993: *Mortality Schedules in China Derived from Data in the 1982 and 1990 Censuses*. Working Paper No. 93-7, Office of Population Research. Princeton: Princeton University.

Coale, A. J. and Hoover, E. M. 1958: *Population Growth and Economic Development in Low Income Countries: A Case Study of India's Prospects*. Princeton: Princeton University Press.

Coase, R. 1960: The Problem of Social Cost. *Journal of Law and Economics*, 3 (1), 1–44.

Colclough, C., Rose, P. and Tembon, M. 1998: *Gender Inequalities in Primary Schooling: The Roles of Poverty and Adverse Cultural Practice. IDS Working Paper 78*, Brighton: Institute of Development Studies University of Sussex.

Conway, G. R. and Barbier, E. B. 1988: After the Green Revolution: Sustainable and Equitable Agricultural Development. *Futures*, 20 (6), 651–71.

Coombs, R. H. and Ahmed, M. 1974: *Attacking Rural Poverty: How Non-Formal Education Can Help*. Baltimore: Johns Hopkins University Press.

Corbridge, S. 1994: Post-Marxism and Post-Colonialism: The Needs and Rights of Distant Strangers. In Booth, 1994, pp. 90–117.

Cowen, M. P. and Shenton, R. W. 1996: *Doctrines of Development*. London: Routledge.

Crafts, N. F. R. 1985: *British Economic Growth during the Industrial Revolution.* Oxford: Clarendon Press.

Crafts, N. F. R. 1998: Forging Ahead and Falling Behind: The Rise and Relative Decline of the First Industrial Nation. *Journal of Economic Perspectives*, 12 (?), 193–210.

Crocker, D. A. 1991: Towards Development Ethics. *World Development*, 19 (5), 457–83.

Crow, B., Thorpe, M. et al. 1988: *Survival and Change in the Third World.* Cambridge: Polity.

Damachi, U. G. 1974: *The Role of Trade Unions in the Development Process.* London: Routledge.

Dasgupta, P. and Maler, K.-G. 1991: The Environment and Emerging Development Issues. *Proceedings of the World Bank Annual Conference on Development Economics*, 1990, Washington, DC: World Bank, 101–31.

Deane, P. 1979: *The First Industrial Revolution.* Cambridge: Cambridge University Press.

Deane, P. and Cole, W. A. 1962: *British Economic Growth, 1688–1959.* Cambridge: Cambridge University Press.

de Mello, L. R. jr. 1997: Foreign Direct Investment in Developing Countries and Growth: A Selective Survey. *Journal of Development Studies*, 34 (1), 1–34.

Deyo, F. C. (ed.) 1987: *The Political Economy of the New Asian Industrialism.* Ithaca, NY: Cornell University Press.

Dick, W. 1974: Authoritarian vs Non-Authoritarian Approaches to Economic Development. *Journal of Political Economy*, 82 (4), 817–27.

Dixon, C. 1990: *Rural Development in the Third World.* London: Routledge.

Dobb, M. 1955: A Note on the So-Called Degree of Capital Intensity of Investment in Underdeveloped Countries. In *On Economic Theory and Socialism*, London: Routledge, pp. 138–54.

Domar, E. D. 1946: Capital Expansion, Rate of Growth and Employment. *Econometrica*, 14, 137–47.

Domar, E. D. 1947: Expansion and Employment. *American Economic Review*, 37, 34–55.

Domar, F. D. 1957: *Essays in the Theory of Economic Growth.* New York: Oxford University Press.

Donaldson, P. 1986: *Worlds Apart: The Economic Gulf between Nations.* Harmondsworth: Penguin.

Donnelly, J. 1989: 'Repression and Development: The Political Contingency of Human Rights Trade-Offs'. In D. P. Forsythe (ed.), 1989, *Human Rights and Development: International Views*, London: Macmillan, pp. 305–28.

Dore, R. 1976: *The Diploma Disease.* London: Allen and Unwin.

Dore, R. 1980: The Diploma Disease Revisited. *IDS Bulletin*, 2 (2), 55–61.

Dornbusch, R., Fischer, S. and Startz, R. 1998: *Macroeconomics*, 7th edn, Boston: Irwin McGraw-Hill.

dos Santos, T. 1970: The Structure of Dependence in Latin America. *American Economic Review*, 60 (2), 231–6.

Dove, L. 1981: The Political Context of Education in Bangladesh, 1971–1980. In P. Broadfoot et al. (eds), *Political and Educational Change*, London: Croom Helm, pp. 165–82.

Drewnowski, J. and Scott, W. 1966: *The Level of Living Index*. United Nations Research in Social Development, report no. 4. Geneva: UNRISD.

Dreze, J. and Mukherjee, A. 1987: *Labour Contracts in Rural India – Theories and Evidence*. STICERD Discussion Paper.

Dreze, J. and Sen, A. 1989: *Hunger and Public Action*. Oxford: Clarendon Press.

Dunleavy, P. and O'Leary, B. 1987: *Theories of the State: The Politics of Liberal Democracy*. London: Macmillan.

Easterlin, R. A. 1967: The Effects of Population Growth on the Economic Development of Developing Countries. *Annals of the American Academy of Political and Social Science*, 369, 98–108.

Ebanks, G. Edward and Cheng, C. 1990: China: A Unique Urbanization Model. *Asia-Pacific Population Journal*, 5 (3), 29–50.

Eckersley, R. 1992: *Environmentalism and Political Theory: Towards an Ecocentric Approach*. London: UCL Press.

Eckstein, A. 1977: *China's Economic Revolution*. Cambridge: Cambridge University Press.

The Economist 1976: 21 January.

Edwards, C. 1992: Industrialization in South Korea. In Hewitt, Johnson and Wield, 1992, pp. 97–127.

Edwards, E. O. 1974: *Employment in Developing Nations: Report of a Ford Foundation Study*. New York and London: Columbia University Press.

Edwards, M. 1989: The Irrelevance of Development Studies. *Third World Quarterly*, 11 (1), 116–36.

Edwards, M. 1993: How Relevant is Development Studies? In Schuurman, F., 1993 (ed.), *Development Research: From Impasse to a New Agenda*, Zed Books: London.

Elliott, J. 1994: *An Introduction to Sustainable Development*. London: Routledge.

Ellman, M. 1989: *Socialist Planning*, 2nd edn. Cambridge: Cambridge University Press.

Emmanuel, A. 1972: *Unequal Exchange*. New York and London: Monthly Review Press.

Enke, S. 1966: The Economic Aspects of Slowing Population Growth. *Economic Journal*, 76 (301), 44–56.

Enke, S. 1971: The Economic Consequences of Rapid Population Growth. *Economic Journal*, 81 (324), 800–11.

Eswaran, M. and Kotwal, A. 1985: A Theory of Contractual Structure in Agriculture. *American Economic Review*, 75, 352–67.

European Foundation 1995: *Public Welfare Services and Social Exclusion: The Development of Consumer Oriented Initiatives in the European Union*. Dublin: European Foundation for the Improvement of Living and Working Conditions.

Evans, P. 1987: Class, State and Dependence in East Asia: Lessons for Latin Americanists. In Deyo, 1987, pp. 203–36.

Falcon, W. P. 1970: The Green Revolution: Generations of Problems. *American Journal of Agricultural Economics*, 52, 698–710.

Farmer, B. H. 1986: Perspectives in the 'Green Revolution' in South Asia. *Modern Asian Studies*, 20 (1), 125–99.

Feder, G. 1983: On Exports and Economic Growth. *Journal of Development Economics*, 12 (1–2), 59–73.

Feder, G., Just, R. E. and Zilberman, D. 1985: Adoption of Agricultural Innovations in Developing Countries: A Survey. *Economic Development and Cultural Change*, 33 (2), 255–98.

Fei, J. and Ranis, G. 1961: A Theory of Economic Development. *American Economic Review*, 4, 533–65.

Fei, J. and Ranis, G. 1964: *Development of the Labour Surplus Economy: Theory and Policy*. Homewood, IL: Irwin.

Fei, J., Ranis, G. and Kuo, S. W. Y. 1979: *Growth with Equity: The Taiwan Case*. New York: Oxford University Press.

Feng, Y. 1996: Democracy and Growth: The Sub-Saharan African Case, 1960–92. *Review of Black Political Economy*, 25 (1), 95–126.

Fielden, K. 1969: The Rise and Fall of Free Trade. In C. Bartlett (ed.), *Britain Pre-Eminent: Studies in British World Influence in the 19th Century*, London: Macmillan, pp. 76–100.

Fields, G. S. 1980: *Poverty, Inequality and Development*. Cambridge: Cambridge University Press.

Fields, G. S. 1991: Growth and Income Distribution. In G. Psacharopoulos (ed.), *Essays on Poverty, Equity and Growth*, Oxford: Pergamon.

Fishlow, A. 1972: Brazilian Size Distribution of Income. *American Economic Review*, 62, 391–402.

Forsyth, D. and Solomon, R. 1977: Choice of Technology and Nationality of Ownership in a Developing Country, *Oxford Economic Papers*, 29 (2), 258–82.

Forsythe, D. P. (ed.) 1989: *Human Rights and Development: International Views*. London: Macmillan.

Forsythe, D. P. 1997: The United Nations, Human Rights and Development. *Human Rights Quarterly*, 19, 334–49.

Foster Cater, A. 1976: From Rostow to Gunder Frank: Conflicting Paradigms in the Analysis of Underdevelopment. *World Development*, 4 (3), 167–80.

Frank, A. G. 1966: The Development of Underdevelopment. *Monthly Review*, 18 (4), 17–31.

Frank, A. G. 1969: *Capitalism and Underdevelopment in Latin America: Historical Studies of Chile and Brazil*. New York: Monthly Review Press.

Frank, A. G. 1984: *Critique and Anti-Critique*. London: Macmillan.

Frobel, F., Heinrichs, J. and Kreye, O. 1980: *The New International Division of Labour*. Cambridge: Cambridge University Press.

Furedi, F. 1997: *Population and Development: A Critical Introduction*. Cambridge: Polity.

Furtado, C. 1964: *Development and Underdevelopment* (English trans). Berkeley: University of California Press.

Gadgil, M. and Guha, R. 1994: Ecological Conflicts and the Environmental Movement in India. *Development and Change*, 25, 101–36.

Gaiha, R. 1995: Does Agricultural Growth Matter in Poverty Alleviation? *Development and Change*, 26 (2), 285–304.

Galenson, W. 1992: *Labour and Economic Growth in Five Asian Countries – South Korea, Malaysia, Taiwan, Thailand and the Philippines*. New York: Praeger.

Garlick, P. C. 1971: *African Traders and Economic Development in Ghana* Oxford: Clarendon Press.

Gauthier, A. H. 1993: Towards Renewed Fears of Population and Family Decline? *European Journal of Population*, 9, 143–67.

George, S. 1993: Uses and Abuses of African Debt. In A. Adedeji (ed.), *Africa within the World: Beyond Dispossession and Dependency*, London: Zed Books/ ADCESS, pp. 59–72.

Gerschenkron, A. 1966: *Economic Backwardness in Historical Perspective: A Book of Essays*. Cambridge, MA: Harvard University Press.

Gerschenkron, A. 1970: *Europe in the Russian Mirror: Four Lectures in Economic History*. Cambridge: Cambridge University Press.

Gertler, P. 1995: On the Road to Social Insurance: Lessons from High-Performing Asian Economies. Paper presented at the International Conference on Financing Human Resource Development in Advanced Asian Countries. Manila: Asian Development Bank.

Gerxhani, K. 1999: *Informal Sector in Developed and Less Developed Countries: A Literature Survey*. Tinbergen Institute Working Paper, 99-083/2, Tinbergen, Netherlands.

Ghai, D. and Vivian, J. (eds) 1992: *Grassroots Environmental Action*. London: Routledge.

Ghosh, P. K. (ed.) 1984: *Multinational Corporations and Third World Development*. London: Greenwood Press.

Ghosh, S. and Pal, S. 1999: *A Theoretical and Empirical Investigation into Regional Growth and Inequality: A Case Study of India*. Cardiff Business School Working Paper no. 99-023.

Gibson, H. and Tsakalotos, E. 1992: The International Debt Crisis: Causes, Consequences and Solutions. In Hewitt, Johnson and Wield, 1992, pp. 41–65.

Giddens, A. 1990: *The Consequences of Modernity*. Cambridge: Polity.

Gillis, M., Perkins, D. H., Radelet, S., Romer, M. and Snodgrass, D. R. 2001: *Economics of Development*, 5th edn. London: W. W. Norton & Company.

Glaeser, B. 1988: A Holistic Human Ecology Approach to Sustainable Agricultural Development. *Futures*, 20 (6), 671–8.

Glewwe, P. and van der Gaag, J. 1990: Identifying the Poor in Developing Countries: Do Different Definitions Matter? *World Development*, 18 (6), 803–14.

Goldsworthy, D. 1988: Thinking Politically about Development. *Development and Change*, 19, 505–30.

Gonzalez, A. and Norwine, J. (eds) 1998: *The New Third World*. Oxford: Westview Press.

Gordimer, N. 1971: *A Guest of Honour*. London: Jonathan Cape.

Goswami, O. 1996: Legal and Institutional Impediments to Corporate Growth. In Oman, 1996, pp. 113–55.

Gottman, J. 1983: Third World Cities in Perspective. *Area*, 15 (4), 311–13.

Griffin, K. B. 1989: *Alternative Strategies for Economic Development*. Basingstoke: Macmillan.

Griffin, K. B. and Enos, J. C. 1970: Foreign Assistance: Objectives and Consequences. *Economic Development and Cultural Change*, 18 (3), 29–58.

Griffin, K. B. and Gurley, J. 1985: Radical Analyses of Imperialism, the Third World and the Transition to Socialism: A Survey Article. *Journal of Economic Literature*, 23 (3), 1089–143.

Grossman, G. M. and Helpman, E. 1991: *Innovation and Growth in the Global Economy*. Cambridge, MA: MIT Press.

Guimares, R. P. 1992: Development Pattern and Environment in Brazil. *CEPAL Review*, 47, 47–62.

Hadenius, A. 1992: *Democracy and Development*. Cambridge: Cambridge University Press.

Haggard, S. 1990: *Pathways from the Periphery: The Politics of Growth in the Newly Industrialising Countries*. Ithaca, NY: Cornell University Press.

Handa, S. 1996: Maternal Education and Child Attainment in Jamaica. *Oxford Bulletin of Economics and Statistics*, 58 (1), 119–37.

Hansen, H. and Tarp, F. 1999: Aid Effectiveness Disputed. Mimeo, Development Economics Research Group, University of Copenhagen.

Harbison, F. and Myers, C. (eds) 1965: *Manpower and Education*. New York: McGraw-Hill.

Harcourt, W. (ed.) 1994: *Feminist Perspectives on Sustainable Development*. London: Zed Books.

Harris, J. and Todaro, M. 1970: Migration, Unemployment and Development: A Two-Sector Analysis. *American Economic Review*, 40, 126–42.

Harrison, P. 1979: *Inside the Third World*. Harmondsworth: Penguin.

Harrison, P. 1993: *The Third Revolution: Population, Environment and a Sustainable World*. Harmondsworth: Penguin.

Harrod, R. F. 1939: An Essay in Dynamic Theory. *Economic Journal*, 49, 14–33.

Hart, K. 1973: Informal Income Opportunities and Urban Employment in Ghana. *Journal of Modern African Studies*, 11 (1), 61–89.

Haynes, J. 1996: *Third World Politics*. Oxford: Blackwell.

Hayter, T. 1971a: *Aid as Imperialism*. London: Penguin.

Hayter, T. 1971b: Aid: Concepts and State of the Discussion. Republished in R. Ayres, 1995, *Development Studies*, Dartford, Kent: Greenwich University Press, pp. 364–9.

Heckman, J. and Klenow, P. 1997: Human Capital Policy. Mimeo, University of Chicago.

Held, D., McGrew, A., Goldblatt, D. and Perraton, J. 1999: *Global Transformation: Politics, Economics and Culture*. Cambridge: Polity.

Helleiner, G. K. 1975: The Role of Multinational Corporations in the Less Developed Countries' Trade in Technology. *World Development*, 3 (4), 161–89.

Helliwell, J. F. 1994: Empirical Linkages between Democracy and Economic Growth. *British Journal of Political Science*, 24 (2), 225–48.

Helliwell, J. F. 1998: *How Much do National Borders Matter?* Washington, DC: Brookings Institution.

Henley, J. S. 1989: African Employment Relationships and the Future of Trade Unions. *British Journal of Industrial Relations*, 27 (3), 295–309.

Henriques, I. and Sadorsky, P. 1996: Export-Led Growth or Growth-Led Exports? The Canadian Case. *Canadian Journal of Economics*, 29 (3), 540–55.

Hettne, B. 1990: *Development Theory and the Three Worlds*. Harlow: Longman.

Hettne, B. 1995: *Development Theory and the Three Worlds*, 2nd edn. Harlow: Longman.

Hewitt, T., Johnson, H. and Wield, D. (eds) 1992: *Industrialization and Development*. Oxford: Oxford University Press and Milton Keynes: Open University Press.

Heywood, A. 1994: *Political Ideas and Concepts*. London: Macmillan.

Hicks, N. L. 1979: Growth vs Basic Needs: Is there a Trade-off? *World Development*, 7, 985–94.

Hicks, N. L. and Streeten, P. 1979: Indicators of Development: The Search for a Basic Needs Yardstick. *World Development*, 7, 567–80.

Hill, H. 1998: An Overview of the Issues. *ASEAN Economic Bulletin*, 15 (3), 261–71.

Hill, P. 1970: *Studies in Rural Capitalism in West Africa*. Cambridge: Cambridge University Press.

Hirschman, A. O. 1958: *The Strategy of Economic Development*. New Haven: Yale University Press.

Hirschman, A. O. 1981: The Rise and Decline of Development Economics. In *Essays in Trespassing: Economics to Politics and Beyond*, Cambridge: Cambridge University Press, pp. 1–24.

Hirschman, A. O. and Rothschild, M. 1973: The Changing Tolerance for Income Inequality in the Course of Economic Development; With a Mathematical Appendix. *Quarterly Journal of Economics*, 87, 544–66.

Holmstrom, M. (ed.) 1990: *Work for Wages in South Asia*. Delhi: Manohar.

Hoogvelt, A. 1990: Extended Review: Rethinking Development Theory. *Sociological Review*, 38, 352–61.

Hoogvelt, A. 1997: *Globalisation and the Postcolonial World*. London: Macmillan.

hooks, b. 1984: *Feminist Theory from Margin to Center*. Boston, MA: South End Press.

hooks, b. and Watkins, G. 1991: *Sisterhood: Political Solidarity between Women*. London: Routledge.

Horowitz, I. L. 1972: *Three Worlds of Development*, 2nd edn. New York: Oxford University Press.

Hoselitz, B. F. 1962: *Sociological Aspects of Economic Growth*. New York: Free Press.

Hoselitz, B. F. 1966: *The Progress of Underdeveloped Areas*. Chicago: University of Chicago Press.

Howell, J. and Kambhampati, U. S. 1999: Liberalisation and Labour: The Fate of Retrenched Workers in the Cotton Textile Industry in India. *Oxford Development Studies* 27 (1), 109–28.

Hughes, H. and Waelbroeck, J. 1981: Can Developing Country Exports Keep Growing in the 1980s? *World Economy*, 4, 127–47.

Huntington, S. P. 1968: *Political Order in Changing Societies*. New Haven: Yale University Press.

ILO 1970: *Towards Full Employment: A Programme for Colombia*. Geneva: ILO.

ILO 1973: *Employment in Africa: Some Critical Issues*. Geneva: ILO.

ILO 1973: *Strategies for Employment Promotion*. Geneva: ILO.

ILO 1974: *Employment, Incomes and Equality: A Strategy for Increasing Productive Employment in Kenya*. Geneva: ILO.

ILO 1976a: *Employment Growth and Basic Needs: A One-World Problem*. Report of the Director-General of the International Labour Office, Tripartite World Conference on Employment, Income Distribution and Social Progress and the International Division of Labour. Geneva: ILO.

ILO 1976b: *Meeting Basic Needs: Strategies for Eradicating Mass Poverty and Unemployment*. Geneva: ILO.

ILO 1995: *World Employment Report*. Geneva: ILO.

International Statistics Yearbooks 1985: Korea, New York Science, Industry and Business Library website.
International Statistics Yearbooks 1990: Korea, New York Science, Industry and Business Library website.
International Statistics Yearbooks 1997: Korea, New York Science, Industry and Business Library website.
Jabri, V. and O'Gorman, E. (eds) 1999: *Women, Culture and International Relations*. London: Lynne Reinner.
Jenkins, R. 1983: *Transnational Corporations and their Impact on the Mexican Economy*. London: Macmillan.
Jenkins, R. 1984: *Transnational Corporations and Industrial Transformation in Latin America*. London: Macmillan.
Jenkins, R. 1986: *Transnational Corporations and the Latin American Automobile Industry*. London: Macmillan.
Jenkins, R. 1987: *Transnational Corporations and Uneven Development*. London: Methuen.
Jenkins, R. 1991a: The Political Economy of Industrialisation: A Comparison of Latin American and East Asian Newly Industrialising Countries. *Development and Change*, 22, 197–231.
Jenkins, R. 1991b: *Transnational Corporations and Uneven Development: The Internationalisation of Capital and the Third World*. London: Routledge.
Jenkins, R. O. 1992a: Industrialization and the Global Economy. In Hewitt, Johnson and Wield, 1992, pp. 13–40.
Jenkins, R. O. 1992b: Learning from the Gang – Are there Lessons for Latin America from East Asia? *Bulletin of Latin American Research*, 10 (1), 1–37.
Jenkins, R. O. 1992c: Re-interpreting Brazil and South Korea. In Hewitt, Johnson and Wield, 1992, pp. 167–200.
Jessop, B. 1999: Globalization and the Nation State. In S. Aaronowitz and P. Bratsis (eds), *Rethinking the State: Miliband, Poulantzos, and State Theory*. Minneapolis: University of Minnesota Press. *http://www.comp.lancaster.ac.uk/sociology/soc012rj.html*.
Jessop, B. 2003: Bringing the State Back In (Yet Again): Reviews, Revisions, Rejections and Redirections. Department of Sociology, Lancaster University. *http://www.comp.lancs.ac.uk/sociology/soc070rj.html*.
Jiggins, J. 1994: *Changing the Boundaries: Women-Centred Perspectives on Population and the Environment*. Washington, DC: Island Press.
Joffe, G. 1992: The Changing Geography of North Africa: Development, Migration and the Demographic Time Bomb. In Chapman and Baker, 1992, pp. 139–64.
Johnson, C. 1985: Political Institutions and Economic Performance: The Government–Business Relationship in Japan, South Korea and Taiwan. In R. Scalapino, S. Sato and J. Wanandi (eds), *Asian Economic Development – Present and Future*, Berkeley: Institute of East Asian Studies, University of California Press, pp. 63–89.
Jones, H. 1990: *Population Geography*, 2nd edn. London: Chapman.
Jorgenson, D. W. 1961: The Development of a Dual Economy. *Economic Journal*, 71 (282), 309–34.
Jorgenson, D. W. 1967: Surplus Agricultural Labour and the Development of a Dual Economy. *Oxford Economic Papers*, 19 (3), 288–312.

Joshi, H. 1980: The Informal Urban Economy and its Boundaries. *Economic and Political Weekly*, March, 638–44.

Joshi, H. and Joshi, V. 1976: *Surplus Labour and the City: A Study of Bombay*. Delhi: Oxford University Press.

Kabeer, N. 1994: *Reversed Realities: Gender Hierarchies in Development Thought*. London: Verso.

Kaldor, N. 1967: *Strategic Factors in Economic Development*. Ithaca, NY: Cornell University Press.

Kambhampati, U. S. 1999: *High-Technology Service Exports from India*. Report to the Department for International Development, London.

Kambhampati, U. S. 2002: The Software Industry and Development: The Case of India. *Progress in Development Studies*, 2 (1), 23–45.

Kambhampati, U. S. and Pal, S. 2000: *Access to Schooling in Rural India: Role of Gender, Household Income and Parental Bargaining*. Cardiff Business School Working Paper, 00:043, Cardiff: Cardiff Business School.

Kambhampati, U. S. and Pal, S. 2001: Role of Parental Literacy in Explaining Gender Difference: Evidence from Child Schooling in India. *European Journal of Development Research*, 13 (2), 97–119.

Kandiyoti, D. 1997: Bargaining with Patriarchy. In Visvanathan et al., 1997b, pp. 86–92.

Kannappan, S. 1985: Urban Employment and the Labour Market in Developing Nations. *Economic Development and Cultural Change*, 33 (4), 699–730.

Karshenas, M. 1994: Environment, Technology and Employment: Towards a New Definition of Sustainable Development. *Development and Change*, 24, 723–56.

Kearney, R. 1990: Mauritius and the NIC Model Redux, or How Many Cases Make a Model? *Journal of Developing Areas*, 24, 195–216.

Keller, B. and Mbewe, D. 1991: Policy and Planning for the Empowerment of Zambia's Women Farmers. *Canadian Journal of Development Studies*, 12, 75–88.

Kelley, A. C. 1988: Economic Consequences of Population Change in the Third World. *Journal of Economic Literature*, 26, 1688–1709.

Kellner, D. n.d.: Globalisation and the post-Modern Turn. *http://www.gseis.ucla.edu/courses/ed253a/dk/GLOBPM.html*.

Kiely, R. 1998: *Industrialization and Development*. London: UCL Press.

Kindleberger, C. P. 1958a: *Economic Development*. New York: McGraw-Hill Book Co.

Kindleberger, C. P. 1958b: *International Economics*. Homewood, IL: Irwin.

King, D. Y. 1981: Regime Type and Performance: Authoritarian Rule, Semi-Capitalist Development and Rural Inequality in Asia. *Comparative Political Studies*, 13 (4), 477–504.

Kingdon, G. 1996: The Quality and Efficiency of Private and Public Education: A Case Study of Urban India. *Oxford Bulletin of Economics and Statistics*, 58 (1), 57–82.

Kingdon, G. G. 1998: Does the Labour Market Explain Lower Female Schooling in India? *Journal of Development Studies*, 35 (1), 39–65.

Kitching, G. 1990: *Development and Underdevelopment in Historical Perspective*. London: Routledge.

Kohli, A. 1980: Democracy, Economic Growth and Inequality in India's Development. *World Politics*, 32 (4), 623–38.

Kohli, A. 1986: Democracy and Development. In J. P. Lewis and V. Kallab (eds), *Development Strategies Reconsidered*, New Brunswick, NJ: Transaction Books, pp. 153–82.

Kohli, A. 1994: Where do High Growth Political Economies Come From? The Japanese Lineage of Korea's 'Development State'? *World Development*, 22 (9), 1269–93.

Kozul-Wright, R. and Rowthorn, R. 1998: Spoilt for Choice? Multinational Corporations and the Geography of International Production. *Oxford Review of Economic Policy*, 14 (2), 74–92.

Krueger, A. and Lindahl, M. 2000: *Education for Growth: Why and for Whom?* NBER Working Paper 7591.

Krueger, A. O. 1986: Aid in the Development Process. *World Bank Research Observer*, 1 (1), 57–78.

Krugman, P. 1998: What Happened to Asia? Mimeo.

Kunst, R. M. and Marin, D. 1989: Notes: On Exports and Productivity: A Causal Analysis. *Review of Economics and Statistics*, 71, 699–703.

Kuznets, S. 1955: Economic Growth and Income Inequality. *American Economic Review*, 45, 1–28.

Kuznets, S. 1965: *Economic Growth and Structure*. London: Heinemann.

Kuznets, S. 1966: *Modern Economic Growth: Rate, Structure and Spread*. New Haven: Yale University Press.

Kuznets, S. 1973: Modern Economic Growth: Findings and Reflections. *American Economic Review*, 63, 247–58.

Kyriacou, G. 1991: *Level and Growth Effects of Human Capital*. Working Paper, C. V. Starr Center, New York University.

Laclau, E. 1971: Feudalism and Capitalism in Latin America. *New Left Review*, 67 (May/June).

Ladejinsky, W. I. 1977: *Agrarian Reform as Unfinished Business: The Selected Papers of Wolf Ladejinsky*. New York: Oxford University Press (for the World Bank).

Lal, D. 1983: *The Poverty of Development Economics*. London: Hobart.

Lall, S. 1975: Is Dependence a Useful Concept in Analysing Underdevelopment? *World Development*, 3 (11), 799–810.

Lall, S. (ed.) 1993: *Transnational Corporations and Economic Development*. London: Routledge.

Lall, S. 1996: *Learning from the Asian Tigers: Studies in Technology and Industrial Policy*. Basingstoke: Macmillan.

Lall, S. 1999: India's Manufactured Exports: Comparative Structure and Prospects. *World Development*, 27 (10), 1769–86.

Lanjouw, J. O. and Lanjouw, P. 1995: *Rural Non-Farm Employment: A Survey*. World Bank Working Paper no. 1463.

Lappe, F. and Collins, J. 1977: *Food First*. Boston: Houghton Mifflin.

Larrain, J. 1989: *Theories of Development: Capitalism, Colonialism and Dependency*. Cambridge: Polity.

Larson, D. A. and Wilford, W. T. 1979: The Physical Quality of Life Index: A Useful Social Indicator? *World Development*, 7 (6), 581–4.

Lavigne, M. 1995: *The Economics of Transition: From Socialist Economy to Market Economy*. Basingstoke: Macmillan.

Leeson, P. F. and Minogue, M. M. (eds) 1988: *Perspectives on Development: Cross-Disciplinary Themes in Development Studies*. Manchester: Manchester University Press.

Leftwich, A. (ed.) 1990: *New Developments in Political Science*. Aldershot: Edward Elgar.

Leftwich, A. 1993: Governance, Democracy and Development in the Third World. *Third World Quarterly*, 14 (3), 605–24.

Leftwich, A. 1995: Bringing Politics Back In: Towards a model of a Developmental State. *Journal of Development Studies*, 31 (3), 400–27.

Lehmann, D. 1990: *Democracy and Development in Latin America: Economics, Politics and Religion in the Postwar Period*. Cambridge: Polity.

Lele, U. and Agarwal, M. 1991: Four Decades of Economic Development in India and the Role of External Assistance. In Lele and Nabi, 1991, pp. 17–42.

Lele, U. and Nabi, I. 1991a: Aid, Capital Flows and Development: A Synthesis. In Lele and Nabi, 1991b, pp. 399–413 repr. in R. Ayres (ed.), *Development Studies*, Dartford, Kent: Greenwich University Press, 1995.

Lele, U. and Nabi, I. (eds) 1991b: *Transitions in Development: The Role of Aid and Commercial Flows*. International Centre for Economic Growth.

Lemarchand, R. 1992: Uncivil States and Civil Societies: How Illusion Became Reality. *Journal of Modern African Studies*, 30 (2), 177–91.

Lenin, V. I. 1899: *The Development of Capitalism in Russia*, 4th edn. Moscow: Foreign Languages Publishing House, 1961.

Lenin, V. I. 1982: *Imperialism: The Highest Stage of Capitalism*. Moscow: Progress Publishers.

Lerner, D. 1964: *The Passing of the Traditional Society*. New York: Free Press.

Lewis, W. A. 1954: Economic Development with Unlimited Supplies of Labour. *Manchester School of Economics and Social Studies*, 22 (May), 139–91.

Lewis, W. A. 1955: *The Theory of Economic Growth*. London: Allen and Unwin.

Lewis, W. A. 1966: *Development Planning*. London: Allen and Unwin.

Lewis, W. A. 1978: *Growth and Fluctuations, 1870–1913*. London: Allen & Unwin.

Lewis, W. A. 1980: The Slowing Down of the Engine of Growth. *American Economic Review*, 70 (4), 555–64.

Lewis, W. A. 1984: The State of Development Theory. *American Economic Review*, 74 (1), 1–10.

Leys, C. 1996: *The Rise and Fall of Development Theory*. London: James Currey.

Lin, J. Y. 1992: Rural Reforms and Agricultural Growth in China. *American Economic Review*, 82, 34–51.

Lipietz, A. 1982: Towards Global Fordism: Marx or Rostow? *New Left Review*, 132, 33–47.

Lipietz, A. 1987: *Mirages and Miracles: The Crisis of Global Fordism*. London: New Left Books.

Lipset, S. M. 1960: *Political Man*. New York: Anchor Books.

Lipton, M. 1968: Urban Bias and Rural Planning. In P. Streeten and M. Lipton (eds), *The Crisis of Indian Planning: Economic Planning in the 1960s*, Oxford: Oxford University Press, pp. 83–148.

Lipton, M. 1977: *Why Poor People Stay Poor: Urban Bias in World Development*. Cambridge, MA: Harvard University Press.

Lipton, M. 1980: Migration from Rural Areas of Poor Countries: The Impact on Rural Production and Income Distribution. *World Development*, 8, 1–24.

Lipton, M. 1999: *Reviving Global Poverty Reduction: What Role for Genetically Modified Plants?* Sir John Crawford Memorial Lecture. Washington, DC: CGIAR Secretariat.

List, F. 1885/1996: *The National System of Political Economy*. New York: A. M. Kelley.

Lofchie, M. F. 1986: Africa's Agricultural Crisis: An Overview. In M. F. Lofchie et al. (eds), *Africa's Agrarian Crisis: The Roots of Famines*, Boulder, CO: Lynne Rienner Publishers Inc., 3–18.

Lucas, R. E. 1988: On the Mechanics of Economic Development. *Journal of Monetary Economics*, 22, 3–43.

Luxemburg, R. 1951: *The Accumulation of Capital*, tr. into English by A. F. Schwarzschild. London: Routledge and Kegan Paul.

Lyotard, J. F. 1984: *The Postmodern Condition*, tr. into English by Geoff Bennington and Brian Massumi. Minneapolis: University of Minnesota Press.

Machlup, F. 1970: *Education and Economic Growth*. Lincoln, NE: University of Nebraska Press.

Maddison, A. 1970: *Economic Progress and Policy in Developing Countries*. London: Allen & Unwin.

Maddison, A. 1982: *Phases of Capitalist Development*. Oxford: Oxford University Press.

Maddison, A. 1995: *Monitoring the World Economy: 1820–1992*. Paris: OECD.

Mahalanobis, P. C. 1953: Some Observations on the Process of Growth in National Income. *Sankhya*, 12, pt 4 (Sept.), 307–12.

Mahalanobis, P. C. 1955: The Approach of Operational Research to Planning in India. *Sankhya*, 16, pts 1 and 2 (Dec.).

Malthus, T. R. 1798: *An Essay on the Principle of Population*. Harmondsworth: Penguin, 1976.

Mankiw, N. G. 1997: Comment. In B. Bernanke and J. Rotemberg (eds), *NBER Macroeconomics Annual*, Cambridge, MA: MIT Press, pp. 103–6.

Marchand, M. and Parpart, J. L. 1995: *Feminism/PostModernism/Development*. London: Routledge.

Marin, D. 1992: Is the Export-Led Growth Hypothesis Valid for Industrialized Countries? *Review of Economics and Statistics*, 74 (4), 678–88.

Marsh, R. 1979: Does Democracy Hinder Economic Development in Latecomer Developing Nations? *Comparative Social Research*, 2, 215–48.

Marx, K. 1859: *Grundrisse: Foundations of the Critique of Political Economy*.

Marx, K. 1867: *Capital*, 1st English edn, Moscow: Progress Publishers, tr. Samuel Moore and Edward Aveling, 1887.

Marx, K. and Engels, F. 1840: *The Manifesto of the Communist Party*. Peking: Foreign Language Press. Ch. 1 in *http://csf.colorado.edu/psn/marx/Archive/1848-cm*.

Mathias, P. 1983: *The First Industrial Nation*. London: Methuen and Co. Ltd.

Mazumdar, D. 1976: The Urban Informal Sector. *World Development*, 4, 655–79.

Mazumdar, D. 1987: Rural–Urban Migration in Developing Countries. In E. Mills (ed.), *Handbook of Regional and Urban Economics*, vol. 2, Amsterdam: North Holland, pp. 1097–128.

McClelland, D. 1961: *The Achieving Society*. New York: van Nostrand.

McGee, T. G. 1971: *The Urbanisation Process in the Third World: Explorations in Search of a Theory*. London: Bell.

McGranahan, D. V., Richaud-Proust, C., Sovani, N. V. and Subramanian, M. 1972: *Contents and Measurement of Socio-Economic Development*, UNRISD, New York: Praeger.

McGrew, A. 2000: Sustainable Globalization? The Global Politics of Development and Exclusion in the New World Order. In Allen and Thomas, 2000, pp. 345–64.

Meadows, D. H. 1972: The Limits to Growth: A Report for the Club of Rome's Project on the Predicament of Mankind. London: Earth Island Ltd.

Meier, G. M. (ed.) 1989: *Leading Issues in Economic Development*. New York: Oxford University Press.

Meier, G. M. (ed.) 1991: *Politics and Policy Making in Developing Countries: Perspectives on the New Political Economy*. San Francisco: ICS Press.

Meier, G. M. and Rauch, J. E. 2000: *Leading Issues in Economic Development*, 7th edn. New York: Oxford University Press.

Michaely, M. 1977: Exports and Growth: An Empirical Investigation. *Journal of Development Economics*, 4 (1), 49–53.

Mies, M. 1982: *The Lace Makers of Narsapur: Indian Housewives Produce for the World Market*. London: Zed Books.

Mies, M. 1986: *Patriarchy and Accumulation on a World Scale: Women in the International Division of Labour*. London: Zed Books.

Mies, M. and Shiva, V. 1990: *Ecofeminism*. London: Zed Books.

Migdal, J. 1988: *Strong Societies and Weak States: State–Society Relations and Capabilities in the Third World*. Princeton: Princeton University Press.

Minier, J. A. 1998: Democracy and Growth: Alternative Approaches. *Journal of Economic Growth*, 3 (2), 241–66.

Mohanty, C. T. 1991: *Under Western Eyes – Feminist Scholarship and Colonial Discourse*. Bloomington: Indiana University Press.

Mohanty, C. T. 1997: Under Western Eyes: Feminist Scholarship and Colonial Discourses. In Visvanathan et al., 1997b, pp. 79–86.

Momsen, J. H. 1991: *Women and Development in the Third World*. London: Routledge.

Moore, M. 1995: Democracy and Development in Cross-National Perspective: A New Look at the Statistics. *Democratization*, 2 (2), 1–19.

Moraga, C. and Anzaldua, G. (eds) 1983: *This Bridge Called my Back*, 2nd edn. Latham: Kitchen Table, Women of Color Press.

Morawetz, D. 1977: *Twenty-Five Years of Economic Development, 1950–75*. Washington, DC: World Bank.

Morris, M. D. and Liser, F. B. 1977: The PQLI: Measuring Progress in Meeting Human Needs. Overseas Development Council, *Communiqué on Development Issues*, no. 32.

Moser, C. O. 1978: Informal Sector or Petty Commodity Production: Dualism or Dependence in Urban Development. *World Development* 6 (9/10), 1041–64.

Moser, C. O. N. 1993: *Gender Planning and Development*. New York: Routledge.

Mosley, P. 1987: *Overseas Aid: Its Defence and Reform*. Brighton: Wheatsheaf Books.

Mosley, P., Harrigan, J. and Toye, J. 1991: *Aid and Power: The World Bank and Policy Based Lending*, 2 vols. London: Routledge.

Mosley, P., Hudson, J. and Horrell, S. 1992: Aid, the Public Sector and the Market in Less Developed Countries: A Return to the Scene of the Crime. *Journal of International Development*, 4 (2), 139–50.

Mosse, J. C. 1993: *Half the World, Half a Chance: An Introduction to Gender and Development*. Oxford: Oxfam.

Mundle, S. 1998: Financing Human Development: Some Lessons from Advanced Asian Countries. *World Development*, 26 (4), 659–72.

Myrdal, G. 1968: *Asian Drama: An Inquiry into the Poverty of Nations*. Harmondsworth: Penguin.

Myrdal, G. 1970: *The Challenge of World Poverty: A World Anti-Poverty Program in Outline*. New York: Pantheon Books.

Nadiri, M. 1972: International Studies of Factor Inputs and Total Factor Productivity: A Brief Survey. *Review of Income and Wealth*, 18 (2), 129–54.

Nafziger, E. W. 1990: *The Economics of Developing Countries*. Englewood Cliffs, NJ: Prentice-Hall.

Nafziger, E. W. 1993: *The Debt Crisis in Africa*. Baltimore: Johns Hopkins University Press.

Narula, R. 1996: *Multinational Investment and Economic Structure: Globalisation and Competitiveness*. London: Routledge.

Nash, M. 1984: *Unfinished Agenda: The Dynamics of Modernisation in Developing Nations*. Boulder, CO: Westview.

Naughton, B. 1995: *Growing out of the Plan*. Cambridge: Cambridge University Press.

Nehru, B. K. 1979: Western Democracy and the Third World. *Third World Quarterly*, 1 (2), 53–70.

Nettl, J. P. 1967: *Political Mobilisation: A Sociological Analysis of Methods and Concepts*. London: Faber.

Newbery, D. and Stiglitz, J. 1981: *Theory of Commodity Price Stabilisation*. Oxford: Oxford University Press.

Nisbet, R. A. 1969: *Social Change and History: Aspects of the Western Theory of Development*. New York: Oxford University Press.

Nolan, P. 1990: China's Economic Reforms. In J. Eatwell, M. Milgate and P. Newman (eds), *The New Palgrave: Problems of the Planned Economy*, London: W. W. Norton and Co., 22–37.

Nolan, P. 1995: *China's Rise, Russia's Fall: Politics, Economics and Planning in the Transition from Stalinism*. Basingstoke: Macmillan.

Norgaard, R. B. 1988: Sustainable Development: A Co-evolutionary View. *Futures*, 20 (6), 606–20.

North, D. 1990: *Institutions, Institutional Change and Economic Performance*, Cambridge: Cambridge University Press.

Nugent, J. B. and Yotopoulos, P. A. 1979: What has Orthodox Development Economics Learned from Recent Experience? *World Development*, 7, 541–54.

Nurkse, R. 1953: Problems of Capital Formation in Underdeveloped Countries. In Meier, 1989, pp. 13–15.

Nurkse, R. 1961: *Patterns of Trade and Development*. Stockholm: Almqvist Och Wicksell.

Nussbaum, M. C. and Glover, J. 1995: *Women, Culture and Development: A Study of Human Capabilities*. Oxford: Clarendon Press.

O'Brien, P. 1975: A Critique of Latin American Theories of Dependency. In I. Oxaal et al. (eds), *Beyond the Sociology of Development*, London: Routledge, pp. 7–27.

O'Connor, A. 1992: The Changing Geography of Eastern Africa. In Chapman and Baker, 1992, pp. 114–38.

O'Manique, J. 1992: Human Rights and Development. *Human Rights Quarterly*, 14, 78–103.

Olson, M. 1993: Dictatorship, Democracy and Development. *American Political Science Review*, 87 (3), 567–76.

Oman, C. (ed.) 1996: *Policy Reform in India*. New Delhi: Oxford and IBH Publishing Co. Pvt. Ltd.

Oman, C. and Wignaraja, G. 1991: *The Post-War Evolution of Development Thinking*. London: St Martin's Press.

Ostergaard, L. 1992: *Gender and Development: A Practical Guide*. London: Routledge.

Ostry, S. 1998: *Globalization and the Nation State: Erosion from Above*. Timlin Lecture, University of Saskatchewan.

Pack, H. 1974: The Employment-Output Trade-off in LDCs – A Microeconomic Approach. *Oxford Economic Papers*, 26 (3), 388–404.

Pack, H. and Westphal, L. W. 1986: Industrial Strategy and Technological Change: Theory vs Reality. *Journal of Development Economics*, 22, 87–128.

Palma, G. 1978a: Dependency: A Formal Theory of Underdevelopment or a Methodology for the Analysis of Concrete Situations of Underdevelopment? *World Development*, 6, 881–924.

Palma, G. 1978b: Underdevelopment and Marxism: From Marx to the Theories of Imperialism and Dependency. *Thames Papers in Political Economy*.

Parente, S. L. and Prescott, E. C. 1993: Changes in the Wealth of Nations. *Federal Reserve Bank of Minneapolis Quarterly Review*, 17, 3–16.

Parish, W. L. and Willis, R. J. 1993: Daughters, Education and Family Budgets. *Journal of Human Resources*, 28 (4), 863–98.

Parker, M. and Wilson, G. 2000: Diseases of Poverty. In Allen and Thomas, 2000, pp. 75–98.

Parsons, T. 1951: *The Social System*. London: Routledge.

Partridge, M. D. 1997: Is Inequality Harmful for Growth?: A Comment. *American Economic Review*, 87 (5), 1019–33.

Pearce, D. W. and Turner, R. K. 1990: *The Economics of Natural Resources and the Environment*. Hemel Hempstead: Harvester Wheatsheaf.

Pearson, R. 1992: Gender Matters in Development. In Allen and Thomas, 2000, pp. 383–402.

Peet, R. and Watts, M. (eds) 1993: Development Theory and Environment in an Age of Market Triumphalism. *Economic Geography*, 69 (3), 227–53.

Perkins, D. H. 1988: Reforming China's Economic System. *Journal of Economic Literature*, 26 (2), 601–45.

Piore, M. J. and Sabel, C. F. 1984: *The Second Industrial Divide: Possibilities for Prosperity*. New York: Basic Books.

Platteau, J. P. 1991: *Formalization and Privatization of Land Rights in Sub-Saharan Africa: A Critique of Current Orthodoxies and Structural Adjustment Programmes*. STICERD Discussion Paper, DEP/34, London: STICERD.

Pohl, G. et al. 1997: *Privatisation and Restructuring in Central and Eastern Europe: Evidence and Policy Options*. Washington, DC: World Bank.

Pomfret, R. 1997: *Development Economics*. London: Prentice-Hall.
Pool, J. and Stamos, S. 1985: The Uneasy Calm: Third World Debt—The Case of Mexico. *Monthly Review*, 36, 7–19.
Portes, A., Castells, M. and Benton, L. A. (eds) 1989: *The Informal Economy: Studies in Advanced and Less Developed Countries*. Baltimore: Johns Hopkins University Press.
Poulantzos, N. 1975: *Classes in Contemporary Capitalism*. London: New Books.
Poulantzos, N. 1978: *State, Power, Socialism*. London: Verso.
Prebisch, R. 1959: Commercial Policies in Underdeveloped Countries. *American Economic Review (Papers and Proceedings)*, 49 (2), 251–73.
Prendergast, R. and Singer, H. W. (eds) 1991: *Development Perspectives for the 1990s*. Houndsmills: Macmillan.
Preston, D. (ed.) 1987: *Latin American Development: Geographical Perspectives*, Harlow: Longman.
Preston, D. (ed.) 1991: *Latin American Development: Geographical Perspectives*. Harlow: Longman Scientific and Technical.
Preston, P. 1982: *Theories of Development*. London: Routledge.
Preston, P. 1985: *New Trends in Development Theory: Essays in Development and Social Theory*. London: Routledge.
Preston, P. 1986: *Making Sense of Development*. London: Routledge.
Proudhon, P. J. 1994: *What is Property?*, ed. and tr. B. G. Smith and D. R. Kelley, Cambridge: Cambridge University Press.
Przeworski, A. and Limongi, F. 1995: Political Regimes and Economic Growth. In Bagchi, 1995, pp. 3–24.
Psacharopoulos, G. 1981: Returns to Education: An Updated International Comparison. *Comparative Education*, 17 (3), 321–41.
Psacharopoulos, G. 1985: Returns to Education: A Further International Update and Implications. *Journal of Human Resources*, 20 (4), 583–97.
Psacharapolous, G. 1994: Returns to Investment in Education: A Global Update. *World Development*, 22 (9), 1325–43.
Psacharopoulos, G. and Woodhall, M. 1985: *Education for Development: An Analysis of Investment Choices*. New York: Oxford University Press.
Pye, L. W. 1965: The Concept of Political Development. *Annals of the American Academy of Political and Social Science*, 358 (March), 1–13.
Pye, L. W. and Verba, S. (ed.) 1965: *Political Culture and Political Development*. Princeton: Princeton University Press.
Ranis, G. and Schultz, T. P. (eds) 1988: *The State of Development Economics: Progress and Perspectives*. Oxford: Blackwell.
Rao, C. H. H. 1975: *Technological Change and Distribution of Gains in Indian Agriculture*. Delhi: Macmillan.
Ravallion, M. 1995: Growth and Poverty: Evidence for Developing Countries in the 1980s. *Economics Letters*, 48 (3–4), 411–18.
Rawls, J. 1972: *A Theory of Justice*. Oxford: Clarendon Press.
Ray, D. 1998: *Development Economics*. Princeton: Princeton University Press.
Redclift, M. 1988: Sustainable Development and the Market. *Futures*, 20 (6), 635–50.
Reich, R. B. 1991: *The Work of Nations*. New York: A. A. Knopf.
Reitsma, H. A. and Kleinpenning, J. M. G. 1985: *The Third World in Perspective*. Totowa, NJ: Rowman and Allanheld.

Reynolds, L. 1983: The Spread of Economic Growth to the Third World: 1850–1980. *Journal of Economic Literature*, 21 (3), 941–80.

Ribeiro Ramos, F. F. 2001: Exports, Imports and Economic Growth in Portugal: Evidence from Causality and Cointegration Analysis. *Economic Modelling*, 18, 613–23.

Rich, B. 1994: *Mortgaging the Earth*. London: Earthscan Publications Ltd.

Riedel, J. 1984: Trade as the Engine of Growth in Developing Countries, Revisited. *Economic Journal*, 94, 56–73.

Robertson, R. 1992: *Globalization: Social Theory and Global Culture*. London: Sage.

Robinson, E. A. G. 1954: The Changing Structure of the British Economy. *Economic Journal*, 64, 443–61.

Robinson, T. W. (ed.) 1991: *Democracy and Development in East Asia: Taiwan, South Korea and the Philippines*. Lanham, MD: AEI Press.

Rodrik, D. 1997: *Has Globalisation Gone Too Far?* Washington, DC: Institute for International Economics.

Rodrik, D. 1998: The Debate over Globalization: How to Move Forward by Looking Backward. Washington, DC: Institute for International Economics.

Rodrik, D. 2000: How Far Will Economic Integration Go? *Journal of Economic Perspectives*, 14 (1), 177–86.

Rodrik, D. 2002: Feasible Globalisations. Mimeo, Washington, DC: Institute for International Economics.

Roemer, J. E. 1995: On the Relationship between Economic Development and Political Democracy. In Bagchi, 1995, pp. 28–55.

Romer, P. 1986: Increasing Returns and Long-Run Growth. *Journal of Political Economy*, 94 (5), 1002–37.

Rosensweig, M. R. and Binswanger, H. P. 1993: Wealth, Weather, Risk and the Composition and Profitability of Agricultural Investments. *Economic Journal*, 103 (416), 56–78.

Rostow, W. W. 1960: *The Stages of Economic Growth: A Non-Communist Manifesto*. Cambridge: Cambridge University Press.

Rowthorn, R. E. and Wells, J. R. 1987: *De-industrialization and Foreign Trade*. Cambridge: Cambridge University Press.

Roxborough, I. 1988: Modernisation Theory Revisited: A Review Article. *Comparative Studies in Society and History*, 30, 753–61.

Roy, P. 1981: Transition in Agriculture: Empirical Indicators and Results (Evidence from Punjab, India). *Journal of Peasant Studies*, 8 (2), 212–41.

Rudra, A. 1982: *Indian Agricultural Economics: Myths and Realities*. Delhi: Allied Publishers.

Ruschemeyer, D., Stephens, E. H. and Stephens, J. D. 1992: *Capitalist Development and Democracy*. Chicago: University of Chicago Press.

Ruttan, V. W. 1977: The Green Revolution: Seven Generalizations. *International Development Review*, 4, 16–23.

Ruy, M. M. 1972: Brazilian Sub-Imperialism. *Monthly Review*, 9, 14–24.

Sachs, J. 1998: International Economics: Unlocking the Mysteries of Globalisation. *Foreign Policy*, 110, 97–111.

Saha, S. 1991: The Role of Industrialisation in Development in sub-Saharan Africa: A Critique of the World Bank's Approach. *Economic and Political Weekly*, 26, 2753–62.

Sarre, P., Smith, P. with Morris, E. 1991: *One World for One Earth: Saving the Environment*. London: Earthscan Publications Ltd and Milton Keynes: Open University.

Saxenian, A. 1999: *Silicon Valley's New Immigrant Entrepreneurs*. San Francisco: Public Policy Institute of California.

Scheuerman, W. 2002: Globalization. In *The Stanford Encyclopedia of Philosophy*, Fall 2002 edn. *http://Plato.stanford.edu/archives/fall2002/entries/globalization/*.

Schmidheiny, S. 1992: *Changing Course: A Global Perspective on Development and the Environment*. Cambridge, MA: MIT Press.

Schmitz, H. 1982: Growth Constraints on Small Scale Manufacturing in Developing Countries: A Critical Review. *World Development*, 10 (6), 429–50.

Schumacher, E. F. 1973: *Small is Beautiful*. London: Blond and Briggs.

Schuurman, F. (ed.) 1993: *Beyond the Impasse: New Directions in Development Theory*. London: Zed Books.

Scitovsky, T. 1984: Comment on Adelman. *World Development*, 12, 953–4.

Scott, J. W. 1988: *Gender and the Politics of History*. New York: Columbia University Press.

Seers, D. 1979a: The Birth, Life and Death of Development Economics. *Development and Change*, 10 (4), 707–19.

Seers, D. 1979b: The Meaning of Development. In D. Lehmann (ed.), *Development Theory: Four Critical Studies*, London: Frank Cass, pp. 9–30.

Selden, M. 1988: *The Political Economy of Contemporary China*. Armonk, NY: M. E. Sharpe.

Sen, A. K. 1977: Starvation and Exchange Entitlements: A General Approach and its Application to the Great Bengal Famine. *Cambridge Journal of Economics*, 1 (1), 33–59.

Sen, A. K. 1981: *Poverty and Famines: An Esssay on Entitlement and Deprivation*. Oxford: Clarendon Press.

Sen, A. K. 1983: Development: Which Way Now? *Economic Journal*, 93 (372), 745–62.

Sen, A. K. 1984: *Resources, Values and Development*. Cambridge, MA: Harvard University Press.

Sen, A. K. 1985: *Commodities and Capabilities*. Amsterdam: North Holland.

Sen, A. K. 1987: *The Standard of Living*. Tanner Lectures. Cambridge: Cambridge University Press.

Sen, A. K. 1989: Food and Freedom. *World Development*, 17, 769–81.

Sen, A. K. 1997: *Hunger in the Contemporary World*. DERP Working Paper no. 8. London: LSE.

Senghaas, D. 1985: *The European Experience: A Historical Critique of Development Theory*, tr. K. H. Kimming. Leamington Spa: Berg.

Sengupta, A. 1993: *Aid and Development Policy in the 1990s*. Helsinki: UNU/WIDER.

Sercovich, F. with Ahn, C.-Y., Frischtak, C., Mrak, M., Muegge, H., Peres, W. and Wangwe, S. 1999: *Competition and the World Economy: Comparing Industrial Development Policies in the Developing and Transitional Economies*. Cheltenham: Edward Elgar and UNIDO.

Servan Schrieber, J. J. 1968: *American Challenge*. London: Hamish Hamilton.

Shanmugaratnam, N. 1989: Development and Environment: A View from the South. *Race and Class*, 30 (3), 13–30.

Sheehan, G. and Hopkins, M. 1978: *Basic Needs Performance: An Analysis of Some International Data*. Geneva: ILO.

Shiva Ramu, S. 1996: *Globalization: The Indian Scenario*. New Delhi: Wheeler Publishing.

Shiva, V. 1989: *Staying Alive*. London: Zed Books.

Shiva, V. 1994a: Conflicts of Global Ecology: Environmental Activism in a Period of Global Reach. *Alternatives*, 19, 195–207.

Shiva, V. (ed.) 1994b: *Women Reconnect Ecology, Health and Development*. London: Earthscan Publications.

Shiva, V. 1997: Women in Nature. In Visvanathan et al., 1997b, pp. 62–7.

Simpson, E. S. 1994: *The Developing World: An Introduction*. Harlow: Longman Scientific and Technical.

Singer, H. 1950: The Distribution of Gains between Investing and Borrowing Countries. *American Economic Review (Papers and Proceedings)*, 40 (2), 473–85.

Singer, H. 1984: Industrialization: Where do we Stand? Where are we Going? *Industry and Development*, 12, 79–88.

Singh, A. 1977: UK Industry and the World Economy: A Case of De-industrialisation. *Cambridge Journal of Economics*, 1 (2), 113–36.

Singh, A. 1979: The Basic Needs Approach to Development vs the New World International Order: The Significance of Third World Industrialisation. *World Development*, 7 (6), 585–606.

Sklair, L. 1993: *Assembling for Development*. San Diego: University of California Press.

Skocpol, T. 1985: Bringing the State Back In: Strategies of Analysis in Current Research. In P. Evans et al. (eds), *Bringing the State Back In*, Cambridge: Cambridge University Press, pp. 3–37.

Smith, B. C. 1996: *Understanding Third World Politics: Theories of Political Change and Development*. London: Macmillan.

Snyder, M. C. and Tadesse, M. 1995: *African Women and Development: A History: The Story of the African Training and Research Centre for Women of the United Nations Economic Commission for Africa*. London: Zed Books.

Sogge, D. with Biekart, K. and Saxby, J. (eds) 1996: *Compassion and Calculation: The Business of Private Foreign Aid*. London: Pluto.

Solow, R. 1956: A Contribution to the Theory of Economic Growth. *Quarterly Journal of Economics*, 70, 65–94.

Soon, T. W. and Stoever, W. A. 1996: Foreign Investment and Economic Development in Singapore: A Policy-Oriented Approach. *Journal of Developing Areas*, 30 (3), 317–40.

Sorensen, G. 1993: *Democracy and Democratization*. Oxford: Westview Press.

Spence, A. M. 1973: Job Market Signalling. *Quarterly Journal of Economics*, 87 (3), 355–74.

Spivak, G. C. 1987: *In Other Worlds – Essays in Cultural Politics*. New York: Methuen.

Stern, N. 1989: The Economics of Development: A Survey. *Economic Journal*, 99, 597–685.

Stiglitz, J. E. 1989: Markets, Market Failures and Development. *American Economic Review (Papers and Proceedings)*, 79 (2), 197–203.

Stiglitz, J. E. 1998: The East Asian Crisis and its Implications for India. Washington, DC: World Bank.

Streeten, P. 1982: A Cool Look at 'Outward-Looking' Strategies for Development. *World Economy*, 2, 159–69.

Streeten, P. 1983: Development Dichotomies. *World Development*, 11 (10), 875–89.

Streeten, P. and Burki, S. J. 1978: Basic Needs: Some Issues. *World Development*, 6 (8), 411–21.

Sunkel, O. 1966: The Structural Background of Development Problems in Latin America. *Weltwirtschaftliches Archiv*, 97 (1), 22–68.

Sunkel, O. 1969: National Development Policy and External Dependency in Latin America. *Journal of Development Studies*, 6 (1), 23–48.

Svejnar, J. and Singer, M. 1994: Using Vouchers to Privatise an Economy: The Czech and Slovak. *Economics of Transition*, 2 (1), 43–69.

Swaminathan, M. S. 1990: *Changing Nature of the Food Security Challenge: Implications for Agricultural Research and Policy*. Sir John Crawford Memorial Lecture. Washington, DC: CGIAR Secretariat.

Swaminathan, M. 1991: *Understanding the 'Informal Sector': A Survey*. Working Paper no. 95. Helsinki: WIDER.

Sweezy, P. and Magdoff, H. 1984: The Two Faces of Third World Debt: A Fragile Financial Environment and Debt Enslavement. *Monthly Review*, 35, 1–10.

Tester, M. 2001: Depolarising the GM Debate. *New Phytologist*, 149 (1), 9–12.

Thirlwall, A. 1994: *Growth and Development: With Special Reference to Developing Economies*, 5th edn. Basingstoke: Macmillan.

Thomas, H. (ed.) 1995: *Globalisation and 3rd World Trade Unions: The Challenge of Rapid Economic Change*. London: Zed Books.

Todaro, M. P. 1969: A Model of Labour Migration and Urban Unemployment in Less Developed Countries. *American Economic Review*, 59 (1), 138–48.

Todaro, M. P. 1985: *Economic Development in the Third World*. London: Longman.

Townsend, J. 1987: Rural Change: Progress for Whom? In Preston, 1987, pp. 199–228.

Townsend, P. 1979: *Poverty in the United Kingdom*. Harmondsworth: Penguin.

Toye, J. 1993: *Dilemmas of Development: Reflections on the Counter-Revolution in Development Theory and Policy*. Oxford: Blackwell.

Turner, R. K. 1988: *Sustainable Environmental Management*. London: Belhaven.

UNDP 1997: *Human Development Report*. New York: Oxford University Press.

UNDP 1999: *Human Development Report*. New York: Oxford University Press.

UNDP 2000: *Human Development Report*. New York: Oxford University Press.

UNICEF 1990: *The State of the World's Children 1990*. Oxford: Oxford University Press.

United Nations 1989, *Report on the World Social Situation*, Geneva: United Nations.

UNRISD 1995: *States of Disarray*. Geneva: UNRISD.

Usher, D. 1981: *The Economic Prerequisite to Democracy*. Oxford: Blackwell.

USJEC 1975: *China: A Reassessment of the Economy*. Washington, DC: Joint Economic Committee of the US Congress.

Visvanathan, N. 1997a: Introduction. In Visvanathan et al., 1997b, pp. 1–6, 17–29.

Visvanathan, N., Duggan, L., Nisonoff, L. and Wiergersma, N. (eds) 1997b: *The Women, Gender and Development Reader*. London: Zed Books.

Wallace, T. with March, C. (eds) 1991: *Changing Perceptions: Writing on Gender and Development.* Oxford: Oxfam.

Wallerstein, I. 1979: *The Capitalist World.* Cambridge: Cambridge University Press.

Wallerstein, I. 1984: *The Politics of the World Economy: The States, the Markets and the Civilizations.* Cambridge: Cambridge University Press.

Wambugu, F. 2000: Feeding Africa: Opinion Interview. *New Scientist,* 27 May, 40–3.

Warren, B. 1973: Imperialism and Capitalist Industrialization. *New Left Review,* 63, 3–44.

Warren, B. 1980: *Imperialism: Pioneer of Capitalism,* ed. John Sender. London: Verso.

Waylen, G. 1996: *Gender in Third World Politics.* Buckingham: Open University Press.

WCED (The World Commission on Environment and Development) 1987: *Our Common Future.* The Brundtland Report. Oxford: Oxford University Press.

Weber, M. 1930: *The Protestant Ethic and the Spirit of Capitalism,* Talcott Parsons. London: Unwin Hyman.

Webster, A. 1990: *An Introduction to the Sociology of Development.* London: Macmillan.

Weede, E. 1983: The Impact of Democracy on Economic Growth: Some Evidence from Cross-National Analysis. *Kyklos,* 36 (1), 21–38.

Weede, E. 1997: Income Inequality, Democracy and Growth Reconsidered. *European Journal of Political Economy,* 13 (4), 751–64.

Weiner, M. and Huntington, S. P. (eds) 1987: *Understanding Political Development.* Boston: Little, Brown and Co.

Weiringa, S. (ed.) 1995: *Subversive Women: Historical Experiences of Gender and Resistance.* London: Zed Books.

Weisbrot, M., Baker, D., Kraev, E. and Chen, J. 2001: The Scorecard on Globalization, 1980–2000: Twenty Years of Diminished Progress. Washington, DC: Centre for Economic and Policy Research.

Weiss, J. 1990: *Industry in Developing Countries: Theory, Policy and Evidence.* London: Routledge.

White, G. and Wade, R. 1984: Developmental States in East Asia: Capitalist and Socialist. *IDS Bulletin,* 15 (2), 1–70.

White, H. 1992a: The Macroeconomic Impact of Development Aid: A Critical Survey. *Journal of Development Studies,* 28 (2), 163–240.

White, H. 1992b: What Do We Know about Aid's Macroeconomic Impact? An Overview of the Aid Effectiveness Debate. *Journal of International Development,* 4 (2), 121–37.

White, S. C. 1999: Gender and Development: Working with Difference. In Jabri and O'Gorman, 1999.

Whiteside, A. 1998: A Global Pandemic. *The Health Exchange,* Aug., pp. 4–5.

Williamson, J. G. 1997: *Industrialization, Inequality and Economic Growth.* Cheltenham: Edward Elgar.

Wood, A. 1994: *North–South Trade, Employment and Inequality: Changing Fortunes in a Skill-Driven World.* Oxford: Clarendon Press.

Wood, A. and RidaoCano, C. 1999: Skill, Trade and International Inequality. *Oxford Economic Papers,* 51 (1), 89–119.

World Bank 1974: *Land Reform*. Washington, DC: World Bank.
World Bank 1975: *Rural Development*. Sector Policy Paper. Washington, DC: World Bank.
World Bank 1983: *World Development Report*. Oxford: Oxford University Press.
World Bank 1987: *World Development Report*. Oxford: Oxford University Press.
World Bank 1990: *World Development Report: What Do We Know about the Poor?* Oxford: Oxford University Press.
World Bank 1991: *World Development Report*. Oxford: Oxford University Press .
World Bank 1993a: *The East Asian Miracle: Economic Growth and Public Policy*. Oxford: Oxford University Press.
World Bank 1993b: *World Development Report*. Oxford: Oxford University Press.
World Bank 1994: *Adjustment in Africa: Reforms, Results and the Road Ahead*. Oxford: Oxford University Press.
World Bank 1995: *World Development Report*. Oxford: Oxford University Press.
World Bank 1997a: *Confronting AIDS: Public Priorities in a Global Epidemic*. Oxford: Oxford University Press.
World Bank 1997b: *World Development Report*. Oxford: Oxford University Press.
World Bank 1998: *Assessing Aid: What Works, What Doesn't and Why*. World Bank Policy Research Report. Oxford: Oxford University Press.
World Bank 1999/2000: *World Development Report*. New York: Oxford University Press.
World Bank 2000/1: *World Development Report*. Oxford: Oxford University Press.
World Bank 2001: *World Development Indicators*.
World Bank, *www.worldbank.org/data/dev/devgoals.html*.
World Commission on Environment and Development 1987: *From One Earth to One World: An Overview*. Oxford: Oxford University Press
Worsley, P. 1965: Bureaucracy and Decolonisation: Democracy from the Top. In T L. Horowitz (ed.), *The New Sociology*, New York: Oxford University Press, pp. 370–90.
Yotopoulos, P. A. and Nugent, J. B. 1973: A Balanced Growth Version of the Linkage Hypothesis: A Test. *Quarterly Journal of Economics*, 87 (2), 157–71.
Yotopoulos, P. A. and Nugent, J. B. 1979: What has Orthodox Economics Learned from Recent Experience? *World Development*, 7 (6), 541–54.
Young, A. 1995: The Tyranny of Numbers: Confronting the Statistical Realities of the East Asian Growth Experience. *Quarterly Journal of Economics*, 110, 641–80.
Young, K. 1997: Gender and Development. In Visvanathan et al., 1997b, pp. 366–74.
Yusuf, S. 1994: China's Macroeconomic Performance and Management during Transition. *Journal of Economic Perspectives*, 8 (2), 71–92.
Zinkin, M. 1978: Aid and Morals: Addressing the Aspirations of the Poor Countries. *Round Table*, 271, 222–8.

Index